Praise for *Nighthawk Alley*

'Marvellous, terrific. A love poem to Boston on top of all its other qualities' – Roddy Doyle

'Not many men tell you about men. This book does and the heart expands' – Nuala O'Faolain

'A beautifully observed, lovingly written first novel, as funny and acutely truthful as it is finally moving' – Joseph O'Connor

'Astonishingly accomplished and evocative. A new and subtle look at Irish immigrants, as humorous as it is sad' –The Irish Times

'Nighthawk Alley is an extraordinary debut ... this has the hallmarks of a modern classic' – Image Magazine

'Glavin's superb use of the vernacular gives an engaging, streetwise rhythm to the tale. Nighthawk Alley is a little gem' – Evening Herald

'A gentle, intriguing novel of decent men's lives at a certain turn of the wheel' – RTÉ Guide

Also by Anthony Glavin

One For Sorrow (1980)

Nighthawk Alley (1997)

The Draughtsman and The Unicorn (1999)

Colours
Other Than
Blue

A NOVEL

For Gib and Kay

Anthony Glavin

With great admiration, affection, nay love, and heartfelt the Thanks for friendship!

**WARD
RIVER
PRESS**

Tony 13 April 2016

Published 2016
by Poolbeg Press Ltd
123 Grange Hill, Baldoyle
Dublin 13, Ireland
E-mail: poolbeg@poolbeg.com
www.wardriverpress.com

1

A catalogue record for this book is available from the British Library.

ISBN 978-1-78199-918-9

Typeset by Poolbeg Press Ltd
Printed and bound by CPI Group (UK) Ltd, Croydon, CR0 4YY

www.poolbeg.com

About the author

Boston-born novelist Anthony Glavin first came to Ireland in 1974, where he lived in Donegal for many years. A former editor of Hennessy New Irish Writing, he also worked as commissioning editor for New Island Books, where he edited among many titles Nuala O'Faolain's international bestseller *Are You Somebody?*. Author of a critically acclaimed first novel, *Nighthawk Alley*, and two short story collections, *One For Sorrow* and *The Draughtsman and The Unicorn*, his stories have been widely anthologised in Ireland, the UK, and the US.

Sadness is surely the secret mother of memory.
                                                Richard Weber

⚬☙‧‧☙⚬

For Mary Alice

AFTERWORD

I

I THOUGHT I was done with this notebook two months ago—until last night's dream of my mother and that crow. Only this time Ma actually managed to stitch its belly up, using that thick waxy thread you get for mending carpets. And it's that dream has brought me back to this notebook one last time.

Here I sit in my Dublin kitchen, a woman of thirty-eight, still dreaming of her mother. Still working the shuttle of memory back and forth across the Big Pond as Pops always called it, from Ireland to Boston where the story begins. And back and forth and back again.

It's Christmas next week, and I've the tree up already. A surprise for Katy when she gets home from secondary school—after which we'll trim it together, as we always do. I just strung the lights this afternoon, to see which bulbs have given up the ghost of Christmas past. It gets dark early now, so I drew the sitting-room curtains before plugging the lights in. Yet when I did, and it all came to life, I suddenly recalled another tree. On Christmas Eve when I was five or six, and sick to my stomach from all the excitement, if not a tummy bug. Ma put a damp face-cloth over my brow and made me lie on the sofa in our living room, opposite the Boston Common with its own coloured

1

Christmas lights and life-sized crib. I could hear Ma in the kitchen as I lay there in the dark beside our lit-up tree, making the shrimp & rice dish she always served on Christmas Eve, and which I never ate. A mellower memory than others that follow here, and I'm happy to have retrieved it.

Nor am I making it up—even if mother is the necessity of invention. Both the lies we tell our mothers, and the world we create as a counter to them. Only I'm getting ahead of myself, for had I known this much to start, I might well have developed a Personality as a child. Gone on to become a weather presenter or chat-show host. Or—who knows—a writer, now that I've scribbled a book-length script? Or I might have left Boston for Barcelona or bella Roma instead of dirty ol' Dublin nearly thirteen years ago. At the very least—had I known this much last year—I wouldn't have sought out Sister Úna. Nor begun this notebook whose Afterword I suppose these final lines are.

It seems so obvious now—the way a truth is so often obvious, once uncovered. Out of sight under your nose, until you suddenly look down and see it. Like the truths that lie buried back there in childhood: out of sight but not out of mind nor memory—provided you know how to read them, how to reassemble the pictures until there's narrative enough to set you free. Or, if not entirely free, more fully back into the Here & Now—and hopefully better positioned to get on with it.

Certainly it's taken me this long to see how large a part mothers play in it all. Even with the help of Constance Fitzgerald, chanting that truth like a one-woman Greek chorus at work these past four years. Constance being one of forty-odd residents at the Fairview Home for the Elderly in Dublin, and Constance at seventy-eight among the oddest. Constance who is always at the front door, asking to be let out so she can go home to take care of the mother she buried in Galway over twenty years ago.

'Nurse, will you let me out? My mother's not well.'

'I haven't got a key, Constance,' Assistant Matron Mary O'Mara tells her.

'Nurse, will you let me out? My mother's expecting me.'

'I'm only junior staff, Constance,' Fiona Flynn, my other Assistant Matron, fibs. 'They don't give the likes of me a key.'

'Sure, what good's a key to anyone?' says Constance, trudging slowly back to her chair in the front day-room.

I used to tell Constance I wasn't trusted with a key either, but I stopped that two years ago when I became Matron. Addled as she is, Constance still knows that I'm Nurse Ratched—the one with the big ring of keys, so to speak. It's funny how the mind works, even for those who seem permanently parked in cloud-cuckoo land. You think a resident is totally out of it, until suddenly they tune back in, like the perfect reception you might briefly get on a bockety old radio in between all the static. And you can get caught out then—if you're not careful with the fibs you tell. For old folks are a lot like children if they catch you dissembling—disposed to dig in or rear up. Get mulish or go bolshie. Or ballistic, like Gemma Dunne does—if she thinks you're having her on. 'Germany Calling' as Mary O'Mara dubbed poor Gemma, with her head full of plots and bombs. So honesty's the best insurance policy—at least some of the time.

Of course, there are those like Larry Ferguson whose wireless mostly pulls in outer space. Tell Larry the world is ending tomorrow, and he'd just fix you with his impossibly bright eyes, like a squirrel on drugs, and ask for seconds of ice cream. Larry who thinks the Home is some 24/7 party he's at, and who's forever asking his visitors—his granddaughters say, or even the staff—for the lend of a fiver so as to get a few drinks. 'He's the original Happy as Larry,' Mary O'Mara laughed her first week at work, and didn't 'Happy-As' stick, too. Larry's not bothered about getting out the front door, but we still keep an eye on him given his habit, on days when he's feeling partied out, of walking about with his penis outside his pants. Another of the forty-odd, no doubt about it. 'It's not the one way we all go,' as Pops used to say.

It was Constance Fitzgerald, however, who kept on like a chorus I couldn't hear, chanting her mantra about her mater. 'I need to go now—my mother needs me.' Most of the residents look the part—that is, patently not going anywhere, God love them. But Constance looks well yet, hair neatly brushed, her cardigan generally clean. Last year a deliveryman mistook her for a visitor and, after wishing her mother a speedy recovery, took the key from behind the potted geranium at Reception and opened the front door. That his own mother must have lived to 150 was all I could think, the fecking eejit. Though he took off after her once he realised his error, along with Polish Petra, one of our care attendants, who glimpsed Constance out front, thank God, and also went after her like a shot. Constance's mother also lies at the heart of it—yet, even with her acting it out, I failed to cop it for myself. Constance with a shawl under her arm—for her mother who's complaining of a chill. Or wrapping a couple of biscuits in a serviette from the afternoon tea trolley: Vanilla Cremes, her mother's favourites. I merely figured Constance for the youngest daughter on whom it fell to care for an ageing mother, and so never got to marry or raise a family of her own. Or so I assumed until a few months ago—when her nephew set us straight. Constance was the youngest, true enough, but it wasn't her mother she had handed over her life for. Which makes the necessity of invention around her mother even more creative. Not to mention sad.

But I didn't understand that straight off. Nor could I as yet read Constance and her confabulations as a pluperfect example of how we weave our own lives against the weft of our mother's. Certainly I didn't know that about myself and Ma—not in any clear sense yet. Indeed I didn't know that at all.

II

All I knew, following Pops' death September before last, was how low I was. Lower than low. Not initially—at the news of his death or the busyness of the burial—but in the months that followed. What the textbooks call 'the anguish, disorganisation and despair stage of grieving' that kicked off with that early Saturday morning phone call from my brother.

'Maeve, it's Brian.'

'Brian—what is it?' As if I hadn't already guessed what had him calling at 2.00 a.m. Boston time.

'It's Pops, Maeve.'

I hate the phone at the best of times—which clearly this wasn't. Brian isn't much better either, and he rang off shortly after saying Pops had died quietly in his sleep at the nursing home, adding to ring him back when I had my flight details. I just stood there with phone in hand, as if my morning had suddenly shattered like a mirror, all bits of glass on the kitchen floor. I began to cry then—quietly—for

Katy was still asleep upstairs, and I've always hated breaking down around her—as if determined to spare her the burden of a mother's unhappiness.

It was a lovely early-autumn morning, and I'd the kitchen door ajar onto the back garden, where Nibbles lay sunning himself atop the coal-bunker. Inside, a wasp buzzed at the window over the sink—what we call a yellow jacket back in Boston. Staring at the Bank of Ireland calendar on the wall, I suddenly realised it was Labor Day weekend back home. And just as suddenly, the fact Pops had died on that holiday—Pops who had never stopped labouring—seemed utterly, cruelly apt. With that, it all came loose deep down inside, pitching me forward against the kitchen table. And when Katy, hearing me, came downstairs to hold me, there was nothing I could do, only put my arms around her too.

I rang Orla then, who promptly offered to stay with Katy while I flew over. I sometimes think how I'd never have survived here in Dublin without Orla, and that Saturday was no exception. She came straight over too, taking a tin of Tasty Treats for Nibbles from her overnight bag, and making a big show of presenting it to K, who absolutely dotes on the cat and is mad about Orla as well.

I wanted to ring Aer Lingus when she arrived, but Orla made me sit and talk about Pops instead. What I said probably didn't make much sense—memories of the battered fedora he always wore, or his Boston Red Sox cap in summer—while Orla made me a cup of tea and Katy got her breakfast, after giving Nibbles his. And when I finally did ring, it was Orla who reminded me to ask for a compassionate fare, something I'd not have thought of myself.

I went down to the Home that afternoon where, as luck

had it, Mary O'Mara was the weekend charge nurse. 'Don't bother coming down,' Mary had told me on the phone, saying she'd change her own roster through the week so as to keep an eye on the day-shift until I got back. But I wanted to look over the roster myself, check a few med charts, and see what else might need looking after before I flew out. And sure enough, Constance Fitzgerald was at the front door as I came in, saying she needed to take her mother shopping. It was my father I had just lost, however, so I didn't hear what Constance was really telling me. 'See if there's anything she'll watch on telly?' I instead suggested to Polish Petra, who was also working that Saturday.

Mary O'Mara had already anticipated all I'd come down to do, so I didn't have to stay long. Even so, Mary didn't start with care plans or purchase orders—all that busyness of denial I had summoned for myself. Instead she put her arms around me, giving me a moment in which to move beyond my disbelief. I've only known Mary two years, but she's nearly as big in my life as Orla is. Deep is what Mary is, and she didn't bother saying much in the office, just rubbed my back as she held me.

Constance was at the front door again as I came out of the office, so I took her down to the newer day-room where she rarely sits, thinking the change might help settle her. As I seated her, the Noticeboard on the wall opposite the big TV caught my eye. The Noticeboard being a large white Formica board designed to help the residents keep track of a few basic facts, like the date and season, written up with a grease pencil. It also used to give 'Today's Menu' until we decided said info only gave a head start to those residents who like to grumble about the food. 'Thought for the Day' is the previous Matron's idea, after she came across 'A

Book of 1000 Inspirations' at a sale-of-work. But most of those are pretty saccharine, so I keep an eye out for better stuff—like song lyrics, a line of poetry, or even an exceptional Chinese-cookie fortune. However, there was nothing exceptional on the board this morning:

DATE: Saturday, 5th September 1987
SEASON: Autumn
WEATHER: Bright & Cool
ACTIVITY: Exercise to music
SONG FOR THE DAY: 'Try to Remember the Kind of September'

Nothing out of the ordinary—which is what gave me pause. Nothing to mark this as the day my father died, back in Boston where we call autumn 'fall'.

Leaving the day-room, I went through the dining room into the kitchen before going back upstairs. Mary O'Mara had said nothing to any of the staff, so I was able to take a quick look around without having to field condolences. Just long enough to see refrigerators and freezer were amply stocked, and all of Happy-As-Larry was safely tucked inside his trousers.

III

The following morning I hugged Katy goodbye and flew off across the wide Atlantic. Early autumn and mid-spring are when Dublin and Boston just might share the same weather map on a given day. Or so it felt after I touched down at Logan that afternoon and stepped out into the same bright blue I'd left behind that morning. Only there was Brian in

8

Arrivals after I cleared Customs, looking so much like Pops, same medium build and thinning sandy hair. Whereas I'm even slighter—like Ma in that way at least—although my red hair comes from her mother, Granny O'Byrne.

Brian got defensive in the car when I wondered was it only Yanks who applaud when a plane touches safely down? He and Cheryl never fly anywhere, so it's hardly like he too claps along like that. But maybe he thought I was putting Americans down—which is silly, seeing as I'm one too. Anyhow, he gave me the funeral details as we came up out of the Sumner Tunnel, explaining how there were already two Tuesday burials at his own Stoneham church, so Pops' Funeral Mass would be next door in Wakefield.

'I don't think Pops gives a hoot,' I said, which made Brian smile.

He looked relieved, too, when I said I could help him sort out whatever Pops had left in his apartment whose lease wasn't up yet, as I wasn't flying back till Thursday. An apartment in the same building where Pops had worked for forty years as Superintendent. The same Park St address where Brian and I had grown up, the Super's son and daughter, just across from the Boston Common, with the gold-domed State House to the north, and the hurly-burly of Tremont St a half-dozen doors to the south.

No. 23 Park St had changed hands five years before, its apartments converted into condos. Pops had finally retired that same year, but the old owners put in a word with the new crowd, who offered to let him a studio-unit fashioned from one of the old, larger apartments. He got it at a reduced rent too, in exchange for taking out the barrels on trash day, and mopping down the lobby daily. And if one of the new condo owners had a plugged drain or faulty socket, Pops also looked after that. Much as when he had been Super, only now he got to charge an hourly rate for labour, plus parts.

Of course Brian had badgered Pops to come out to him and Cheryl in Stoneham, but he wouldn't leave Boston in a fit.

'What would I do in Stoneham all day? Visit the zoo?'

'Actually there's talk of the zoo closing,' Brian said.

'There you are!' Pops replied, resting his case.

Nor had he seemed down in the dumps those last years without Ma. He still had a few pals, a couple of other Supers, whom he met for coffee most mornings in one of the sandwich shops along Tremont or Boylston St. As a child, I don't remember Pops much in the Common or Public Gardens, which were like a front yard for Brian and me growing up. But in retirement he visited them daily, reading his newspaper on a bench beneath a huge willow by the Swan Boats in clement weather.

When he fell ill two years ago, I flew over to ask would he come back to Ireland. Not to his Mayo, which he had left over forty years before, but back to what was now my Dublin.

'So you can wheel me out every morning?' he smiled. 'Along with the other crinklys?'

'I mean home to me and Katy,' I laughed, though we both knew a care facility was likely not that far down his road. 'On the other hand, we've nearly all women at the Home,' I kidded him. 'Who knows, you might meet a rich widow?'

'One with a pension for the blind?' he smiled. 'Give me a cage in Stoneham Zoo any day.'

The Home is at times something of a zoo itself, but telling Pops that wouldn't have helped my case. Nor could I easily picture him in the same frame as, say, Kitty the

Conductor, her top unbuttoned and singing 'Look at my titties, they're all my own!' as Nurse Ethel makes a beeline towards her.

'Still, I could keep an eye on you,' I said. 'If you had to go into care for a spell.'

'For a spell,' Pops laughed softly—as if either of us believed a brain tumour might mend like a broken leg. 'Thanks, Pet, but I'm berthed on this side of the Big Pond for the duration.'

I left it, for there was never really any arguing with him. Mostly because he generally refused to argue—which is probably how he managed Ma down the years, those years she wasn't lost to depression, or the two occasions on which she went altogether mad.

Later that June I flew over again, to find him thinner, his speech occasionally slurred, his left arm out of commission.

'It's shaped like a starfish,' Dr Alper told me after I made an appointment. 'Which is why it affects him differently at different times. Right now you see a slight paralysis on the left side of his face, but that could disappear by next week, and his balance be affected instead.'

'Can you operate?' I asked, even if I knew the answer.

'No, not where the tumour is situated.'

'Chemo or radium?' If nothing else, nursing leaves you less in awe of the doctors you encounter. But Dr Alper, who had followed Pops for years, didn't mind questions.

'We're hoping so, Maeve, but it may not be feasible, given its advanced stage.'

'So what's the prognosis?' I finally asked.

Dr Alper got up and walked from his desk over to the window. I had my answer then, before he turned and said, 'Likely six months at most'.

Back home in Dublin, I lay in bed imagining it. Not

spiny and stiff, like the starfish we found on Revere Beach as kids, but soft and luminous, its ghostly arms radiating out from its hub. I knew better of course, having seen textbook illustrations of malignant astrocytoma, but I preferred envisioning it that way for Pops' sake. Or my own, as I could not hold the thought of him suffering. 'I've two rich widows at work,' I wrote on a postcard, 'fighting over you already!'

But that August, six weeks after my last trip over, Pops went into a Wakefield nursing home instead, one town over from Brian and Cheryl. Where he died just a fortnight later. 'In his sleep,' as Brian had informed me over the phone. Died without my being there—same as I hadn't managed when my mother died, the early morning phone call on that occasion coming from Pops himself.

The viewing was on Monday at Mahoney & Sons Funeral Home, followed by the funeral Mass Tuesday at the Mater Dolorosa Church. 'Sounds like an Italian restaurant,' Mahoney Jr had chanced, which prompted Brian to tell of an Irish-American workmate who requested that a crêpe-paper Irish flag be draped over his father's casket. The funeral director provided a tricolour all right— green, white, and red—dispatching the deceased as a Son of Italy. For our part, Brian and I rode behind Pops' hearse in a black limousine with two orange Mahoney & Sons pennants stuck on either side of the bonnet, the tiny flags snapping smartly in the breeze as we passed derelict red-brick factories basking in the sun. The Mater Dolorosa had the same red-brick depressed look too, sweet wrappers and old newspapers blown up against the chain-link fence around the parking lot.

Inside however was another story: statues everywhere, the walls plastered with holy pictures and floridly painted floral motifs. Reading the brass nameplates on the front pew where Mahoney Jr had ushered us—Korzec, Lenki, Zalinski—it struck me how James Anthony Maguire of Louisburgh, Co Mayo, late of 23 Park St, Boston, was being mourned in a Polish-American church in a suburban parish, eulogised as a good father and good Catholic by a priest who had never met him. Which made me wish the funeral had been back in Boston, at Holy Cross Cathedral like Ma's, or even the Arch St Chapel amid the bag ladies and commuters.

'Does it matter we're sending him off as a Son of Poland?' I whispered to Brian, who whispered back something about kielbasa. Nor would Pops have given a hoot what church—Polack or Pater Doloroso. Though he might have smiled at the idea of a Mater D—an irony utterly lost on his daughter that September. As was Constance Fitzgerald, chanting like a Daughter Dolorosa back at the Home—offering me yet another clue I utterly failed to read.

I rang Katy that evening in Dublin, who told me of her first day back at school. And how Nibbles wouldn't touch his regular food after the Tasty Treats from Orla. All quiet on the home front, so. As for the Home front, Mary O'Mara had warned me not to even think about checking in long-distance from America.

The day after the funeral was lovely too, bright and not quite as cool. That afternoon Brian and I went over to Pops' apartment, where I tried to recall which tenant had lived in the second-floor apartment out of which his glorified bed-sit had been fashioned. But it hadn't belonged to any of those tenants I remember best—like Mrs. Lunenburg, Captain Evarts, or Miss Chauncy say—whose apartments I could still pick out. Not to mention our own

Apt 1A. I wondered would Brian remember, but he seemed his old irascible self that afternoon, and I didn't want to annoy him further with an invitation to stroll down memory lane. Much as I used to worry about irking him with some query or question when we were kids. He got that from Ma, I think, a pool of irritability not that far beneath the surface, where anything might set it rippling.

It took no time to pack Pops' few effects into a couple of suitcases and cardboard cartons. Not much to collect from what was basically a large single room, with a tiny kitchenette and tiny bathroom in opposite corners. A musty medicinal smell greeted us as we came in, and I cast a practised eye over half-a-dozen vials atop the dresser. Next to the pills were two ballpoints, his black wooden Rosary beads, a tin of shoe polish, and a spare pair of reading glasses. Plus a small photograph of Ma I didn't remember, taken in her thirties I'd say, seated on what looked like a bench in the Public Gardens. And over the dresser the same colour portrait of JFK that had hung inside our Apt 1A with its small brass plate etched 'Superintendent' on the door.

I'd only broken down twice—in my Dublin kitchen after Brian's call, and again at seeing Pops laid out in Mahoneys'. But as I looked at his dresser—its bits & bobs like a makeshift shrine to an ordinary life—I felt the same sudden sharp stab. Followed by a few tears which of course disconcerted Brian.

'You OK?' he asked, putting a hand on my shoulder.

We had embraced at the airport, but we were never a demonstrative family, always somewhat body-shy. The few times ever I was in my parents' bed, sick with a flu, I always saw my mother take her clothes behind the closet door to get dressed.

'You know he's better off,' Brian said, proffering a platitude and the truth both, as he handed me a tissue from the dresser.

'I know he is.' And then, to put Brian at ease—but also because I've been years in Ireland—I told him a story. A story Assistant Matron Fiona Flynn had recently told us at the Home. Of an uncle who broke down at seeing his wife laid out in the funeral parlour, leaning over the coffin and taking her face in his hands, as his children looked on distraught. 'It's all right, Daddy,' one of his daughters tried to console him. 'It's not all right!' sobbed her father. 'She has my teeth!'

'At least Pops got buried with his,' smiled Brian, who heartened me by telling a story in turn. About his boss Hank who went fishing with a brother on Spy Pond in Arlington. As Hank fiddles with the outboard motor, his brother ties his own dentures onto Hank's tackle for a laugh, then lowers the line back into the water. 'Well, I've a bite anyhow,' Hank announces, reeling in. 'Ah, fuck me!' he says upon seeing the teeth which he figures have fouled his line, before throwing them back into the water like you do an undersized fish.

Which prompted me to tell Brian how our eighty-three-year-old Kitty the Conductor sometimes places her dentures in the fish tank by the front door at work. 'One way to keep them clean,' Brian laughed, though Pops simply put his in a glass of water on his bedside table. He then told how Cheryl's Dad stashes his in his pockets, only to slap them back in his mouth—festooned with bits of lint or pipe tobacco—if the doorbell rings or he's heading out.

It was a lovely exchange, almost like playing ping-pong with my brother again, though the white-enamel kitchen table where we used to clamp the net was far too short for

15

a proper game. Nor am I very good at telling stories aloud—even if I often segue from one to another in my head, same as I did playing by myself as a kid.

IV

As it happened, those stories we swapped on Park St were as much of an Irish wake as our Pops got. Just a few mourners showed the afternoon Brian, Cheryl and I sat with his remains at Mahoney & Sons: two of Cheryl's sisters which was nice, seeing it was Labor Day, plus a couple of Brian's workmates. Then, just before we left, Buddy Grimes, one of Pops' old pals, turned up, having made his way up I-93 to pay his respects. Buddy was one of that small circle of Pops' friends, mostly all Irish-born. Several worked in hotels downtown, the Ritz or the Parker House, while Buddy was Super of a large apartment building on Commonwealth Ave near Kenmore Square. They would play poker every other Friday night, nickel & dime pots, and every few months the game came to our apartment. I can't see cards being played in a film that I don't recall those nights, the cigarette smoke trapped beneath the green-enamel lampshade over our kitchen table, and brown, long-neck bottles of beer, Pabst Blue Ribbon or Narragansett, at everybody's elbow. Or the ice-cream floats Pops always made us before his pals arrived— vanilla ice cream frothing over the top, bubbles of ginger ale that broke on your tongue as you took a sip.

Even Ma liked those poker nights, I think, though she skipped the ice cream. And disappeared into the living room once the men arrived, to watch TV same as she did most evenings. But she seemed more relaxed those Friday nights, as if the kitchen conviviality— laughter, banter or a muted curse when the cards hadn't come—had permeated the entire apartment the way, say, the smell of a pie baking does. Later on Ma would pass out the sandwiches she'd already made, ham & cheese or egg salad on Wonderbread, while maybe laughing at something Buddy or Mike Sullivan had said.

Funny enough, Buddy didn't look that much older that afternoon than he had on those long-ago poker nights. Same long nose and big ears with bushy tufts of grey hair sticking out like an untrimmed hedge.

'I'm sorry for your troubles,' he said as he shook our hands.

'Still playing cards?' asked Brian then, able to chat more easily with Buddy than he often can with me.

'It was good of you to come all this way,' I told Hugh, aware our waking Pops that far from Boston had put a journey on an old neighbour. Though where we had lived— smack downtown beside two huge public parks—was hardly a neighbourhood. Fact is, No. 23 was the only residential building on Park St, and the nearby Arch St Chapel seemed more train station than church, with its timetable of Masses and folk constantly rushing in and out. Nor had we had any other family in Boston—or America for that matter—both parents from Ireland, and Ma's brother, Uncle Dinny in Chicago, nearly twenty years dead.

The only other mourners that afternoon were two elderly women in dark gabardine coats too heavy for early September. I tried to place them among the residents at No. 23 as they knelt at the casket, but they didn't look at all familiar.

'So sorry for your troubles,' they then told us, scurrying off before we could get their names.

'How do you think they knew Pops?' I asked Brian.

'From his obituary,' Brian laughed. 'Which is how they organise their afternoons out.'

'They're just making the rounds?' I marvelled.

'Compulsive mourners,' Brian's Cheryl said. 'We'd two of them at my father's funeral. "Did he die at a ball game?" one of them asked my mother. "No, he died at home!" my mother all but spat.'

'At least we don't have to pay them,' Brian said. 'Like the Greeks who hired women to show up shrieking and tearing their hair.'

'Beats staying at home and watching "Oprah", I suppose.'

'Not much to do in Stoneham,' Brian smiled, 'once you've seen the zoo.'

On the way back to their house, Cheryl told of an aunt who had kept a scrapbook for family obituaries.

'Like a goddamn Final Ledger,' Brian laughed.

'Some folk get a scrapbook entry,' I said, 'and some an airport named after them. How fair is that?'

'I don't think Pops minds,' Brian said.

I didn't think so, either. But I still wished it had somehow been the brass Superintendent plaque from Apt 1A instead of the cheap nameplate which Mahoney Jr had affixed to Pops' casket.

'You and Cheryl seem to be doing well,' I offered when Brian and I nipped out later to the supermarket. But 'Uhh' was all he said which I took for an affirmative. I remember reading somewhere how seventy-five per cent of communication is supposedly non-verbal, but with Brian it feels more like eighty-nine per cent. Or maybe we're just not simpatico enough to comfortably pursue much conversation. Anything to do with feelings, basically.

I scarcely know Cheryl, as I was already in Ireland when

they got together. My age exactly, she works as a dental hygienist. She's lovely—petite, curly black hair and big green eyes—though not pushed about her appearance in that jeans & sweatshirt way a lot of American women have. Brian and she bicker a good bit, but then many couples do. Brian making fun of her ornaments, china shepherdesses and unicorns, while she mocks his lava lamp with its syrupy, red liquid that breaks up into these blobby aneurysms which bob up and down.

'It's like watching goldfish,' Brian says that evening, 'only you don't have to feed them.'

More like watching giant leeches, I opt not to say as I was leery of taking sides. I don't tell the one either about how lava lamps are a lot like men—nice to look at, but not very bright? Instead I tell Brian how Fiona Flynn at work sent her husband out to buy a new pair of goldfish before their four-year-old Tommy discovered his old pair had died. Only for Tommy to catch his father an hour later, coming in the front door with the replacements in a plastic bag. 'What are you doing with my goldfish, Da?' he asked, saucer-eyed. 'Just took them out for a walk, Son!'

Brian and Cheryl haven't any kids, whether from choice or not I don't know. But I don't think of them as a 'childless couple' any more than I want to be seen as a 'single mother'—which I guess is what I felt Brian was doing when the matter of Pops' estate came up the afternoon we cleared out his effects. If 'estate' is not too grand a word for the Shawmut Bank passbook Brian found in the small desk where Pops always sat the last Thursday night of each month when we were kids. 'Doing the books!' he called it, as he sorted through various receipts for floor wax, mop heads and light bulbs, and entered figures carefully in a ledger. The passbook balance was around $9,500, though it beats me how Pops managed to save that on what was never much of a salary, whatever about a piddling once-off lump sum when the building was sold, instead of a proper pension to supplement his Social Security.

'Why don't you take that?' Brian said, holding the passbook out. That he genuinely meant it, too, didn't make hearing it any easier.

'Why don't you fuck off?' I said, by way of demonstrating what twelve years in Dublin has done for my vocabulary. I've paid my way and Katy's from the start, I almost added but thankfully didn't. 'Pay the funeral expenses first,' I instead said, 'and we'll divvy it up then.' I waited for him to flare back at me, but when he didn't I chanced, 'Ma should've let him buy that copper stock.'

'That mine probably clapped out years ago,' Brian said, managing a thin smile.

It had been a running joke between our parents—times when they were able to share a joke. About the hot tip Pops got on a Montana copper mine a few years after they married. 'We'd have a suite of rooms year-round at the Ritz,' Pops used to tell us, 'had your mother only handed over her egg money when I needed it!' The Ritz being the Ritz-Carlton Hotel, a quarter-mile or so west of our front door, nearly alongside the Common.

Frank McCann, one of his poker pals who worked maintenance there, gave Pops any 'New York Times Sunday Magazine' the chambermaids found in the rooms. We weren't a 'New York Times' household by any stretch, but Pops loved the Sunday crossword, and would work on it all week until he had it done or nearly. I was helping Pops with it by the time I reached high school, and have been mad keen on crosswords since. Two or three other nurses are as bad at the Home, and we share the 'Irish Times' puzzle at the table beside the kitchen which doubles as a nursing/tea station. I also gave Alice May, one of my favourite residents, the odd word as she did the same puzzle in her own copy of the 'Times'. A crossword is a good indicator of memory function in the elderly, and I used to tease her when she got stumped. 'Think, Alice May, think! You used that word twice only yesterday.'

I had forgotten to request vegetarian meals however, and so sat eating just the boiled carrots again on the flight back to Dublin. When Katy at age ten announced she was a vegetarian, I decided I was too, as it's easier to cook the one menu. But I'll still eat biscuits with gelatine, whereas Katy, now sixteen, scours labels like an Ayatollah looking for an apostate. Anyhow, carrots eaten, I took Pops out of the LL Bean bag Brian had given me and tucked him under the seat in front. Mahoney Jr had presented us the ashes in a heavy oak box, like a miniature casket, but when Brian mentioned I was taking them back to Ireland, he gave us a lighter metal urn instead. And oddly enough, though I lay hands on the dead from time to time at work, I wanted nothing to do with shifting Pops' ashes from box into urn. I had to ask Brian what they were like, however, once he had the job done.

'Sorta like beach sand, only grey.'

'Beach sand?'

'Yeah, a bit coarser maybe.'

'Like beach sand?' I repeated. 'Like Louise?'

'Louise?' Brian puzzled. Then smiled—as big a smile as I saw that week. 'Yeah, just like Louise.' The same Louise who expired at a tender age in a yarn Pops loved to tell, no matter how loudly we protested. The same Louise who had asked her heart-broken sweetheart to scatter her ashes along the beach, where he returns one evening to discover—and here Pops always broke into song — 'how every little breeze seems to whisper Louise!'

'They charge you extra for safe handling if you declare the ashes,' Mary O'Mara had advised, 'so just carry them on as hand luggage.' Mary, who along with Orla had advised on most of what needed doing before I flew to Boston, bar booking a meatless meal.

'Is there nothing you don't know, O'Mara?' I'd asked her at the Home that Saturday.

'We seemed to always have an uncle or aunt who died out in New York or Toronto on our mantel back in Listowel,' she replied. 'Waiting for the family plot to be opened the next time one of us died here at home.'

I kissed Brian goodbye at the Departures gate, showed my boarding pass to an official, then walked through the metal detector which I always think looks like a doorjamb awaiting a door. I didn't know what Airport Security would make of the X-rayed urn inside my bag as it trundled along the conveyor belt. Nor what I'd say if they queried me. Though probably not what I felt like saying—'Just give me Pops back, and I'll fuck off friendly.'

'Don't worry,' Brian had said, 'it'll just look like a flower vase full of cocaine'—which prompted me to slip Pops' death cert into the LL Bean bag, just in case. But the tired-looking black woman on a stool by the TV screen passed no comment, and I retrieved Pops before somebody's black leather attaché case trundling along on the belt behind could give him a knock.

'Sleep well,' I told him two hours later somewhere high above the Big Pond, before turning off our overhead lamp, though I knew sleep wouldn't come for me.

V

Life resumed in Dublin then, as if it ever pauses. Katy still abuzz with her new school year, and business as usual at the Home. Everything much as it had been, only I felt as if all my energy had vanished, leaving me less inclined towards life. The Noticeboard at the Home told its story:

DATE: 28 October 1987
WEATHER: Bright & Breezy
ACTIVITY: Exercise to music
WORDS FOR THE DAY: 'I saw old Autumn in the misty morn'

but my interior season felt more like winter—dull and dampened—no matter how brightly the sun shone. All activity cancelled due to lack of interest, any Thought for the Day too depressing to contemplate.

Katy and I went down to Wicklow the Saturday after I got back, but the morning sun playing on the golden, red and green-flecked foliage of a beech-lined road near Glendalough, with 'Ave Maria' playing on the car radio, looked—nay, felt—like all the sorrows of the world were somehow suspended there.

All part of the grieving process, I told myself, but sometimes what you <u>know</u> is f-all help with what you <u>feel</u>. Like your head and heart speak separate tongues altogether. I've always been capable of crying at the drop of a hat—over the silliest film or at Katy's school concerts, say. Apparently a matter of 'unexpressed grief' according to a magazine I once read—a sadness that you've seemingly never 'processed'—as if grief were a kind of cheese or dairy spread. But now my eyes filled up any time day or night. Simply waving Katy off to school was enough to set me off—as if each time she headed out the door were itself some kind of leave-taking.

Mornings were especially hard—awake but not wanting to get up, no different to half the old ones at the Home. 'Breakfast time!' Mary O'Mara coaxes those residents reluctant to rise. 'You don't want the bed to get a grip of you.' Telling us how her mother used to warn them of Biddy the Bed down in Kerry. 'Biddy Na Leaba who took to her bed at sixteen and stayed there till she died an old woman. The bed got a grip of her and that was that.'

'Did she never get up?' I asked.

'Only late at night my mother said, after the others had gone to bed.'

OK, Maeve the Mattress, I'd tell myself, you'd better shift so. And shift I would—get breakfast on, Katy out to school, and myself off to the Home. But it wasn't getting any easier, and Christmas coming up didn't help either. Certainly not my favourite time of year—not since Katy got big, anyhow. Too big to take to see Santa's Workshop in Clerys' window, or queue for Santy himself at Arnotts, where we once nipped into the loo afterwards for a pee, only to discover there wasn't any toilet paper. 'Never mind, Mama!' said Katy, all of five. 'We'll just jump up and down!'

'Will you get up and open your present, Mama?' K inquired when last Christmas finally arrived, the first since Pops died.

'Let me open my eyes first, Pet, then I'll get up.'

'That'll be as big a miracle as Jesus being born,' sniped Katy, making me laugh despite myself.

As did Nora Cricket at the Home on Stephen's Day. 'Sure, Christmas is as far away now as it ever was!' she informed me in the day-room, head cocked like a ninety-year-old robin. So sanguine is Nora always, which prompted Mary O'Mara to christen her after your man, Jiminy. Which helps distinguish her from our other Nora, Nora Doherty, even though Mary has most of us calling <u>her</u> Nora Doorstop, given her fondness for wandering off with same.

I was ambivalent about nicknames, which I felt ran counter to good nursing practice. It's hard enough to hang onto your dignity in a Home, though the staff would never use the names within earshot of the residents. But I hear them now more as a compassionate coping strategy for the sadness and frustration that comes with the nursing territory, rather than something which objectifies those in our care.

It was New Year's Day, however, that frightened me into doing something about myself. I always take down the tree on the 1st, the first of my New Year's resolutions effected, I suppose. I can't abide a Christmas tree up past its time—unlike Ma who'd leave ours up into February if she were low enough, branches drooping and needles carpeting the floor. Once I was old enough, I'd ask permission to strip it myself, unwind the lights and lift off the ornaments, taking especial care with the one red glass reindeer and the blue glass goose, my favourites. Afterwards Pops would take the tree out into the alley by our building to join four or five others in a mini-grove amid the trash cans.

I'd had to bribe Katy when she was little to let me take it down that early, but this year she lent me a hand, lifting a large silver ball which we'd hung well out of Nibbles' reach. 'I'm going to tell your future, Mama,' holding the globe up to my face.

'Don't,' I shook my head.

'Yes, Mama,' K insisted. 'Look into my crystal ball.'

'No, Katy, I don't want my future told.'

'I see a bright, new – '

'Oh stop, Katy!' I shouted. 'Just stop!' And, bursting into tears, I fled the room.

It'd be hard to say who was more stunned—but I felt just dreadful, never mind ashamed.

'I was only teasing, Mama,' Katy said, in tears herself, when I returned shortly to apologise.

'I know you were, Pet. I don't know what came over me.'

There's nothing worse than losing it with your child. Not your temper, though that's awful too, but losing control, not being able to act the adult. Though K's usually well able the odd time I prove too tired & emotional. 'Mama, you're simple!' she informed me two years ago when Seán and I broke up, and I'd gone out for milk, only to walk around Fairview Park and come back empty-handed.

And Katy was prepared to let me off easy again last New Year's Day. 'Que será, será, Mama?' she smiled. 'Like you used to sing to me?'

But the thought of those long-ago bedtimes, her tiny self tucked beneath the covers, utterly finished me. Sitting down beside the bloody tree, I proceeded to sob my heart out.

'It's all right, Mama,' Katy put her arms around me. 'It's all right.'

But it certainly wasn't all right—even as I assured K it was. For I could hear the anxiety in her voice, even as I struggled to mask it in mine. And that worry was what finally had me begin thinking about making a change. My mother's unhappiness may have burdened me, but I was determined Katy would not carry mine.

Of course, it was Sister Úna who later pointed out how it was coming up to Christmas that my own Ma had died.

VI

It was Mary O'Mara who got me to go see Sister Úna. After I finally confessed how miserable I was, in Gaffney's pub across from the Park, one afternoon after work. 'Miserable' because I hate 'depressed', which I guess I associate with my mother. And while I've had my miserable moments down the years—miserable stretches even—I prefer to think of it as 'melancholy'. Or 'melancholia' even, which has a nice 19th-century ring to it, far less clinical than depression. All of which I poured out to Mary after work.

'I don't want to start on Prozac either,' I said, blowing my nose.

'And lose your sex drive too?' Mary smiled. 'Certainly not!'

'Mine got mislaid aeons ago,' I said. 'But I don't want to take a pill to make me happier.' Which was a bit rich, I know, given all the tablets we dispense at the Home to keep the residents on the rails.

Mary told a story then—like Mary often does—of their neighbour Bridey who called into the house in Kerry the morning after they had buried Mary's mother. 'You'll be wanting these now,' Bridey announced, putting a blue glass bottle on the shelf over the range. And so Mary's father and her two grown brothers had sat around the kitchen, knocking back Valium with whiskey. 'Those tablets are

27

mighty stuff altogether,' her father told Bridey a few weeks later, handing her back the last of the vial.

I can't imagine now running the Home without Mary, and it's not just her Scorpio knack for organisation either. As it happened, Kitty O'Dea had lost her teeth yet again the morning Mary interviewed, and we were hunting for them everywhere. Worse yet, Nora Doorstop had joined the search, moving through the front rooms in tiny steps, like a run-down Eveready rabbit. It had been that mad for a few months, as we hadn't the right balance among the clientele. You want a proper mix of ambulatory and chair-bound for starters. Yet not too many among the mobile who want to get home to turn the oven off, or into town to meet the daughter who actually emigrated to Sydney twenty years ago. Or wanting to collect the mother like Constance Fitzgerald, or just walk into the sunset as Carmen Cassidy used threaten whenever she was low, though Carmen never gave a minute's trouble. Nor do you want too many either like Nora Doorstop, who perpetually motor around the place, unable to stay seated. Nor too many who need help eating, if you hope to get everybody fed. And enough able to get some of their clothes on or off, mornings and evenings, so you can help the others get up or into bed.

It's a tricky ratio to get right, and it was decidedly wrong around the time Mary started with us two years ago. I liked her immediately from the interview, a big, dark-haired woman of forty, with a soft Kerry accent and that fresh complexion some countrywomen manage to keep even after coming up to Dublin.

'You're American,' she said straight off, although I sometimes pass for Irish, given my red hair and over a dozen years in Dublin.

'Boston,' I agreed.

'"There goes the Boston Burglar!"' Mary lilted. Her father's favourite song, she explained, whenever he got merry.

I admired that, as singing a snatch of a song for a stranger—never mind at a job interview—is nothing I could do. Even if Pops was like that, both confident and full of musical bits. Anyhow, I was giving Mary a quick tour of the Home, when she pulled up short at the large fish tank in the hall. To admire its occupants, I thought, only Mary was pointing at the confetti-like coloured pebbles on the bottom. And there beside the plaster mermaid were Kitty's dentures, grinning up at us like a drowned Cheshire Cat.

That alone suggested just how good Mary might prove. As good as two nurses, forever anticipating and keeping track, so that things seemed to settle down from her first week on the job. But it was another month before I realised I'd taken on someone truly gifted, the afternoon she came out and told me Mildred Lacey was for death.

'Do you think so, Mary,' I said. 'Her blood pressure's down, and we got a good amount of water into her this morning.'

'I can smell it.'

'Sorry?'

'I can smell the death.'

To be honest, I didn't know what to say, but at handover that afternoon I remarked on how Mildred seemed that bit stronger. Her vital signs didn't change that evening either; yet Mary, who was working a double shift, called the family around ten and her son and daughter were at her bedside when Mildred died two hours later.

'A kind of musk,' Mary volunteered the next day when I finally asked about it. She didn't say more, nor did I ask for any, as that kind of thing generally unnerves me. Like the little girl Ma spied on the lobby stairs back on Park St, which spooks me yet.

We went for our first drink after work a few weeks later in Gaffney's. There Mary told how her mother had come to her in a dream the previous year, telling of the cruise she planned to take. 'I don't want to lose you.' Mary gave her a hug. 'Do you really want to take this trip?' 'We all have to take it the once,' her mother replied. 'And I must go it alone.' And so she had three days later, peacefully, asleep, in the full of her seeming health.

And it was in Gaffney's again last January that Mary mentioned a nun she knew who works as a counsellor and who, she said, was very good.

I liked the idea of a counsellor as I definitely didn't want to see a shrink. And I liked the idea of talking to another woman. But a nun?

'I don't think a nun's the answer,' I told Mary. 'Any more than Prozac or Valium cocktails.'

'Sister Úna,' Mary said. 'I'll give you her number tomorrow.'

She gave me the number too—only I didn't ring it for another two weeks. Seeking out someone to talk about myself just seemed too daunting. And Sister Úna being a religious made me even more apprehensive, the way you felt as a kid as you knelt waiting to confess. Even if it's years since I gave up Confession for a bad thing. More a collapsed than lapsed Catholic, though I still go to Mass the odd time, though never on a Sunday, which was another of Pops' favourite tunes. Anyhow, I'm long past believing in the Obligation & Sin stuff, even as I try to puzzle out exactly what I do believe. I did better when Katy was little, getting us out to Mass most Sundays. But then at breakfast two years ago Katy announced she was finished with the Church. 'Just don't broadcast that in religion class,' was all I said, as K set off in her convent-school blue-striped blazer and navy skirt. A smashing outfit really, far better than the white uniform I put on every day. Jim O'Connor, who owns the Home, suggested I wear a blue uniform when he made me Matron. But that felt like pulling rank, so I just said I preferred the white.

Anyhow, I was surprised to see Sister Úna herself in mufti—mauve tweed skirt and matching jacket—when she answered her door that first afternoon. No sign of Sister Amadeus's black habit or white-winged war bonnet which had me terrified my first week at the Holy Cross Grammar School back in Boston. A small woman in her late fifties, greying hair cropped short and kindly blue eyes behind rose-framed glasses, Sister Úna looked more like a librarian or piano teacher—apart from a tiny cross on her blouse. Moreover, she did teach once—psychology, not piano—at Maynooth and UCD both.

She'd a nice quiet manner, too, which made me want to relax, even if I couldn't. The PC, CD player, and bookcases in her study also felt like a million miles from the nuns with chalk who first taught me to read and write.

'Tell me a little about yourself, Maeve,' she said. 'Then tell me how you're doing.'

So I did. I told her of growing up the child of Irish immigrants in downtown Boston, the Super's daughter at No. 23. Of two childhood summers spent in Donegal, of getting through high school into college, of becoming pregnant with Katy the year I finished my nursing degree. Of how K and I came to Ireland just over two years later, living first in what had been a gardener's cottage on a large estate in Meath, where I nursed nights at Our Lady's Hospital in Navan. Of coming to Dublin then, the year after my mother Rose died of a heart attack at age fifty-five back in Boston. And of working here first as agency nurse, then at the Mater, before going into geriatric care. I even spoke a little about Eddie, Katy's father, and how I've had a couple of medium-term men in my life at several junctures since, but no truly long-term relationships. If I hurried that bit, Sister Úna looked comfortable enough. I told then of how I felt Katy had managed OK growing up fatherless in Ireland, and how much I loved her—even if it was sometimes like guerrilla warfare now she was in her teens. And, finally, of how my father had died almost five months before, and how I hadn't felt right since.

Which is why I was surprised when Sister Úna said, 'I wonder, Maeve, about your mother?' after we'd talked some more.

'My mother?' I said, wondering had she been truly listening.

'Yes, it's your father you've recently lost,' Sister Úna allowed, 'but sometimes a death summons up other unfinished business.'

At which there suddenly flashed onto the silver screen inside my head this scene from a Bergman film I'd seen back in college. A scene where Death in a hooded black robe plays chess with some poor mortal. Only Sister Úna's 'unfinished business' sounded more like Death rigged out in a pin-striped suit, like a banker, say, foreclosing on a mortgage.

'Maybe,' I conceded, 'but it's my father I'm missing so at the moment.'

To be honest, I thought Sister Úna miles off the mark, asking about Ma who was twelve years gone. And while I liked her, and found her easy to talk to, I doubt I'd have bothered to make another appointment—if she hadn't suggested the notebook.

'Do you want to try keeping one?'

'Like a diary?'

'Not exactly,' Sister Úna said. 'More like a jotter for anything you want to note down. About your father, or Boston growing up. Or how you're feeling on any given day?'

I must've looked worried then, because Sister Úna smiled. 'I wouldn't want to see it—it's a notebook for you alone.'

'Not a homework copy so,' I laughed.

'No, Maeve,' she smiled again. 'Not that kind of homework.'

Of course I'd no idea that afternoon of the part this notebook would play. How the opportunity to write it all down would make all the difference. Along with just the opportunity to write in itself. I must have known something, however, for I didn't pick up any old jotter at Reads on Nassau St the following day. Rather I splashed out on this large, lined journal with a lovely linen cover decorated with yellow fleur-de-lis. The kind of journal I'd often wished I had a reason to buy. I also treated myself to a Parker fountain pen and a fancy bottle of light blue ink. And finally a boxwood ruler with brass ends to draw a kind of Noticeboard heading for each entry. All of this cost nearly twenty pounds, which I hoped might make me actually sit down and write—if only to justify the expense.

I haven't written here in a couple of months. Just these final pages over the past few nights, an Afterword of sorts, which I'll probably tear out and slip in at the front. Although I'd like to write something else again—maybe later on? A story, perhaps. A proper story, I mean, seeing this notebook tells a kind of story. At least I believe it does, though I haven't read it over yet. But I probably owe it to myself to do that now.

PART I

CHAPTER 1

DATE: 25 January 1988
SEASON: Winter of Our Discontent
WEATHER: Cold & Overcast
ACTIVITY: Notebook Writing
THOUGHT FOR THE DAY: Sudden Prayers Make God Jump

Talking to myself in a notebook seems madness, but I'll give it a go this evening anyhow. 'What are you writing, Mama?' Katy asked as she headed upstairs with her homework after helping with the washing-up. 'Just something for work, Pet,' I fibbed, feeling as if I were back in school myself.

Where to begin is the obvious problem—apart from the Noticeboard above. I've often thought of hanging one here in our kitchen—with MOOD instead of WEATHER, and a line each for Katy, Nibbles and me. And maybe a WORD FOR THE DAY, like Miss Dewey did back in high school English class? The bit about God jumping has been knocking about in my head since I saw it in the loo in Gaffney's the afternoon Mary told me about Sister Úna, though I've resisted so far putting it up on the Noticeboard at work.

Graffiti would work well there all the same. I mean the good graffiti, not the dreadful stuff I saw once in Mulligan's, chancing a quick pee in the Gents' on account of the queue for the Ladies', while Orla waited outside to waylay any fella headed in. So awful I quickly stopped reading the inside door of the stall. Good graffiti I love however, the way it unexpectedly pops up, like a message out of the blue. Which is another of the zillion things you leave behind when you're old and out of circulation in a Home. OK, you mightn't hear the residents reminiscing about graffiti, but something like 'I'd Give My Right Arm to Be Ambidextrous' would surely brighten their day more than 'Early to Bed & Early to Rise' from our 'Book of 1,000 Inspirations'. Anyway, I didn't want to begin here with just the date, like in the diaries I kept off & on growing up. Marked with dire warnings to brother Brian: 'PERSONAL DIARY OF MAEVE MAGUIRE. If you read this, you'll feel tremendous guilt!!'

Where to begin so? 'Set the scene!' Miss Dewey always insisted when she assigned a descriptive essay. 'Paint the reader a picture.' So the lobby probably makes the most sense—even if I'm the only reader. To begin at the ground floor as it were: the lobby of 23 Park St with its white-and-black tiled floor, dark walnut wall panels, and three hanging lamps. The same floor my father swept daily, scattering what looked like green sawdust, only oily to touch and smelling like pine and paraffin, in front of his push broom. I recently came across the word for that tiled pattern—'tessellation'—and wondered did Pops know it, as he too was keen for an unusual word. Like the one I found on a scrap of paper behind our building at age six. Part of a seed packet, only I hadn't known that.

'Chrysanthemum,' Ma laughed when I showed her it.

'You'd make a cat smile, so you would.'

I probably pointed out cats couldn't, being ever so earnest at that age. But it's nice to have a memory of Ma laughing all the same. And I often remember it, given how often bunches of Mums come into the Home.

Our apartment was just off that lobby with its tessellated floor. A two-bedroom unit, the larger of which Brian and I shared until he turned seven and Pops partitioned it in half. Like the Berlin Wall, Pops joked, though that was lost on me. We each had a window onto the backyard with its clothesline and storage sheds, behind which rose another row of high-rise buildings. The front apartments that overlooked the Common had the superior view, but the Super's family would hardly have been allotted one of those.

The six granite steps at the front of the building weren't a real stoop—that is, no tenants sat there in summer sipping a beer, and Brian and I were not allowed to hang out there either. Had we lived in an actual neighbourhood, those steps might have served as a kind of front porch, but our downtown location and the gentility of our residents ruled that out.

Staying off the front steps was all part of being the Super's kids. Staying off the apartment elevator was too, but not making noise absolutely headed the list of prohibitions. 'Keep your noise down!' was a favourite mantra of Ma's. 'Keep your noise down!'—which we generally did, certainly never making as much noise as Ma the year she went mad for the second time, and took out both living-room windows with her sweeping brush, the panes of glass as they shattered echoing yet.

'Do you want your father to lose his job?' Ma sometimes added to her stricture about noise. And what would happen after he lost his job didn't bear thinking about.

I was something of a scaredy-cat growing up, worrying about atomic bombs and polio, never mind the darker dark inside our bedroom closet at night. Or the Blessed Virgin who liked to pop up when you were alone, as Sister Amadeus said had happened to St Bernadette. Or the toilet snake that Manny, Pops' helper, talked about, until Brian informed me, "It's a tool, Stupid, not a reptile!" Or the terror of tsunamis, though like 'tessellation' I didn't have that word yet. Just a morbid fear of tidal waves that I got from God knows where.

I was also terrified of our elevator after I overheard Pops telling his poker pals about the cadaver dressed up in a hired tuxedo which a couple of final-year med students had left propped up for him inside the elevator one night at the Harvard Medical School, where he moonlighted for a time as night watchman. I didn't dream of the living dead that night, but I wasn't able to go near our own elevator for months after.

The nightmare that did plague me back then was a far more abstract affair: a black background with a little white fence, like linked croquet-hoops, which marked off a rectangular garden-like plot with a few red and blue flowers. A white fridge door then floated up from the black, before it opened onto a close-up shot of cogs and wheels, like giant clockwork gears. By this time I'd be terrified, sobbing aloud, which would bring Pops from my parents' bedroom. Years later I recognised something of that dream in a Paul Klee painting—a black field with stylised coloured flowers. But only now do I see how it was almost always my father who arrived to comfort me.

The thought of Pops' losing his job no doubt helped us keep our noise down. Both our parents were immigrants after all, Irish who had known a kind of poverty. And some of that reality—that you can be without work, without prospects, without a full larder—was handed down, I think, to us growing up. Like the Saturday morning walking back from Haymarket Square when Brian threw a half-eaten apple into the gutter, and Pops snapped, 'You'll follow the crows some day for that!'

Which isn't to say our parents were anyways mean. Frugal surely, but in fairness there was never a surplus of cash to hand. Ma also worked part-time as a poorly paid clerk at Jordan Marsh department store. We had the apartment rent-free, but we still paid for utilities, which meant Pops never left a room without turning out a light. Which, who knows, might explain why Brian keeps every light in his house on—or so it seemed last September—as if a police interrogation were underway in every room. We weren't allowed pets either, which in turn might explain why, like Katy, I absolutely dote on Nibbles. I was given two goldfish once, after weeks of pleading for a parakeet, but after finding them belly-up in the bowl one morning I didn't bother going back to Woolworth's for a refill. Small wonder brother Brian has settled for a lava lamp—a light he can keep on and a blobby pet he doesn't have to feed.

Being kids, we sometimes chanced hanging off the iron railings on the front steps. Or if Pops were out and Ma occupied, we might play 'Jordan Marsh' in the elevator, once I got over my fear of that tuxedoed ghoul. Taking turns as the elevator attendant, who called out the various floors—Ladies' Wear or Men's Fashion—as the other got on and off to shop. We couldn't play Jordan's for long however, lest one of the crankier tenants should end up waiting on the elevator, and subsequently complain to Pops.

Well, that's enough scene-setting for one evening. Especially as I don't really see any point to this at all. Besides, I've my ironing to do, Katy's French to review, and 'Captain Corelli's Mandolin' awaiting me upstairs. So, goodnight, Notebook, as I used tell my Diary, and don't take it personally if I never come back.

CHAPTER 2

DATE: 29 January 1988
WEATHER: Frost on the North Side of Hills
ACTIVITY: Unblocking the Toilet
THOUGHT FOR THE DAY: Go With the Flow

Well, today was my second appointment with Sister Úna, about which I'll fill a page or two here, before I throw my hat at the whole affair. I expected her to ask about growing up in Boston, but she wanted instead to hear about my life in Dublin and my work at the Home. Don't talk to me about the Home, I felt like saying, given the day we'd had there—a day which started with the arrival of a new resident, which you always want to go well. Alice May Murphy from just down the road in Killester. Only I'd forgotten to ask Leo Healy, our porter, to come in early to help with Alice May's things for her room, one of three singles in the new wing.

It took me six months as Matron to persuade Jim O'Connor, the owner, to allow a resident bring in a favourite chair, or hang a favourite picture on the wall. A few personal belongings help make a room look less like a hospital or Holiday Inn, and a few nail holes aren't

43

anything a dab of Polyfill won't fix for the next occupant. Being a Super's daughter only helps on this job, and Leo the Porter just laughs when I ask him to put a drop of oil on a squeaky door-hinge which he has yet to hear.

After Leo finally gets Alice May's few pieces, including two cartons of books, into her room, I ask Fiona Flynn to make the usual inventory list against any lost-property claims. I also know Fiona will do her best to help Alice May settle in, whereas Nurse Powers, who is also on, merely ticks off knickers and nighties like you were coming into a refugee camp, not a Home.

Leo the Porter then discovers a toilet overflowing in the new wing, into which Kitty the Conductor has successfully stuffed three or four Kango pads. I leave Leo to sort that, so I can ring Mrs. Sheehan at the Nursing Agency to send us somebody for Polish Petra who's called in sick again. Meanwhile Germany Calling is up in arms, insisting the Pakistani boy had snuck into her room again last night, and was rooting through her bedside drawers.

'Who was it, Gemma?' I ask.

'That Pakistani, or Indian, Muhammadan—whatever he is!'

'Can you describe him?'

'What do you mean—"describe him"?' Gemma snaps. 'You know who I mean! The little darky who's always sneaking around with a white towel on his head.'

'Gemma is playing Hide & Go Sikh again,' I warn Mary O'Mara, before I tell Rosie the Agency Nurse which residents still need to get dressed before we've a full-scale mutiny on our hands. I like Polish Petra, but as this is the third time she's been out sick this month, we're going to have a little talk.

I don't tell Sister Úna any of this of course—just set the

scene for her with a general description of the Home and its clientele. Formerly three separate terraced houses, the Home sits on a quiet Fairview road just back from Dublin Bay. Rowan trees at the front with bright red berries in summer, and a large garden at the back, above which the DART runs on its embankment. A small office with a reception counter sits just inside the front door; to the left are two bedrooms which serve as a sick bay, and to the right two large adjoining day-rooms. At the back is a large two-storey extension Jim built five years ago, a year before I arrived as a staff nurse, with bedrooms on both floors, plus a kitchen and dining room downstairs, and a third day-room which opens onto the garden.

The new day-room with its cathedral ceiling is my favourite part of the house, not counting the garden. Tall corner-windows flood the room with sunlight on good days, and there's a TV on one wall, and the large Noticeboard opposite. I know the Noticeboard is a help to the residents, but I also feel its insistence on a single reality can be overdone. Like last week, when I heard one of our younger Care Assistants, Clodagh Corcoran, quizzing Kitty the Conductor.

'What day is it, Kitty?'

'Monday.'

'No, Friday, Kitty. And what month is it?'

'August.'

'No, it's January.'

'January,' repeated Kitty.

'And what's next month?'

'April.'

'No, Kitty. It's three months till April.'

'That crazy young wan says it's three months till April,' I overheard Kitty telling Nora Doorstop afterwards. 'And it's the Queen of the May after that!'

'Don't annoy yourself or Kitty,' I tell Clodagh later. 'What odds to her if it's Friday or Monday?'

What odds to Germany Gemma either, who has Hindus going through her handbag one day, and the IRA plotting beneath her bed the next. I'm terribly fond of Gemma, even if she's a handful-and-a-half. A small, frail woman who won't use a walker, no way! Her head is full of palace coups, but at least she's engaged—albeit in a world with its own Noticeboard:

DATE: 12th of Never

SEASON: Plague and Pestilence

WEATHER: Sturm und Drang

ACTIVITY: Mayhem & Murder

THOUGHT FOR THE DAY: Ready, Take Aim, Fire!

Still you sometimes encounter an impossible patient whom you can handle more easily than others. Like Mrs. DeCosta at MGH in Boston, my first year nursing, whose petulant neediness drove the rest of the staff crazy. 'Nurse, I have to pee!' Then 'Oh Nurse, I can't pee!' once they got her to a commode. Then 'Whoosh!' all over the sheets as soon as they got her back in bed. And here at the Home it's Gemma with whom I have the knack most days, for all her intrigues and paranoia. Meantime, another nurse is doing the same with a patient who drives you spare. Like the way Mary O'Mara manages Kitty the Conductor whom I'll confess I christened as such—after her habit of hollering 'Choo-Choo on the Track!' whenever the Angelus sounds on telly or radio. The same Kitty who called me 'a big piss-pot' just yesterday, throwing in 'You big shite, you!' for good measure. Or the way Fiona Flynn handles Nora Doorstop, who I can rarely get to settle. And the opposite is sometimes true, too. A special client who gives you something back, a sense of kinship or an insight into yourself, as if they've somehow turned up just for you.

Of course Gemma, Kitty and the two Noras are only four of our forty current occupants: thirty-six females and four males. About half are originally from the country— like Tom the Teacher—who came up to Dublin to work, rear families, grow old, wear out. Occasionally we get somebody who ventured farther afield, like our newcomer Alice May, who yesterday told me she was thirty years in America before returning to Dublin. Or Germany Gemma who was in London during the War, and where, judging from her current Pakistani pal, she appears to be hanging out yet. Anyhow, as nursing homes go, we're certainly not the worst. Nobody here would choose to end their days with us, of course, but that's life for you.

'You enjoy your work?' Sister Úna asked this evening.

'I do,' I said. And I honestly do. I sometimes miss the clinical aspects of a hospital ward, but you get more of a chance here with those you nurse. Most of whom will be there the next morning, please God, whereas it's like conveyor beds on a hospital floor. And while it's not easy for them, most of our residents are troupers, giving it their best. Simply endeavouring to endure, to see a life out, a life in many senses already largely lived. 'The staff are mostly great,' I told Sister Úna, 'and we have a laugh most days.'

Besides, I was on a fast track to nowhere as a hospital nurse. Having trained in the States felt like two strikes against me when I came over. And a university degree on top of that made me at best suspect among those charge nurses it didn't absolutely threaten, while being an unwed mother put paid to my chances with more than one. Plus shift-work can be brutal, especially now there's a shortage of nurses and the wards are all understaffed. In any event, I began to see hospital nursing for what it truly is—a younger woman's game. And so I interviewed at the Home where Jim, impressed by my BSN, hired me as a staff nurse, then appointed me Matron two years on.

Nursing, be it in Boston or Dublin, is largely the same drill, though the different terminology sat oddly at first. Casualty for Emergency, roster for schedule, or different proprietary names for meds—like Stadol for Toradol. Or Matron instead of Charge Nurse, suggesting a bigger bust than I've ever boasted. Ward Sister was another that took getting used to, as Sister in Boston always signified a nun. Like Sister Amadeus or Sister Teresa back at Holy Cross Grammar School.

'Thank you, Sister Úna,' I said this afternoon when our session ended. Thanks for listening, I suppose, as I'm damned if I know what good this is doing.

'How is the notebook going?'

'Shaping up to be a bestseller,' I laughed ruefully.

'Next Wednesday so, Maeve?' Sister Úna smiled.

CHAPTER 3

DATE: 31 January 1988
LONG-RANGE FORECAST: Same As It Ever Was
ACTIVITY: Self-Pity
THOUGHT FOR THE DAY: A Good Man Is Hard to Find

Of course there's a large part of my life in Dublin I can't share with Sister Úna, easy as she's proving to talk to. More a missing part of my life—the fact I'm living on my own. Well, not on my own—as I've Katy, the love of my life. But there's no man in the picture anywhere. I don't really want one under our roof, where Katy, Nibbles and I are fairly set in our ways. Nor have I ever had a live-in lover since Katy was born. But still I'd fancy a fella in my life.

It's not something I constantly think about, not like men who reportedly think of sex every seven minutes. And about their relationships every seven months. But I still feel the lack at the oddest times, like today when Clodagh Corcoran linked both Tom the Teacher and Happy-As by the arm on their way to dinner. 'I want two fellas,' she smiled at them. 'What's wrong with that?' Clodagh who is so sweet she deserves a dozen fellas queuing up. Her lovely brown curls, and the buckets of confidence so many young girls seem to have these days. Yet something in that exchange had me suddenly longing for just one fella, though he'd want to be at least half Tom's or Larry's age.

It's not the kind of thing you can explain to a nun, however. Too much like telling a vegetarian you could murder a rasher sandwich. I've Orla and Mary O'Mara of course, whom I can talk with when the man-thing truly has me down. But that's the point, I guess. That being on my own does get me down.

I did mention Eddie—Katy's father—the first session we had. How I'd realised marrying him would be a huge mistake, so I broke it off, two months pregnant and all. But Eddie was the only fella I really mentioned. Not that there've been legions in the sixteen years since. Nobody my last two years in Boston, and just Peter the Landlord up in Meath, my second year in Ireland. And only Seán as far as real relationships here in Dublin go, as opposed to flings, which number two or three. Though I'd prefer to forget—not tally—those.

It's over two years now since Seán went out to Saudi. We were together for three years before that, as in sleeping together. Though only at his flat, and never sleeping over, as I always made it home to Katy and the baby-sitter.

I get frightened sometimes when I realise it's been two years since Seán. Frightened to think this might be the way it's going to stay? While Katy, who celebrated her Sweet Sixteenth three weeks ago, is heading in the other direction. She's not boy-crazy yet—and I doubt she'll lose her head that way. Too much a Capricorn, cautious and choosy both. Nor overly interested yet—or so she professes. Not interested in any of the local talent, that is—as opposed to whatever film star is flavour of the month. Or maybe she takes that line out of respect to her old-maid mother? Still, she always quotes my Aunt Chrissie if I ask her about a beau: 'Men is worms,' she reminds me—as if I've reared a real man-hater. Which isn't so of course. A feminist hopefully, but what other kind of daughter could you possibly raise? Yet I fear it's going to feel a bit painful when the lads do start calling round.

What hurts already is feeling I've forgotten how to get a fella. As if I've actually forgotten the moves. Like yesterday afternoon, when I was waiting on Orla for a coffee in Bewley's on Westmoreland St, before I headed back home to get the dinner on. There was a nice-looking guy at the next table—blue eyes, fair hair just starting to go grey. I'd first noticed him wiping some crumbs off his jumper, thinking there was something nice in how he did it, not too fastidious, just taking care. A few minutes later he asked to borrow my paper for the cinema listings. It should've been easy then to exchange a few words at least, but I couldn't even manage that.

What's worse, I can't most times be bothered to figure out the next move. As if I haven't the energy for it all. And if I were looking for the unrivalled Mr. Right, how likely is he to surface in a pub or coffee shop? Although there's more chance of that, I guess, than his turning up at work. Unless Bertha the Bag has a smashing son in the French Resistance, sallow-skinned with a dark beret and bedroom eyes. If Bertha's truly a partisan, that is. Germany Gemma of course swears she is, whispering to me about the military intelligence Bertha keeps in a notebook inside her bag. You might well wonder what's in that bag, the way Bertha worries over it, but I doubt it's to do with covert operations. Nor do I really believe in a Mr. Right, even if Bertha had a son, which she hasn't. Nor am I keeping an eye out for a Mr. OK, either. It's just that being on my own seems to weigh more since Pops checked out.

I write here more like I'm telling a story than making notations—notes in a notebook. 'Notes on a Life' by Maeve Maguire—is that what I should call these pages?

CHAPTER 4

DATE: 2 February 1988
SEASON: Spring—In Ireland Anyhow
WEATHER: Bloody Freezing
TAUNT FOR THE DAY: Ding-a-Ling-a-Ling, Your Hair's on Fire!

I finally got a chance to chat with Alice May this morning, whose pictures, reading chair, floor lamp, and small bookcase have nicely transformed her room. I'm keen to see her books, but don't want to be too familiar too soon, so I admired her pictures instead. One, a desert water-colour by Georgia O'Keefe, I really liked. Alice May said it reminds her of the countryside around Tucson, Arizona, where the brother she used to visit still lives. I don't look for a life story in one go, but I learned that much today. Plus how she herself lived for years in St Louis—like Arizona, another part of America I don't know at all.

We also talked about the Home: whether she's warm enough at night, and is there anything she absolutely hates to eat? We get a lot of complaints about the food, but there's no winning really, given the taste buds for sweet and salty are what atrophy first, while those for sour and bitter at the back of the tongue function well into old age.

However Alice May said she wasn't a bit fussy about her food. Something in the way she said it too reminded me of Ma—the way she tossed her head maybe, because she looks nothing like Ma at all.

Anyhow she seems to have settled in well, even if it's early days. If anything, she seems a bit too fit for us: very steady on her feet, and all her wits about her. Certainly her reasons for coming into care are not as readily apparent as with, say, Constance Fitzgerald, constantly seeking her mother, or Kitty the Conductor, who mistook a storage heater at home for her bed, and sat on it long enough to badly burn her bottom. Or poor Nora Doorstop who asks her daughter nearly every visit, 'Tell me who I am?' Or Happy-As Ferguson who was giving out at home about the lodgers he imagined were living in his attic. 'I want them out by spring!' he used to holler at his wife.

Today's the first day of spring in Ireland, seven weeks earlier than it arrives in Boston. Certainly the flowers come on earlier here—the first of the daffodils across the road in Fairview Park preparing to toss their sprightly heads by the end of the month, even if my heart won't dance with them. A poem Miss Delaney drummed into us back in seventh grade, same as Katy learned it here. My daffs on the Boston Common and hers in Fairview Park.

Whatever the date, today is fiercely bitter, and spring won't really begin to feel like spring for another two months. New England weather is notoriously changeable, but even New England spoils you for what passes as spring here. As for summer, I still like the one about the Irish farmer asked by a tourist what the summer had been like? 'I don't know,' says the farmer, 'as I was shaving at the time.'

Today is also St. Brigid's Feast Day. A lot of the Boston-

Irish girls back in seventh grade chose Brigid for their Confirmation name. But I took Maria, brainwashed by 'West Side Story' and 'The Sound of Music' both. Plus I liked the alliteration—Maeve Maria Maguire—and briefly took to signing myself as M^3 after Miss Normile introduced us to the power of three in ninth grade. Certainly I wasn't interested in making myself any more Irish than I already was. Maeve Maguire plus my ginger mop did the job nicely, thanks very much. 'Maeve, Maeve, will ya be my slave?' as Richie Traynor used to shout in the schoolyard. When he wasn't hollering 'Red, Red, Wet the Bed! Wiped It Up With Gingerbread!'

'Why'd you have to give me such a stupid name?' I'd reproach Ma, saving my tears until I got home. Though my parents at least spared me its other spellings: Maev, Medb, Medbh, or Meadhbh, God help her. Even so, nobody in America could take the name down over the phone or decipher it as written. A Maeve by any other name would spell far sweeter, I used to think, nor can it be turned into something else, like the Rose that Ma had made of her own Róisín.

For that matter, I could have blamed Ma for my red hair too. I didn't however, just wished I'd got her lovely shade of chestnut. 'Donn dearg' in Irish, according to Katy of all folk, who inherited it herself. Of course I'd have had to blame Pops too, who contributed a recessive gene from some ginger-haired Mayo Maguire. It took me years anyhow to make peace with my hair. What I hated most was the attention it drew, the way total strangers might remark upon it in a shop, patting me on the head. Or the way teachers invariably commented on it the first day of school each year, making me want to disappear under my desk.

So making myself even more Irish via the Sacrament of Confirmation was not what I wanted at age twelve. The same age at which everything about your parents begins to mortify you. Like their accents which I suddenly found excruciating, as if they had only recently acquired a West of Ireland twang. Boston has a great reputation as an Irish-American city, but that wasn't our experience growing up. Had we lived in South Boston, Jamaica Plain or West Roxbury—before the Boston-Irish fled them for towns like Milton and Weymouth—me and my head of red curls might have felt more at home.

Instead a feeling of not quite fitting in flavoured our childhood—the Super's kids—to be seen, not heard—and not to be seen either playing on the front steps or in the elevator. It must have felt the same for Brian although, like so much else, we never really talked of it. We were not hugely close as kids, apart from a couple of years when I was eight and nine. I idolised him of course, if only because he was two years older. And we certainly played together—by default, there being only two other children briefly in the building. Alison, a year or so older, whom I never really liked—even before she told me that her mother paid her to play with me. There was also her brother Paul, around Brian's age, but he and Alison only lived at No. 23 for six months or so. After I turned eight, I was allowed to join Brian playing on the Common, where we met a few other children on the slide and swings. Presumably they lived downtown too, though like Alison and Paul most likely attached to families only passing through, for they always disappeared before any real friendship had a chance.

In bad weather, however, we played indoors like kids do. Inside Apt 1A, or sometimes chancing a quiet game further afield, as our large lobby, elevator, marble stairs, and six floors offered more scope than a three-storey tenement. More scope, but nothing as exotic as Eloise enjoyed. Eloise who lived on the top floor of the Plaza Hotel in a picture book I brought home from the library more than once. Eloise who roamed her hotel from top to bottom, getting up to mischief wherever she went. That's what I envied her most—not living in a hotel or that she got to keep pets, a dog and a turtle—but the fact she was bold. That she raised hell in her innocent way, and didn't care.

Had I remembered, I'd have read 'Eloise' to Katy when she was little. Not that Katy especially needed an Eloise to emulate. Not my Katy, who was allowed make as much noise indoors as she wanted, or nearly. Katy who came in from playing one summer evening at age six, bubbling her delight over one of the other girls, a few years older, out on the road.

'You like Liz Kelly?' I asked.

'Oh, yes, Mama!' K enthused.

'And why is that, Precious?'

'Cuz she's not a bit ladyish. She's loud, and she threatens people!'

By no means, though, did Brian and I spend all our time at home. There was school: the nuns at Holy Cross until third grade, and John Adams Grammar School on Arlington St after that. I was fairly terrified of the nuns at Holy Cross, apart from Sister Anastasia in second grade, who had a lovely smile and used divide us into two lines either side of the classroom for a spelling bee. We hadn't words much bigger than c-a-t or d-o-g, which Sister had us learn by rote. Bobby Nixon who sat next to me had no trouble memorising, only he was clueless about phonetics. 'P-e-a-s!' he'd chant. 'P-e-a-s spells pigs!'

Sister Anastasia would just smile and correct Bobby,

whereas Sister Amadeus would've sorted him out proper. Like she had the Casey twins, Maura and Clare, in first grade for talking: buttoning them into their winter coats, then hanging them from two hooks in the cloakroom. And Donna Donovan, whom she locked in the supplies closet, whereupon Donna promptly wet her pants.

In third grade I got Sister Amadeus again. Most parents only gave out if you got in trouble at school but, after spotting my tears one October afternoon, Pops sat me at the kitchen table until I told him all. There wasn't much to tell—only how I loved the sweet pungent smell off the mimeo sheets Sister Amadeus handed out, something like alcohol or aftershave in the duplicating fluid which left the paper slightly damp. And how I'd had a math worksheet pressed to my face, inhaling deeply, when Sister caught me a vicious clip on the ear.

Two days later Pops had Brian and me out of Holy Cross and enrolled in John Adams. That caused a row at home, but Pops stuck to his guns. 'That kind of bulldozing is over,' he told Ma. Well, I don't remember exactly what else he said, but 'bulldozing' was his favourite word for any abuse of power by Church or State. He was a devout Catholic, but with a strong anti-clerical streak, and the bulldozing probably harked back to his own youth in Mayo. If so, I never thought to ask him about it in later years, nor do I remember hearing anything about the Church in Mayo, apart from his disgust at how the priest always read out the amount each family gave in the Annual Collection.

In fact I don't recall Pops ever saying much about Mayo. Just him shaking his head when I asked once whether he missed Ireland.

'How come?' I persisted.

'When you're marching, you're not fighting,' he offered.

I puzzled that one for ages, until the 1970s when it suddenly came back to me as I stared at the BE HERE NOW banner at my weekly Zen group in a loft on Boylston St. Come to think of it, a number of Pops' sayings were not unlike Zen koans. Nothing as far out as 'the sound of one hand clapping', but word riddles in their own way. ''Twas walking quickly lost the ducks,' he often remarked, 'and time enough that found them.' Or 'The less you spend, the more you win, the day you lose' which I puzzled over for hours.

Of course there was so much more I might've asked— about Ireland or himself—all the things you only think of asking when it's too late. As if there's always time enough, to find the ducks and whatever else.

CHAPTER 5

DATE: 6 February 1988

ACTIVITY: Hibernation

WEATHER: Grey With Drizzle

THOUGHT FOR THE DAY: See You in the Spring,
When the Bed Gives Way

I'm not long up, as the bed got a fierce grip on me this morning. It didn't help that today's an evening shift, which I do every fortnight—to keep an eye on how things are ticking over nocturnally at the Home. At the same time, it's not natural to get up mornings in the dark, even if you're not feeling down. Which is why our Palaeolithic forebears slept twelve hours in winter—precisely what our post-industrial bodies still crave this time of year. It's written in the DNA, so it is—Do Not Disturb Till Noon. You seldom saw signs of a fire lit in a neighbour's house in Kerry before ten o'clock, Mary O'Mara says, unless there were kids to get out to school. That said, her mother felt the bed was a dangerous place—winter or summer: 'Were you to spend a week in bed, you wouldn't be fit to leave.' Like Biddy the Bed, who took a notion, then took to her bed.

I only lay on for an hour so. Fit to finally rise but no ways fit for life—or so it feels this weather. Too weary for the bloody struggle. Hearing Katy below at her breakfast made me feel guilty at not being up to see her off and finally shifted me. Indeed when I dare stare directly into the darkness, I see K is the only reason I have for keeping on, for not checking out myself. I get out of bed, put on the same clothes I took off last night, though what I really want is the T-shirt Eamon Kerr had on yesterday: WHEN IN ROME, PUT UP WITH IT. Except the grey dullness inside, that interior winter, feels more a kind of Hell than Rome.

'You have to attend to what you're feeling, Maeve,' Sister Úna tells me. 'You can't just sweep it aside, or sideline it with work.' Well, here it is for the record: I don't feel like I'm able for it anymore. Filling pages about how I fitted in, or didn't fit in, back in Boston—when I haven't even the energy for the Here & Now. Never mind trying not to worry whether it's maybe twice writ in my DNA— the inability to get out of bed—seeing it was sometimes afternoon before Rose rose when she too was lower than low.

CHAPTER 6

DATE: 10 February 1988
WORD FOR THE DAY: Xenophobia
ACTIVITY: Tank-Spotting
THOUGHT FOR THE DAY: Send Lawyers, Guns and Money

The Here & Now of Gemma Dunne meantime is truly something else. Like a perpetual State of Emergency which had her on sentry-duty at cockcrow this morning. In the front day-room where Nurse Ethel Lyons found her slipper-less in her nightie, her walking stick across her knees like a loaded musket.

'Did you hear the traffic all last night?' she inquired as Nurse Ethel walked her back to her room. 'I couldn't shut my eyes.'

'The traffic is desperate,' Ethel agreed. 'And not just at rush hour.'

'I'm not talking about that traffic!' snapped Gemma. 'This was military traffic. Heavy trucks and tanks.'

'She was on about the invasion all morning,' Nurse Ethel told me. 'Asking Bertha the Bag if she'd had any warning from her pals in the Resistance.'

'Are we winning or losing?' I laughed, invading Germans

being a change from thieving Pakistanis anyhow. Xenophobia with a historical subtext.

Xenophobia came up recently in the 'Times' crossword too, but it was only this afternoon I suddenly thought of Manny at No. 23, forever complaining about the Dutch elm beetle or the Norway rat—as if those countries were personally responsible for their respective pests. Manny who showed up every few weeks to give my father a hand with the heavier tasks. Like stripping the wax on the hall floors, or painting a vacated apartment before new tenants took possession. Stocky, swarthy Manny was a few years older than Pops, bald but for a few wispy grey curls above his ears. I don't remember his last name—if I knew it—but he looked like he hailed from somewhere on the Mediterranean, Greek or Sicilian maybe? He had a Mediterranean temperament anyhow—voluble and volatile—and often cursed in front of Brian and me, which always gave me a thrill. 'I'm like horseshit,' he'd mutter going up and down the stairs. 'All over the place.'

Manny also periodically fumigated against cockroaches. Decked out in a pair of yellow goggles with a spray-tank strapped to his back, he looked like a deep-sea diver selling door-to-door. 'It's the Bug Man!' he'd announce in his high-pitched voice, rapping on each apartment door with the spray-gun nozzle, before letting himself in with Pops' master key.

Whatever his own ethnicity, Manny was 100% American and 100% certain about the source of most of America's ills. The Asian flu and Japanese beetle spoke for themselves, but not everybody knew the rats around Boston were mostly Norway rats. He knew his stuff, too, telling Brian how the Norway rat actually came from Central Asia. 'Only it must have jumped onto a Norwegian ship.'

'That's bullshit,' he corrected Brian once, who had claimed Pops' poker-pal Mike Sullivan had to carry a rifle against the humongous rats in the MTA tunnels near North Station. 'Sewer rats don't run much over two pounds.' Nor did the German cockroach, its proper name, grow to any great size in Boston either. Thanks to Manny, I also knew silverfish were primarily starch-eaters which thrive on the seizing in book-bindings and cardboard boxes. 'You mean a silverfish,' I informed my friend Vivian Henry, who had taken to calling me a bookworm.

Full of such facts I was—how roaches take comfort in clutter, and can go forever on no food.

'They live off their own,' Manny explained.

'You mean they're cannibals!' I asked.

'Let's just say they don't waste food.'

There was little Manny didn't know about rats or roaches, and he shared it all with us. What's worse, I still recall most of it. How the warfarin we dispense at the Home as an anti-coagulant is also the active ingredient in rat poison. How a cockroach who loses its head can survive for nine days before it starves to death. Or how the cockroach evolved sooner than most fauna, which makes them among the oldest creatures on earth. 'You remind your daddy to call me in three weeks,' Manny would say, as he sprayed the walnut baseboards in the lobby. 'Three weeks is the hatching cycle for cockroach eggs.'

Brian also tagged after Manny, who told how posh Beacon Hill, just a few blocks from us, had more rats per square foot than many poorer neighbourhoods, including Mattapan where Manny lived. Ma didn't mind either if we hung around Manny, who was one of the few folk she seemed easy with. Still B got into trouble at supper one night, after he informed us that roaches are mostly what a rat eats.

'That'll do, Brian,' Ma said.

'Manny told me a neat way to kill a rat,' B persisted. 'Feed it Coca-Cola!'

'Why for?' I asked, already annoyed at Brian who had spent the afternoon watching Manny paint the iron railings out front, while I got to help Ma sort the laundry.

'It dies,' Brian said, 'cuz it can't burp!'—which saw Ma send him from the table.

B got into trouble another time after Manny spotted him opening the lobby mailboxes, à la the Hardy Boys, with one of my bobby pins. All Brian wanted to do was inspect everybody's post before replacing it, but Manny must have had a quiet word with Pops. The first Brian knew of it, however, was the next evening when Officer Feeney knocked at our apartment.

'You're wanted in the living room,' Ma told Brian, who was doing his homework at the kitchen table.

'Is Brian in trouble?' I blurted, but Ma merely shushed me.

Heretofore Feeney had been the friendly face of the law, a pal of Pops whose beat included our end of the Common. Pops only wanted to throw a fright into Brian, but Feeney's recitation of a Federal statute on interfering with the US mails had me quietly sobbing in the kitchen, until Ma said, 'Snap out of it, Maeve.'

It's not that Ma was callous or cruel—more that she lacked the patience—that plus something else, some kind of maternal wherewithal, with which to handle my fears and neediness. Which is why it was generally Pops who appeared when I awoke from my black nightmare with the white fridge door. Or Pops who, often as not, tucked Brian and me in when we were small. 'Meet you under the apple tree!' his parting words as he turned out the light. 'Nobody needs three parents!' I sometimes rebuked B when he ordered me around, but in truth it sometimes felt like we'd only the one full-time on the job ourselves.

Yet what mother can possibly have patience all the time, as I know full well now? Certainly not I, and certainly not the night Katy—all of four—lay sobbing her heart out over some gargantuan injustice.

'You need to stop that now,' I barked, 'and go to sleep!'

'You don't understand very much about childhood!' K shot back through her tears, fixing me with a look I'll never forget.

I was cut to the quick, but it's more likely motherhood I don't fully comprehend. Motherhood from either side.

CHAPTER 7

DATE: 12 February 1988

THOUGHT FOR THE DAY: Age Makes a Winter in the Heart

WEATHER: Rain on the Glass

It's generally quiet from half-ten, after we've tucked the last of the residents in. And though I worked an evening just last week, I don't mind covering tonight for Mary O'Mara who had tickets for the Abbey. And I can even write for a few minutes here at the teacup-and-wrapper-strewn table which serves as a nursing station.

I finally asked Alice May tonight could I look at her books. It's a bad habit of mine, and I have to check myself if I see a bookshelf in somebody's home. Of course you can also learn something about folk by having a quick look at their medicine cabinet, albeit at the risk of suddenly having to picture them with piles, or worse yet, discovering something else even less your business—like vials of Valium or Viagra. But all I gleaned tonight was how well-read Alice May is: Jane Austen, leather-bound Shakespeare, and Margaret Atwood whom I've always meant to read. I also got some more of her own story as we chatted—the years she worked in St Louis as a librarian, and how Johnny, the brother in Tucson, has a small ranch just outside the city.

'Is he still there?' I asked.

'He's still there,' Alice May smiled. 'Sure, you could live forever in that dry heat, provided it didn't kill you first!'

Apparently St Louis is terribly humid in summer, not unlike Boston which she in turn asked me about. So I told her a little about growing up there—if far less than I've written here these past few weeks. Filling page after page, more pages than Sister Úna foresaw me doing, I'm sure. Problem is I write like I think, one thing on the heels of another. 'You're all over the place, Maeve!' Miss Dewey wrote on my high school essays. 'Stay focused!' Then again, we Cancerians are notorious for wanting to relive our childhood and hang onto our memories forever.

It's nearly eleven and time to go home anyhow. Katy waits up when I work an evening shift, and I don't want her bleary-eyed tomorrow on my account. And a miserable night it is too, the rain beating on the French doors to the garden. Which reminds me—I also learned why Alice May, who seems still so able, has come to us. While I find these winter mornings impossibly hard, for Alice May it's the opposite. 'It's the night-time, Maeve,' she said, tossing her head, reminding me of Ma again. 'I can no longer do the nights alone.'

CHAPTER 8

DATE: **14 February 1988**
SAINT FOR THE DAY: Valentine
ACTIVITY: Wearing My Heart on My Sleeve
QUESTION FOR THE DAY: Will You be My Valentine?

My darling daughter left a card and Toblerone bar on the kitchen table this morning, making me wince at having forgotten hers. She's off chocolate herself, so I nipped into town after work to pick up a card and a pair of socks, all hearts & cupids. Seán made a fuss our first year together, but I told him not to bother the next, as Valentine's Day for grown-ups is all about marketing, full stop. Still K and I've always exchanged cards, and I was hugely touched by hers this morning.

Back in Boston we swapped cards at school, though not with everybody. Which meant worrying all week, unless you were popular, about how many cards you'd receive. Worse was fourth grade, where Miss Balfe had one of her pets reach into a big pink-paper-trimmed hatbox and read out each envelope, while the class kept score. Worse yet, Ma refused that year to buy the little packs of Valentines you got at Woolworth's. Instead she gave Brian and me some coloured construction paper, along with scissors and a jar of glue. 'It means more if it's home-made,' she said when I protested. It meant more all right: it meant you were too mean to buy proper cards, it meant hours cutting and pasting, and worst of all, a hand-made card meant you were <u>different.</u>

Valentine's was the only time we were allowed eat candy in school. Chewing gum wasn't allowed either; 'Throw out that gum unless you've enough for everybody!' Miss Parsons in fifth grade would declare, until the day Salathiel Edwards, a quiet new black student from somewhere down South, stood up and passed out a stick of Juicy Fruit to everybody from the five packs he'd swiped from a corner shop on his way to school.

Of course Ma was right about home-made meaning more. And how it's the thought that counts—which she likewise proclaimed whenever I fretted over the present I had for somebody's birthday party. She was right there too—even though I couldn't know that as a child. But I knew enough to make Katy's birthday cards when she was little, drawing a bird or bunny on the front and a bit of silly verse inside. And it was a smashing hand-made card I got this morning, two bears in a woods, propped against the cornflakes box.

CHAPTER 9

DATE: 17 February 1988

THOUGHT FOR THE DAY: Absence Makes the Heart
Grow Sadder

QUESTION FOR THE DAY: Come si chiama?

I got a jolt this morning, drawing back my bedroom curtain to discover Mrs. Sheedy's apple tree gone from her back garden. Strange how an absence can work like a presence— a stump and wood chips scattered round like fallen petals instantly summoning forth the bent and gnarled tree I'd taken for granted most mornings. Bare-limbed in winter, then a first flush of leaves come spring, followed by apple blossoms. Mrs. Sheedy told me once how Mr. Sheedy had planted it when they moved in fifty years ago. Last autumn she mentioned it was bad with canker, but I had no idea it would have to come down.

A postcard looked up at me from the scatter rug beneath the mail slot as I came downstairs a few minutes later. From Pops? I thought—heart lifting for a split-second—before I remembered. A Lanzarote beach scene, only I couldn't think of anybody holidaying in the Canaries. Addressed to Mrs. Mahon at No 8 in fact, but the tears had begun by the time I saw that, so I just sat down on the stairs and wept.

Yesterday morning was a bit easier, thankfully. A walk in the Botanic Gardens with Orla, followed by coffee back at her place. Sunday mornings are truly special, all shuttered shops along quiet streets, like being on a film set for early-risers. Orla and I visit the Bots a lot, just around the corner from her flat in Glasnevin. Orla whom I met almost eight years ago at our Italian class in the Instituto di Cultura on Fitzwilliam Square. Not that far from Gael Linn on Merrion Square, where I'd attempted Irish the previous year, hoping I might help Katy with her homework. I gave it up after a few weeks, however, no more able to get my tongue around it than I had that first Donegal summer with Aunt Chrissie and Uncle Hughdy.

Italian, though, I'd wanted to learn since hearing the fruit & veg vendors at Haymarket Square where Pops took us Saturday mornings, whenever he got fed up with the potatoes from The Economy Market in the West End. It sounded a beautiful tongue, as if the stout women in their plastic aprons, and equally stout men in porkpie hats, were singing to—rather than shouting at—one another. Spuds selected, Pops would treat us to a hot chocolate or cannoli at a little Italian café beside the market.

That Eddie, Katy's father, was Italian was another reason for the Instituto lessons. Or Italian-American as I've learned to say over here, whereas in Boston folks blithely declare 'I'm Italian' or 'I'm Polish'. And of course 'I'm Irish' too!—even to somebody like Pops or Ma who actually were. 'From County Kerry!' they might add—when they actually hail from Everett or Arlington. But Eddie at least had a genuine Italian grandmother at home, his Nonna, who'd maybe a hundred words of English, but who took a real shine to me, and always shouted 'Bella la mia Rosa!'

whenever Eddie brought me round. We broke up before Katy was born, but some allegiance to both what was—that is, Eddie & me—and what is—namely my darling daughter—saw me enrol in Conversazione I, where I ended up beside Orla Aherne that first evening. Orla who told me after class how she wanted Italian to converse with the rich Signore she felt certain her future held. Only she wasn't clear whether her Mario would have his millions made from olive oil or Chianti.

'I'll settle for Federico with a Ferrari franchise,' I told Orla that night, though I've an eye out for a Captain Corelli now after finishing that novel. With or without mandolin, seeing how I failed to stay the course with Seán and his bloody bodhrán. Orla and I however have remained fast friends long after those Italian lessons ended.

A systems analyst for the Department of Health, she used to say 'I configure' to any bloke who tried to chat her up. As if to say 'Go figure' or 'Cop yourself on!' Yet computers are far from what's she truly into—stuff like the Tarot, I Ching and palmistry being what really makes her tick. Scatty, like Pisceans are, but a great pal. Her Mario never materialised, but she dated Silvio, an Italian accountant attached to Citibank, for a few months after our lessons ended. 'An Italian, sì,' she afterwards redefined her goal. 'An accountant, no grazie.' 'I Think, Therefore I'm Single' was always her motto, but she and her Irish fella Jack have been together two years now, and I won't be surprised if they eventually tie the knot.

There was no talk of anything like marriage yesterday, though. Just our usual chat, even as I struggled to keep up my end. Despite the Bots being only lovely—sunny with that rich smell of damp earth you get in early spring. A heron flopped onto a tall pine where its partner had already perched as we walked along the Tolka, the ground beneath ringed by fabulous swathes of purple crocuses and a scattering of snowdrops. The very spring blooms you find in the Boston Public Gardens, only you don't see them there till the end of March. And it was lovely to see the first flowers, the green growth promising what's to come, but I feel like I'm taking it on faith alone.

CHAPTER 10

DATE: 19 February 2010
SONG FOR THE DAY: 'Sometimes I Feel Like a
Motherless Child'

I was running late for Sister Úna yesterday afternoon, as
Carmen Cassidy was in a bad way. She's on morphine for
an abdominal tumour, but still has a good deal of
discomfort. Poor Carmen knows what's what, I believe,
though Dr Hogan in his wisdom hasn't told her yet. Not
that most folk at the Home don't know what's what—even
if the individual expiry dates vary. Of course we all face the
same brutal cut-off, but it's the old, not least those in care,
who stare it in the face.

As does Carmen, I suspect, though she wasn't saying as
much. Just quietly wet-eyed in her wheelchair, her face
crumpled up in pain. Or in sorrow, perhaps, for she said
her stomach was OK. But you can't comfort somebody in
the midst of the day-room, so I wheeled her along to her
bedroom, asking Clodagh en route to bring her a cup of
tea. As we waited, I asked Carmen about her bedside
photos, three brothers and a sister. All of them with the

77

same sallow aspect and dark eyes that have Germany Gemma convinced Carmen is Spanish. Unless it's her name, though I doubt Mr. and Mrs. Cassidy had Bizet's gypsy in mind when they christened their daughter. 'Your one from Spain,' Gemma Dunne calls Carmen when she can't remember her name.

'They all died in the month of April.' Carmen gestured at the photos.

'That's right,' I said. 'I remember your sister's passing last year.' I also remember the knock it gave Carmen, making me think April's imminence is possibly what's playing on her now. Only I don't say any such thing, of course.

I don't mention a family portrait Assistant Matron Mary O'Mara spoke of last week either, even if Carmen's photos bring it to mind. An old snapshot of Mary's mother's family, all seven brothers and sisters, taken in Kerry for some occasion. Only the photograph came back from the chemist's showing six siblings only, with the youngest brother, Mossie, missing. It wasn't a question of his being cropped off either, as there was an expanse of empty cottage wall either side. It simply looked like Mossie wasn't there, although Mary's mother insisted he had been, recalling how shy Mossie had even linked her arm. Then one afternoon a fortnight later they found Mossie, still astride his bike along the road, left foot propping him up against the grassy bank. Another brother brought a chair down from the cottage, onto which they lowered his remains. Mary said her mother had feared for Mossie ever since the photograph, fears she only spoke of after the funeral. How the photo had foreshadowed—without so much as a shadow—his imminent departure. I can't really believe that—even if it unsettles me writing it down. Yet had I grown up in Donegal like Ma, might I be better able for such supposition? Or were I gifted even—if a gift it was she had—to hear a phone before it rings, or espy a small girl on the stairs inside a Boston apartment where no other small girl apart from myself resided.

'You haven't said much about your mother, Maeve,' Sister Úna said yesterday, when I finally got to my appointment.

Why my mother? I wanted to say again. Why my mother, when I'm here to talk about my father? Though losing Pops means I've now lost them both—which is possibly why I fill these pages with whatever memory comes to mind. As if I don't want to entirely lose that Boston childhood. There's no denying the pleasure of writing some of it down, nor the feelings it sometimes brings up. Something like homesickness but not exactly. I mean it's not like I miss Boston day to day. Dublin is where K and I live, the Home is where I work—for the moment anyhow.

Yet even now—as with Sister Úna—I veer off the subject of my mother. If only because I'm not sure what there is to say—beyond the simple facts. What I sketched for Sister Úna yesterday: that Ma wasn't a terribly easy person, though I loved her and believe she loved me.

'In what ways not easy?' Sister Úna asked.

'She hadn't much patience,' I said, even if I know now the patience that mothering requires. 'Nor was she very demonstrative,' I added. 'Not warm really, though that was just her nature.' That's what I tell myself now anyhow—whereas I used worry it was something about myself. Some thing that kept my mother from taking me wholeheartedly to her heart? 'Maternal ambivalence,' I tell myself now, parroting what I learned in Psychology 101.

'You mentioned she suffered from depression?' Sister Úna prompted.

'She was actually bi-polar,' I said. 'Hospitalised twice

after psychotic outbreaks.'

Sister Úna lifted her head. 'You haven't mentioned this before, Maeve?'

'I didn't think of it, no,' I said—suddenly on the defensive. And thinking how utterly implausible that sounded.

'Not even when you spoke of your own melancholy?' Gently—as if she could see me stumbling.

'But it's my father's death has me this low,' I protested. 'That's why I came to you.'

'Yes,' Sister Úna said. 'But sometimes a loss brings up other, older sorrows.' When I said nothing, she continued. 'It's like our occasions of sorrow are somehow linked deep down, like subterranean pools that feed one into another.'

I liked that—underground pools of sorrow—but then I've always admired a strong metaphor. Probably another reason I'm hanging in with Sister Úna, who it happens lectured in First-Year English as well as psychology. But Sister wasn't resting on her similes yesterday.

'Does your mother's illness ever worry you?'

'For myself?' I said—too quickly.

'Yes,' Sister nodded.

'Not really,' I replied. 'Though my brother had a manic breakdown five years ago. I might feel myself speeding up a little in early spring, but I worry far more about Katy and her mood swings.'

'So you don't worry about mania?' Sister Úna asked, like a lawyer leading a witness.

'No. And I never really worried before about the other pole either,' I said, hoping to get a step ahead of her. 'I've had my miserable moments,' echoing what I told Mary O'Mara six weeks ago in Gaffney's, 'but I've never been clinically depressed heretofore.'

What staggers me however is what I next told Sister Úna. As if I'm forever doomed to play the daughter—a daughter nearing forty whose mother is twelve years in her grave. And not just playing the daughter—but an aggrieved daughter, too. Yet how else do I explain what I told Sister Úna? Unless I just needed to veer off once again, offer something in a minor key to mask the major chord which Sister Úna had struck.

'I'll never forget what Ma said to me once. I was reading—as always—but I even remember the book, "Gone With the Wind". Curled up on the couch at age twelve, lost in the story.'

Ma resented my reading, I think, for books were something I'd discovered on my own, with a big assist from Mrs. Lunenberg on the third floor. Maybe it was the escape Ma envied, the paths elsewhere books can provide, for she herself read little, preferring the TV and radio. Anyhow, I can't recall what the problem was that afternoon. She wasn't fond of my few school pals, but maybe she felt I should be out playing, not languishing indoors, nose in a book. But I remember her declaration, word perfect, like a judgement being handed down. 'I think, Maeve, you need to develop your Personality.' Pronouncing it like it had a capital P.

'I rebelled of course,' I told Sister Úna. 'Not like most kids do—by smoking or bad company, both of which might have helped to develop a Personality. Instead I rebelled by sticking my nose farther into books, any book, any chance I got, for another five years.'

'You might have done worse,' Sister Úna smiled.

'I could've done worse,' I conceded. I might've done drugs, drink or lots of boys. But sometimes I think I might've developed an interesting Personality too, had my mother not put me off.

CHAPTER 11

DATE: 23 February 1988

T-SHIRT FOR THE DAY: Wrinkled Was Not One of the Things I Wanted to Be When I Grew Up

Polish Petra has a Personality all right, and good English besides. Tall, twenty-four, with a blond ponytail and a lovely, full figure, as if she hails from a long line of healthy peasant stock. A great worker when she turns up, but she rang in sick again yesterday, so I confronted her this morning.

'You might as well still be with the Agency, seeing I'm always ringing Mrs. O'Sheehan to cover for you.'

'I don't want to go back to Mrs. O'Sheehan,' Petra said quickly. 'It's much nicer working here.'

'You need to show up when you're rostered so.'

Petra flashed me a 100-watt smile of reassurance before going off to get her assigned breakfast trays. I don't blame her either for not wanting to go back on the Agency game, as Mrs. O'Sheehan is a right rip, capable of going from Zero to Bitch in two seconds flat. I worked for her three months myself when first we came over, before Katy and I moved out to the gardener's cottage in Meath. Nearly thirteen years ago, though Mrs. O'Sheehan greets me on the phone like a long-lost daughter still. Even so, I'm wary of her. And I waited until Polish Petra had been coming to us for six months before I offered her a full-time position. Poach one of Mrs. O'Sheehan's crew too quickly, and you'll get no Agency nurse the next few times you ring up short-handed.

I love the way Petra's cheeriness brightens up the Home, and I'd nearly pay her to come live with me on Cadogan Rd. She goes out clubbing a bit, so sometimes has a story from some late-night joint on Leeson St. And it was I, not Mary O'Mara, who christened her Polish Petra—Gdansk being more exotic, I guess, to somebody from Boston than Ireland. Although I can hear Pops laughing at the idea of anybody finding Poland exotic, given the slagging the Poles got in Boston. Anyhow, the male residents all love blond, buxom Petra, and she flirts back at them, though she has to watch Happy-As who likes to go hands-on any chance he gets.

We've currently four men on the rolls: Happy-As, Tom the Teacher, Pat the Pope, and Eamon Kerr. Eamon is a dour old Dub who often shuffles around the Home with his own Thought for the Day—like IF ALL'S NOT LOST, WHERE IS IT?—emblazoned on the T-shirts his son sends over from Florida. Only I had to censor Eamon the morning he appeared proclaiming EAT RIGHT, EXERCISE, AND DIE ANYWAY. There's probably a huge Elder T-shirt and sweatshirts Industry in Florida, given its demographics, and they make you smile too, seeing HE WHO LAUGHS LAST THINKS SLOWEST on dry old Eamon who hasn't a funny bone in his body. Or so I thought, until Nurse Ethel reported finding Eamon a second time last week with his penis outside his pants.

'You told me yesterday it had died,' she remonstrated after she had him put himself back in.

'It did,' Eamon replied. 'And today's the viewing.'

I was too tired last night to write anything, even if my head was full of stuff. Writing the past must be what brings it back. All that about Manny the Bug Man whom I hadn't thought of in yonks. Or Mrs. Lunenberg in Apt 3C whom I mentioned to Sister Úna and thought about on my way home. Of how often I'd wished she'd been my mother, and how guilty I always felt with that thought. Mrs. L who invited Brian and me in for milk and oatmeal cookies, and who introduced me to a world of books beyond 'Eloise'.

Mrs. L was—or so it seemed—everything my mother was not. Above all patient—not harried and always hurried. And comfortably quiet as opposed to garrulous or tongue-tied—both of which Ma could wax when nervous in company. Mrs. L was also old, as a child thinks anyone over fifty is. Somewhere in her sixties, with grey hair in a neat bun, and a grown-up daughter in NYC.

She always had a pleasant word for us, and continued to ask me in even after Brian had outgrown cookies & milk. Sometimes I got to water her houseplants with a small brass can whose thin spout curved like a flamingo's neck. Other times I just sat in her living room looking at cartoons in 'The New Yorker', until one day Mrs. L handed me 'What Katy Did'. 'Try that, Maeve,' she said. 'My own daughter liked it immensely.' Tomboy Katy whom I adored, the eldest of six, whose mother dies when she is eight. It took me several visits to finish, a half-hour or so each time, the longest I could be away from Apt 1A without having to tell my mother some story unless she were working at Jordan Marsh. Ma would forbid me to visit Mrs. L if she knew, which is why I declined her suggestion I take the book home. And maybe Mrs. L figured that much out herself, because after I finished her daughter's copies of 'Mary Poppins' and 'Anne of Green Gables', she told me about the BPL—the Boston Public Library—just a stone's throw down Boylston St. And being Mrs. L, she told me about the John Singer Sargent paintings above its main staircase too.

'Have your mother take you sometime, Maeve,' Mrs. L suggested.

Ma wouldn't take me there in a fit, but emboldened by my secret life in Apt 3C I kept at her until she finally allowed Brian walk me there. And the next day again, with our Boston Edison bill, so I could establish my residency and get a library card.

'My mother works,' I informed the librarian, who'd said they didn't issue cards to eleven-year-olds—even those accompanied by thirteen-year-old brothers.

'Well, just this once,' she relented—which is part of why I've a soft spot for librarians since. Like Alice May at the Home whom I'm mad about already.

Of course Apt 3C was everything I'd have liked our own to be. Its furniture even older than ours, only stylish, not dumpy, the sofa and chairs upholstered in a satiny fabric—what I know now is brocade—affixed by brass tacks with roundy tops. Sometimes there was an art book on her coffee table, which I'd look at once I finished 'The New Yorker' cartoons. And paintings on the wall—actual paintings, not cheap prints like the one we had downstairs of a New England covered bridge in autumn. Plus a small lithograph I used to stop and stare at just inside her door— a winter scene with windmills and tiny figures skating along a frozen canal, the women with strange, winged hats, a man falling arse-over-teakettle, as Pops used to say, his tiny skates pointing at the sky.

Best of all was a cabinet full of china and crystal, except for one shelf halfway down where a selection of seashells sat on a thin layer of beach sand: mussels, scallops, razor clams. It looked the loveliest thing, and I marvelled at having something like that in your living room.

'They're from Maine, Maeve,' Mrs. L told me. 'From the salt-water farm where my mother grew up.' She took time too to explain what a salt-water farm was—time my mother rarely seemed to have for answering questions. Telling how she herself had been raised in New Hampshire, where her father had run the local ice-house. 'Dublin, New Hampshire,' she said, 'just like Dublin, Ireland.' Of course Dublin meant nothing to me then, as my parents were both from the West of Ireland and Dublin could have been on another planet for all I knew.

Mrs. L explained what an ice-house was too, showing me a black & white photo of a large barn-like building of unfinished planks. Only bigger than a barn, more like a windowless warehouse, with a steep chute descending from a door covered with what looked like a blanket. 'Canvas,' Mrs. L said, 'to keep the heat out in summer,' before describing how a workman would send a huge cake of ice thundering down the chute onto a platform, where another worker sluiced the sawdust off with a bucket of water, following which a third chopped it into smaller blocks with an axe.

'What was the ice for?'

'For the icebox in your kitchen, Maeve.'

'Didn't you have ice-cube trays?' I asked Mrs. L—who never once asked was there no end to my questions? Instead she explained how what we still called an icebox had been—before the electric fridge—precisely that. How the freezer compartment held an actual chunk of ice that slowly melted down to nothing. At which point the iceman cameth in his truck to deliver another chunk. 'Provided you had an icebox,' Mrs. L added, 'because not everybody could afford one.' That was another thing I liked about Mrs. L. That while she'd grown up with certain comforts— and possessed paintings, fine books, and a sense of place— she still knew not everybody lived like that. Which allowed me in turn not to feel always like the Super's daughter around her.

'It's an ice-house,' I told Pops later that afternoon, showing him the ice cubes that I'd covered in oatmeal, then stacked beneath an upside-down shoebox that was already ringed by a circle of melting water on our white enamel kitchen table.

'It's a nice house indeed,' Pops joked, 'but you had better clean it up before your Ma gets home from work.'

CHAPTER 12

DATE: 24 February 1988
VERSE FOR THE DAY: 'Every Old Man I See Reminds Me
of My Father'
GRAFFITO FOR THE DAY: Things Are Going to Get a Lot
Worse Before They Get Wojus

Mrs. Sheedy's AWOL back-garden apple tree still catches my eye first thing these mornings, its empty oval of dark soil on green grass fixing me as I part the curtains to see what the weather holds. Or precisely what version of grey & miserable is on offer—though I tell myself at least the lawn stays green through an Irish winter. Most mornings a wood pigeon sits in the large sycamore two gardens over. There's something deceptive about how large they look from a distance, silhouetted on a branch, whereas close-up they don't seem so big, albeit bigger than the pigeons I tried to feed on the Boston Common after I finished 'Mary Poppins'. Sneaking heels of bread out past Ma, who always gave out about how filthy pigeons were. I wasn't much of a Bird Woman though, as the pigeons made me too nervous when they clustered round.

Anyhow I'm trying to sit—sit as in 'meditate'—for ten minutes each morning. After I fight free of the bed, and before I go down to put the porridge on. It's been a few years since I've tried meditating, but I decided this week to give it another go. Even if so far I just sit rather than <u>sit</u>—my mind too trammelled to let go. Spying Pops at a bus stop on my way to work yesterday didn't help either. Until I remembered again—and Pops turned into just another older man in a fedora.

I also try each morning to remember my St John's Wort. I told Sister Úna straight off I didn't want to go on anything like Prozac. 'I can't dispense anything like that, Maeve,' Sister Úna had replied, 'as I'm not a doctor.' Which of course I knew, being a nurse. But after hearing of Ma's psychiatric history, Sister suggested I try St John's Wort for my melancholy. I don't mind taking herbal remedies, though I doubt it'll do anything for me. Any more than talking to Sister Úna really has. I knew about hypericum, the psychotropic element in St John's Wort, but I hadn't known the flower was associated with St Colmcille. 'It grows wild in Donegal,' Sister Úna said, which persuaded me to give it a go. If only because Colmcille was said to have lived for a time in Glenmore, like my mother. Or her brother, Uncle Hughdy, who pointed out a stream to Brian and me, the summer we went over, where he said the Saint used to drink. 'After a feed of dillisk off the rocks by the strand,' Hughdy added, like it had happened only yesterday.

Mary O'Mara is a big one for herbal cures, and says half of Germany is on St John's Wort for depression. She swears by ginkgo also, for the memory. Which I should probably be taking too—if only to remind me to take the hypericum, three times a day, with food. I laughed when Mary mentioned the ginkgo, reminded of the first time I ever heard of the tree. In the BU library my sophomore year, where I sometimes managed to sit across the table from Dan Oliver, a fellow nursing student whom I fancied like mad, only I was too shy to do anything about it. Anyhow, one April evening Dan suddenly pointed out the library window, 'Oh, look, a ginkgo.'

'Oh, where?' I raced over, thinking it some kind of exotic bird. Nor could I cover up my error, which gave Dan a good laugh.

That was the only mistake I ever got to make with Dan, who ended up going out with my pal Laurie our senior year. But I don't intend making even one tiny misstep with Jim O'Connor at the Home, who startled me yesterday by asking me out for a drink at the end of my shift. I begged off, saying I'd the dinner to get on at home. Of course he maybe just wanted to hear how I'm getting on as Matron? But fact is I'm married enough to this job already, without being courted by the boss.

CHAPTER 13

DATE: 26 February 1988

SEASON: Spring

WEATHER: Wintery showers

THOUGHT FOR THE DAY: Praise the Lord & Pass the Ammunition

'I'm not going to Berlin,' Germany Calling whispered to me this afternoon in the front day-room.

'Berlin, Gemma?'

'The woman in charge of propaganda told me a car's leaving in five minutes, and there's a seat for me if I want to go.'

That Jim had hired a Minister for Propaganda was news to me—rather than another nurse's aide on the 8-3 shift which is more what we need. But Gemma was clearly looking for a response.

'You're staying put?' I offered, aiming for something neutral that might still satisfy as I took her empty glass. Sundays we always dole out a glass of sherry after dinner, for those still able to handle a drop. And like my evening shift every fortnight, I try to work a Saturday or Sunday once a month, just to keep an eye on the weekend routine.

'Do you see that one?' Gemma whispered again,

pointing at Nora Cricket. 'With the German Secret Service!'

'Is that right, Gemma?'

'That was German, too,' Gemma said, pointing at the sherry bottle on the trolley.

'Is that so?'

'It's very exciting,' she beamed up at me, 'having a drink with the enemy!'

You could write a book about the Home, so you could. I know that's a cliché, how everybody says the same about their job or family. And I couldn't really write a book—having read enough of them to know it's not a matter of simply setting things down, no matter how funny or bizarre. But a lot of what goes on here at the Home feels akin to fiction. OK, you won't find betrayal, sex or intrigue rife among the crinkly set, but there's a richness to lives already largely lived, and occasional comedy too as the curtain comes slowly down. And no shortage of psychodrama either: Constance who's closing in on eighty, yet still looking after her Mammy, or the early morning Dublin traffic transmogrifying into German tanks for Gemma.

Or Happy-As Ferguson, who never did a day's work according to his wife.

'How do you feel he's settled in?' I inquired after Larry first came to us.

'Oh, it's no bother to him,' Mrs. Ferguson assured me. 'After the life that man's led, you don't think he'd imagine himself anywhere unpleasant?' Telling me of the corner shop they'd had in Phibsboro, despite Larry's best efforts to both drink and gamble it away.

Still, you have to admire the patience most of our residents bring to the task at hand. Those like Tom the

Teacher or Alice May who have their faculties yet. Quietly enduring hour after empty hour in the day-room, negotiating the interminable stretches between meals and cups of tea from a trolley. Only a few like Alice May and Veronica Egan still read, which helps pass the time. There's a TV of course in either day-room, but few bother with it. Instead they simply sit, waiting out the endless hours that outnumber the activities—bingo, sing-song, or seated exercises—we schedule to break up the monotony. Or the occasional visit from a child, grandchild, former neighbour or old friend who's still managing life outside. Which is why I occasionally pause in mid-flight, struck by something approaching heroic in such endurance, in the perseverance all around me. Something beyond mere resignation that sees them through the homestretch: a sense of spirit that offsets their years and diminished capacity.

Of course, having your wits about you can be a disadvantage in a Home. Like Bertha the Bag, who shares with Kitty the Conductor, and gets upset every time Kitty puts on Bertha's best blouse. 'Don't worry,' I want to tell Bertha. 'Kitty generally has her top off and titties airing by dinnertime.' Were Bertha less alert, she might not notice when Kitty goes foraging in her wardrobe. Though God help Kitty if she ever makes a move on Bertha's bag, which Valerie on nights says Bertha is now taking to bed with her. Matching roommates is always tricky, except for Eva and Enda Glynn, an obvious pairing, seeing how they shared a room some sixty years ago. And no doubt fought like cats over clothes the way sisters can.

Though it's clearly better Bertha cares enough yet about her clothes to cause a row—as indifference would be worse, any throwing in of the towel. Which is why you end up respecting a lot of the very behaviour that drives you mad.

Those residents who insist you put in the milk first before you pour their tea. Or somebody, half-frozen, who refuses to put on a jumper because its colour clashes with their skirt. Habits and predilections that have long defined a body, and which they have every right to insist on yet. Even those lost in the fogs of dementia, stripped of both past and present, usually manage to hold on to something integral— to fly a flag, however tattered, of self. Most often it's just pure attitude—attitude maybe all that remains after self gets stripped back to the bare wire. It can be positive or negative—a beatific smile they had as a child, or a violent kick—but it survives.

I never had a sister nor roommate, so I've only recently experienced clothing raids, as Katy makes the odd foray into my wardrobe. Better yet, I sometimes find myself fancying something of hers now that we take the same size. She's within a half-inch of me at 5'5" and clearly destined to be taller, her height coming from Eddie, though she has my Ma's lovely 'donn dearg' hair. She's going to have a fuller figure too, about which I already have to reassure her. Telling her 'You're lovely, Pet' only last night as she stood frowning at her hips and breasts in front of my bedroom mirror.

That anxiety might set off alarm bells, only K has always loved her grub too much for me to overly worry about anorexia or bulimia. What used worry me, however, was the way she used to call every meal 'breakfast' at age two. Telling the child-minder 'I want my breakfast' whenever her lunch was slow in coming. Or hollering 'When's breakfast?' at suppertime—which had me convinced I'd be reported to social services for neglect. I can see her so clearly yet, shrieking like a seagull whenever she saw a pink slice of watermelon in our Somerville kitchen. Or tilting her head back like a baby bird for steamed clams dipped in butter. Yet eating disorders are only one of a myriad worries that come with having a child. From a lorry running a red light to leukaemia, an endless list I try to lay down when sleep won't come, or these mornings when it departs too soon.

CHAPTER 14

DATE: 27 February 1988

THOUGHT FOR THE DAY: Errare Humanum Est!

WORRY FOR THE DAY: Qual la nonna, tal la nipote?

Fact is, I lay awake for a time last night, worrying over Katy, who I most often think is doing OK. She's far moodier this year though—touchy as in touch-me-not—and her mood-swings have me praying she won't end up going her Granny's way. She's also cheekier, though cheek doesn't worry me. 'Get da boat!' she sometimes barks—by way of telling me to bug off. We're still capable of a good heart-to-heart though, and have always talked far more than Ma and I ever managed. Like the afternoon she came home from 6th class, feeling she hadn't any friends, that she wasn't able for her differences, and so on. It took me straight back to Boston: to that very age when I felt the same way, only I wasn't much able to share it with my mother. But being there for K, and having K hopefully still able to spill things out to me, is all of what matters now.

Certainly the few friends I made in grammar school never met with Ma's approval, and so I rarely brought anybody home to play in our apartment. Vivian Henry came over a few times when we were in Miss Parsons' 6th-grade class. Heavily perfumed, thickly powdered Miss Parsons who rarely ever blew her nose, rather spat into a handkerchief she kept up her sleeve. 'Too many of you children hang onto one another in the corridor,' she reminded us weekly. 'I don't want to see any of you touching as you walk.' 'The careful seldom err' was another favourite of hers until Vivian, whose parents taught college, raised her hand one day to say the careful actually pronounce 'err' to rhyme with 'her', not 'hair'.

The afternoon of our school trip to the Museum of Fine Art Vivian came home with me. Someone had used the word 'fuck' that morning outside the museum, which made all the boys laugh, yet nobody would tell me why. Back home, though, Vivian took a paper napkin from our kitchen table and quickly sketched two stick figures coupling.

'That's 'fuck',' Vivian said, handing me the napkin.

I took a quick look before tearing it up in disgust. Then, looking over at Vivian, I giggled and shook my head. And shake my head now—to think of our innocence.

I went over to Vivian's apartment on Commonwealth Ave a few times that year. Hers was a far grander flat than ours, spacious rooms all airy and light, oriental carpets underfoot, and a piano cum music stand in the living room. Each visit Vivian took a purple aluminium pitcher from the icebox and poured herself a glass of some cool-looking purple drink. 'It's my medicine,' she announced, 'so you can't have any.' It was only grape-flavoured Kool-Aid, I think, but that shade of purple has remained for me the colour of all things mysterious and forbidden.

One afternoon I accidentally got the upper hand of Vivian, who probably liked playing with me because she could manage me at will. 'You've germs all over you,' I informed her on that visit, parroting what I'd read somewhere. 'Same as me,' I quickly added, after Vivian burst into tears and raced into her father's study. I stood outside, confidently awaiting corroboration, only to hear her father lie through his teeth: 'Of course you haven't germs, Sweetie. Now run along and play.'

Ma collected me at Vivian's that afternoon, standing awkwardly just inside the door, even though Mrs. Henry had asked her into the living room. She had her keys in her hand for some reason, which she kept putting up to her mouth, and which I kept wishing she wouldn't. Mrs. Henry always wore these flowery dresses, down to her ankles nearly, and all of it—the large flat, the carpets, the fact Mrs. Henry taught piano—was too much for my mother's confidence.

Yet there I lay last night, entertaining one worry about Katy after another, like a string of tabloid terrors, while trying to remind myself of how able my daughter is, not the sometimes loner her mother was back in Boston. Buoyed by the world of books as I was, but not as isolated, rock posters along with paperbacks in her bedroom, and her right ear already pierced twice—as if, unlike myself, she's able to meet her adolescence at least halfway. I also remind myself how Katy *is* of this era, and how that hopefully helps make her not so much inured to, as inoculated against, its worst excesses. Which set me thinking, just as sleep came, how that's precisely what Gemma Dunne needs. Not an inoculation so much as a booster shot—to bolster the defences she once had against the trials of wartime London, even if there were no German tanks outside her door there either.

CHAPTER 15

DATE: 29 February 1988
SHIBBOLETH FOR THE DAY: During Leap Year the Ladies
May Propose

What if you could literally leap over a year? I could do without this one anyhow—though I know that's foolish, given this year, this month, this day, is all I have. Or this morning, hard as it was. I attempted a brave face at breakfast, sunny-side-up like the egg Katy had instead of porridge. I doubt I fooled her though, so able is K at reading me, same as I took the measure of Ma's mood, day in, day out. She asks do I see the crescent moon, like a bright fingernail on the dark sky over the large sycamore, where the wood pigeons usually sit. Pointing a few minutes later to the first pink streaks to the east, what our Latin teacher Mr. Barry, translating from the Greek, used call 'the rosy-tipped fingers of dawn'. I know she's monitoring me, so I try to brighten up as I look out the kitchen window where Nibbles waits to be let in. And brighten me it does— to have Katy doing for me what I so often did for her. Pointing out the morning or evening star, the first daffs, a jet reflecting the sun, a robin at the back step. Never mind the flora and fauna around the gardener's cottage at Balkill House our first two Irish years, the peacocks peering in our kitchen window.

As soon as K's off, however, I sit down and weep. The sadness coming in waves, from deep down inside and so far back. Crying for Pops, Uncle Hughdy, Aunt Chrissie, myself and Katy. Frightened I may be going the same way Ma went—and so locking Katy into a similar mother & daughter dance. But feeling like I'm crying too for the entire cast at the Home, or the shooting victim and the earthquake homeless on this morning's news, wracked by an indiscriminate sorrow that makes no sense.

Mornings are worst though, and once again I get my keel down as I walk to work. 'You'll need to keep your keel down,' Mr. Evarts from Apt 4D would inform Brian and me on a windy day, though we hadn't a breeze as to what he meant. Captain Evarts as Brian called him, a small, dapper man with white hair and trim moustache, who set out in spring in a blue blazer, white slacks, and a sailing cap for the Charles River Boat Club where he kept his boat. I don't remember in what book I finally encountered 'keel', around age eleven, and finally understood what counsel Captain Evarts was offering.

I even tried sitting for a few minutes this morning before heading to work—as if trying to broker a ceasefire with the Here & Now. I've never sustained the practice for more than a few months, apart from the year Katy turned eight. But I've never let go of wanting to meditate either since starting back in college. The chance it offers you to tune out—as if all your chores are done—and simply sit, watching your breath as your mind empties. There seemed, too, a kernel worth cracking in the precepts our teacher Alan offered at the start of each session, though to be honest what I best remember are the Zen jokes some of us occasionally swapped after class. Like what did the Zen master say to the hot-dog vendor? 'Make me one with everything!' OK, not side-splitting stuff, but more laughs than you found in the Baltimore Catechism growing up. And a few laughs are what I could sorely use this weather.

CHAPTER 16

DATE: 5 March 1988

THOUGHT FOR THE DAY: What Goes Up Sometimes
Stays There

'Films have been made of a lesser day!' as Pops used say.
And come to think of it, lifts often feature in a film—
thrillers mostly—somebody racing upstairs or down, either
chasing or fleeing someone else in a lift. Though our
excitement began when our lift stopped, trapping Nurse
Flynn with Tom the Teacher, Carmen Cassidy and Veronica
Egan between the ground and first floor, the only run it
makes. It could have been worse—say Nurse Ethel who's
claustrophobic or Nurse Powers who I worried last week
might be drinking—and not Fiona Flynn who, like Mary
O'Mara, is as good as it gets at the Home. Or it could have
been clientele like Germany Calling, not Veronica who's all
day quietly reading, nary a complaint, just her sad sweet
smile. And Carmen who parks her wheelchair beside
Veronica in the day-room and gives as little trouble, not
even after Dr Hogan finally told her about her tumour.

'There's something wrong with the lift, Matron,'

Clodagh informed me around ten o'clock, though Leo the Porter had already prised open the first-floor outer door by a few inches, allowing us to peer down into the lift shaft.

'Are you all right?' I called down to Fiona who reassured me that Tom and Veronica were carefully seated on the floor, and Carmen in her wheelchair, same as she'd be anywhere.

'All we lack is a deck of cards,' Fiona laughed which heartened me a little.

'I'd better ring Otis,' I said to Leo, Otis being the same crowd who serviced our lift for Pops back in Boston.

'Right you be, Nurse Ratched!' Leo grinned.

I rang Otis, explaining how we needed the lift to get our charges down to their dinner at midday. 'They promised an engineer within the hour,' I told Leo, who spared me the Nurse Ratched this time. He's great, Leo is. In his late twenties and happily married with two young daughters, which doesn't stop him from flirting with the nurses, myself included. A tiler by trade, he began with us last year, saying he was keen to cut back on the ceramics. I smiled when he said that, for Pops used to say the same thing about painting—how too much time staring at a wall was bad for your head, and made most painters either barmy or boozers in the end.

We only need a twenty-five-hour per week porter which suited Leo, who's doing a night-course in Building Management at Bolton St. I smiled to myself when he told me that, imagining what Pops would say about having to go to college now to become a Superintendent. Anyhow Leo has worked out a treat. Shows up daily, does the job, yet takes the time to chat with the clientele. And needless to say the old dears are all mad about him.

An Otis van must have been around the corner, for an

engineer arrived minutes after I rang and quickly sorted the problem: a short circuit in something called the car gate-switch. Which meant we had Fiona and her charges sprung before we needed to start shuttling the rest of the regiment down to their dinner. We had a wheelchair waiting for Veronica, who looked a bit wan as Fiona helped her out, but Tom and even poor Carmen looked like they'd been away on holiday, and laughed heartily at the sign Leo had stuck up outside the lift: FREE THE FAIRVIEW FOUR! And I was free too after dinner, a couple of hours owed me, plus an afternoon appointment with Sister Úna. But worn out as I am by such a thrilling—nay, uplifting—day at the Fairview Home for the Elderly, I'll leave that encounter till tomorrow.

CHAPTER 17

DATE: 6 March 1988

MEMORY FOR THE DAY: The Hills of Donegal

I hardly wanted to talk about the Home after our trapped-in-the-lift morning, so I told Sister Úna instead of my first trip to Ireland, the summer I turned ten. Of how travelling from downtown Boston to Donegal in the early sixties had been like journeying to another planet. Neither parent came over with us, there never being money enough for that kind of holiday. Instead Brian and I were put on a plane in Logan, to be collected in Shannon by Aunt Chrissie and a neighbour with a car. Wide awake when we landed, I crossed the airport tarmac staring up at a sky unlike any I'd ever seen, giant clouds scudding past as the sun broke through, highlighting distant trees and the greenest fields I'd ever seen.

We stood for a few moments inside the small terminal, myself clinging to Brian, something he'd never have allowed at home. Until a woman looking like a younger version of Ma detached herself from the crowd behind the red-braided rope and came up to us. 'You must be Brian?'

said Aunt Chrissie whom we'd never met, 'and this is Maeve,' shaking both our hands before handing our baggage tickets to the neighbour whose name I don't recall. But whom I must have stared at surely, as I can see his ruddy, bloodshot cheeks yet, unlike any face I'd seen, not even on a bum sleeping rough on the Boston Common.

And I still remember the journey from Limerick up to Donegal, crammed into the back seat of an old Morris Minor that seemed as foreign as everything else: the narrow winding roads, or the pungent smell of what I didn't know yet was turf smoke in the small villages at which our driver periodically stopped. Twice we followed him into tiny shops, where unsliced loaves of bread sat unwrapped on the counter. Shops with what I didn't know yet was a pub attached, if only a darker room further in, where our driver knocked back what looked for all the world like the biggest glass of creamy root beer. Equally foreign was the way people said 'Cheerio' which we knew as a breakfast cereal, or the cup of tea and tomato sandwich which Brian and I got in the second shop, both of us exchanging a quick glance at the bizarre idea of tomato on its own, but both too timid and mannerly to chance asking for a peanut butter & jelly sandwich instead.

The rest of the journey was a blur, as the nervous excitement which had me wide awake at Shannon gradually gave way to utter exhaustion: being jolted awake on the bumpy roads, marvelling momentarily at sunlit hedgerows, then nodding off again. Or waking again to marvel at our driver, steering with his head stuck out the window into a fine mist, to afford a better view of the road ahead I thought, but suspect now was more a stratagem to keep himself awake after an extended pit stop in what must have been Bundoran, where Brian and I were allowed down onto what we'd have called a beach, not a strand. To throw stones into the breakers, while I tried not to cry at our being the breadth of that same ocean from Pops and Ma.

Two hours after Bundoran, we reached Glenmore, itself fifteen miles west of Killybegs. Aunt Chrissie's cottage, which had been Ma's home too, sat up a long lane a mile southwest of the small village, the sea just visible a further mile west. But it wasn't the sea we stared at that afternoon, rather at Uncle Hughdy, who came out of a large shed (or byre as we later learned to call it) just as we pulled up. Stockier than his sisters, he spoke sharply to the black & white dog that had chased our car up the lane, then shook our hands as Chrissie had done. He just stood there then, his face nearly as florid as our driver's, weathered by extremes of wind and rain you simply don't get in Boston. We just stood there too, trying not to stare at his tweed cap, the white collarless shirt under a maroon sweater, or his dirty trousers tucked into a pair of muddy black rubber boots.

Inside the cottage we met our Granny, as Brian and I would call her. A tiny woman with a large dark wen on her brow, she sat beside the range and stared right back at us. I couldn't take my eyes off her, hunched in her chair like the old woman you'd encounter in a folk or fairy tale. Wearing a couple of old cardigans and dark skirt, whatever hair she had left hidden beneath a scarf. The very hair I'd inherited, though I doubted hers had much red anymore.

Sister Úna wanted to hear more about Granny, but I hadn't much to tell. Just how she'd suffered a stroke that had taken most of her speech, although her eyes were still unbelievably bright. How she didn't rise till afternoon, and once installed in her chair, mostly sat there quietly, watching the kitchen activity like an old bird, now and again muttering something I could never decipher. That first night however, she seemed like something straight out of Grimms'—as did everything else: wooden table and chairs, a hearth brush made from chicken feathers, or the two china cats above the range which looked to be the only ornaments in the house. There were strange sounds too: the sheep calling out as they grazed the lane, and inside the cottage the Irish that Chrissie and Hughdy mostly spoke to one another.

We had our first fry that evening: eggs that Chrissie gathered from a nest in the byre to my amazement, plus plump pink sausages utterly unlike the shrivelled brown specimens we had in Boston, and tomatoes fried in the same pan, which Brian and I both left on our plates. We were put to bed immediately after that, exhausted by the car journey, jet lag, and the weirdness of it all. Chrissie and Granny slept in the upper bedroom behind the range, while Brian and I each had a small single bed in the lower bedroom, where Uncle Hughdy also slept. There was a strong musty smell to the bedding, even though Chrissie had the blankets airing on a rack over the range when we arrived.

'Are you 'uns still awake?' Hughdy asked when he came in to bed. Too tired to sleep, both Brian and I answered yes, so Hughdy led us in a prayer:

'Now I lay me down to sleep,
I pray the Lord my soul to keep.
And if die before I wake,
I pray the Lord my soul to take.'

Moments later I pulled the bedclothes over my head to muffle my sobs, terrified the Lord might take me at my word—that I was in any way willing to die. Too tired to cry, I cried anyhow, wishing I were back home.

CHAPTER 18

DATE: 12 March 1988

ACTIVITY: Digging for Buried Treasure

Germany Gemma told me the Yanks were taking Berlin today, as I took her and Veronica down to dinner. It must be something in the drinking water, for Kitty the Conductor has hung up her railway hat and tries to kneel now whenever she hears the Angelus, as if she were back in her childhood kitchen. Plus Veronica hasn't slept well since her lift ordeal, and we've had difficulty persuading her back into it. Fiona Flynn suggested giving her a tray in one of the upstairs day-rooms, but I worry we might never get her downstairs again if we do.

'It's like falling off a horse,' I encourage her. 'You have to get right back on.'

'Don't be such a horse's ass!' Germany Gemma tells me on one arm, while Veronica trembles like a leaf on my other as we inch aboard.

The rest of the Fairview Four fared better though. Even Carmen, albeit failing rapidly, seemed livelier the following day, as if the break in routine—or in Carmen's case, one last adventure—were as good as a tonic. And you'd swear thirty minutes in the lift took thirty years off Tom the Teacher, who's been as bright as a button all week. 'Will we take the stairs?' he jokes now at dinnertime. 'Or will we chance the lift?'

Tom is a dote, full-stop—so it's especially nice seeing him this buoyed up. He's from Tipperary, which he left nearly sixty years ago to come up to Dublin to teach in a National School out in Swords. Yet there's little air of the schoolmaster about him, apart from a charming habit he has of presenting the odd fact out of nowhere—like a magician pulling a rabbit from a hat.

'Did you know nylon take its name,' he inquired yesterday, 'from New York and London both?'

'Indeed I didn't, Tom.'

'Aye, discovered simultaneously in both cities.'

Like most of Mary's nicknames, Tom the Teacher has stuck. Per Mary, you were known only by your nickname down the country, like Pat the Pope who came to us already christened. Or Watty the Wire up in Glenmore, who according to Uncle Hughdy could do any kind of fencing job. Which is only one of a myriad memories that have flooded back since I told Sister Úna about Donegal last week. Memories like Brian outside the cottage that first morning, holding his baseball glove and ball, God love him. June it may have been, but June in Donegal: cool, wet, and the ground still muddy from heavy showers the previous night. What sounded like buckets of rain being hurled at the bedroom window, a howling wind clenching the cottage in its fist, until I finally fell asleep. 'A big wind,' Hughdy said at breakfast, and it had sounded big all right.

That first morning we tried playing with a pair of

untamed cats that raced around the byre, stopping only to rub affectionately against each other. The cats never let us near all summer, and Lolly the sheep dog also ignored us outdoors. But inside the kitchen he'd lie at our feet and let us scratch him behind the ears, the closest thing to a pet we ever had.

The cottage had only recently lost its thatch to fibreglass sheets that creaked in the sun each morning as I lay on in bed, trying to summon nerve enough to negotiate another day in an utterly alien world. Kids adapt quickly though, and within a few weeks we had fairly settled in. We were given chores—mine included helping Chrissie with the washing up, while Brian went out a few times a day with a bucket for turf from the stack beside the byre. Chrissie also showed me how to tease the wool she spun into yarn which Hughdy then wove into tweed come wintertime in his loom shed beside the lane. There was also a butter churn which Chrissie and I cranked forever, whenever she had enough cream set by. The home-made butter tasted a bit off to me, however, which meant I ate my bread, both home-bake and shop-loaf, dry.

Brian and I also had plenty of time to play, there being no TV in the house, just an old radio which Chrissie called a wireless. There were no other children nearby, the nearest neighbour ninety-year-old Annie Gillespie who lived with her son Francey. We weren't allowed down the road to the sea by ourselves, but were let roam the hill behind the house, and the even bigger hill across the road, provided we kept an eye out for bog holes.

It's hard to imagine a landscape—or an experience—so different to our Boston. And there are moments I recall so clearly yet—rainbows like coloured brushstrokes on the mountain opposite, or sunlight that broke through clouds to highlight swathes of heather and bracken like a spot lamp. Or stopping on the hill simply to listen to the wind in the grass. Of course I didn't know to call things by their proper names yet—bracken was 'ferns' to me—but I was slowly getting to know the things themselves.

We even grew accustomed to our Auntie and Granny, though it was not until my second visit three summers later that I really began to know Chrissie. She was sometimes cross, but seldom went 'missing' like Ma so often did—lost in a fog of her own making. Plus Chrissie asked countless questions, about Boston, our apartment, or Ma's job at Jordan Marsh. I wanted to ask as many questions back of course, only I hadn't the nerve. Like why had she never visited us in Boston, what games did she and Ma play as kids, or why did Granny wear a scarf indoors? Yet Chrissie liked having us to talk to, I suspect, for Granny was beyond meaningful speech and Hughdy never spoke a lot inside the house. But you sensed she wasn't maybe used to speaking much, as she had this habit of pausing, wide-eyed, when searching for a word, like she'd actually see it when it came to her. That she was Ma's sister fascinated me however, and I used secretly stare at her, noting how much like Ma she looked at the corners of her eyes, the same pert nose. And trying to imagine what it had been like, growing up together, and had the two brothers and two sisters got on at all?

We also grew used to Uncle Hughdy, who might have as easily been a Martian when he stepped from the byre that evening we arrived. Or the following morning when he came in from milking the cow, wearing a long dark coat stained with clabber and turf mould. Though I only knew then to call it dirt—as dirty as the clothes on the winos whom I always gave a wide berth to on the Common, especially after one of them exposed himself to Vivian and myself one afternoon, his thing hanging out of his trousers like an old turkey neck.

To be honest I was terrified by Hughdy at first. Not just his prayers about dying, but his bulky shape and large, gnarled, nicotine-stained hands. Plus his silences, beyond a few words in Irish to his mother and sister, and the way he tended to avoid eye contact, same as ourselves. Certainly it took longer to get a sense of him, as he was seldom in the house. I'd have thought he'd never been out of Donegal either, when he in fact he'd been ten years in Birmingham, before taking the ferry back from Holyhead 'with only a week's wages in his pocket'. But all that Chrissie only told me years later, along with how he'd only given up the drink upon returning to Glenmore.

By our third week however Brian and I were confident enough to follow him and Lolly up the hill after sheep. And up to the bog on the mountain opposite, where we helped turn the turf he'd cut in April and thrown along the bank. It was a hot dry week early in July, which pleased Hughdy no end. 'Sure, they're turning up like sausages,' he declared, pouring out tea from a lemonade bottle Chrissie had slipped into an old sock to keep it warm. 'Getting a skin on them at last,' he enthused, then handed us each a hard-boiled egg. It was lovely up there on the bog, skylarks singing themselves silly out of sight overhead, the sea all shimmery and turquoise in the distance. And warm enough to make you drowsy, only I was afraid of falling asleep in case Brian was right about how the sun on the glasses I'd got that spring might make me burst into flames.

It was on the bog that week we three finally became friends, even if we didn't talk much. Hughdy loved the tiny transistor radio Ma had sent over for him, and propped it carefully on a few lumps of turf. Brenda Lee had a big hit that summer, and Hughdy loved her voice so much he cut her name into the turf bank so as to remember it. And you could still make out the lettering in August, when we returned to load the turf onto the trailer which Watty the Wire pulled behind his tractor down to the byre for Hughdy to build the stack.

It was at that stack one evening that Brian and I saw a small animal with a light brown coat darting among the sods: half the size of the grey squirrels on the Boston Common—the only wildlife we knew—and quicker too, bounding off the stack into a stone ditch like it had no backbone at all.

'A weasel,' Hughdy said after we ran to where he was shovelling up clay around the spuds beside the loom shed. He let us have a turn with the spade then, pointing out how the stalks no longer drooped in the heat, which made evening the best time for that particular chore.

That night in the cottage Hughdy spoke as much as he had all summer. 'The weasel can whistle,' he informed us. 'If one's in trouble, a whole crowd of them gathers.' As a youngster he'd seen thousands of them swarming over a tossed ditch. 'Thousands,' he said, sounding like he meant that many, not just a lot. 'Thousands, maybe more. Running in and out of the ditch, like the one yous saw today.'

Brian and I were only getting used to the way Chrissie and he talked – 'press' for closet or 'rasher' for bacon, but 'ditch' for a stone wall made no sense at all.

'It must have been a funeral,' Hughdy said, 'for when one dies, they all gather.'

'Will you stop before you have the child frightened!' Chrissie said as she saw me shudder.

Paying his sister no mind, Hughdy explained how they whistled by putting their tails in their mouths. How a weasel was good to have around the place as they kept the rats down. And how a purse made from their skin would never be empty, only you'd never kill a weasel for it.

Possibly because neither Brian nor I laughed at the weasels, he began to tell us other stories in the evening, too. Like the man up the Glen who Hughdy swore could bring the sea into your kitchen, and have you up on the table for fear of the waves. Or the fairy shilling a stranger woman gave to a man who'd helped carry her basket over the road. No matter how often he spent the coin then, it turned up always in his pocket. And later on Chrissie told us how the shilling man had been a near neighbour, his daughter still alive, a priest's housekeeper somewhere in the county. I loved how the stories invariably featured some part of Glenmore, an actual rock or bend in the road that made them seem realer than real. Of course I still went to bed most nights half-terrified, fearful of meeting a thousand weasels or a pooka in my dreams. And while I never dreamt of those, I did have my old nightmare once, though it seems silly something as mundane as a fridge full of cogs & wheels could have me sobbing for Pops as both Hughdy and Brian hovered overhead, telling me to hush.

'It was just an old dream,' I told Chrissie the next morning, afraid she might stop Hughdy telling us stories altogether. I had already re-read the two paperbacks I'd packed when Ma wasn't looking, and there was nothing else to read in the cottage—beyond 'The Messenger' and 'Ireland's Own'. Nor other kids to play with, even if that wasn't such a big change from Boston. Entire days came when I moped around, days when the weather turned, and Glenmore suddenly seemed the dreariest place on the planet. And I still got homesick, missing both Ma and Pops, usually at bedtime. And again on the misty morning I found Hughdy spraying his potatoes against the blight, the tank strapped to his back reminding me of Manny waging war on the cockroaches at No. 23.

But most of the time I was content. Chrissie was teaching me how to knit and while she was often quiet like Ma, I was learning to relax within her silences. And Hughdy too—once he got used to the idea of us, and vice versa—helped to truly make that summer. Even if I still struggled to understand him a lot of the time. 'Stupid as mud is, there's a trade to it,' he might declare, clearing a drain in the field below the cottage. A field that he insisted on calling a 'park', though it looked nothing like the Boston Public Gardens. Just rushes and ragwort in lieu of the lovely flowerbeds I waited on each spring to bloom. I didn't understand what Hughdy meant about shovelling mud, but it sounded the kind of thing Pops often said. Word puzzles which I'd repeat in my head in bed until I finally had them figured out.

'There's something wrong with that front wheel,' he shouted another evening as Brian cycled Hughdy's ancient Raleigh up the lane, 'it keeps coming round on ye!' For once I got a joke before Brian—who jumped off straight away lest he damage the bike further. But he laughed too once he got it, while Hughdy quietly smiled.

A few nights before we left, Hughdy told us one last story. 'Did yous ever hear about the O'Byrnes and the evil fairies?' he began, while rubbing some of his minced-up plug tobacco between his massive palms. Never before had he given a name to a story, but I was too keen for him to continue to notice that straight off. His smelly old pipe lit, he went on to tell of this buried treasure lying unclaimed on a Donegal hill.

'How come?' interrupted Brian.

'I'm coming to that part now,' said Hughdy who never hurried. 'There was a kind of a curse, you see, attached to the treasure by these evil fairies. Three O'Byrnes have to die digging it, before it can be unearthed.'

Suddenly I saw THE O'BYRNE FAMILY, GLENMORE, CO DONEGAL, IRELAND in my own neat lettering on an envelope last December, after Róisín O'Byrne Maguire had given in, and let me help her address her few Christmas cards.

'Are you, my Ma and Chrissie from that same family?' I blurted out, forgetting Uncle Dinny out in Chicago.

'Aye, now you have it,' Hughdy said, giving me a queer stare.

I looked over at Aunt Chrissie then, who as a rule paid little attention to Hughdy's yarns. But this time Chrissie stared right back, before giving her head a little shake, like a raven in the know.

If I was spooked, Brian was nearly jumping out of his skin. 'Have you dug it up yet, Hughdy?' he shouted.

'I'm after telling you three O'Byrnes have to die digging it,' Hughdy said, fixing him with the same odd stare. 'Only two have died so far.'

That shut Brian up good. Nor did Hughdy say anything for a time.

'Do you know where it's buried, Hughdy?' I finally asked.

'Oh, aye,' said Hughdy. 'I do, surely.'

'Will you show us?' Brian asked, almost whispering now.

'Oh, aye, someday maybe,' Hughdy replied. 'If you come back another summer.'

CHAPTER 19

DATE: 13 March 1988

SENTIMENT FOR THE DAY: Home, Sweet Home

I took up with Sister Úna this afternoon from where I left off here late last night. Telling how Ma had seemed easier when Brian and I came home from Donegal that September. Asking how our school day had been or had we much for homework—the kind of stuff mothers do without thinking, only ours didn't always think to. Who knows, perhaps the break from looking after us, plus the time with Pops, had been all she needed?

Anyhow, upon hearing me describe the hug we got from Ma at Logan Airport—as if she'd truly missed us too—Sister asked was her well-being possibly the reason my father had sent us off?

'It might've been,' I said, surprised. 'Certainly Ma seemed happier. Not just to have us home, but also in herself. Even going out to the pictures once or twice with some of the other women from work.' And perhaps that had been Pops' intention all along—as two plane tickets to

Ireland, even a child's fare, was a lot of money we hadn't got, and better spent surely on my mother's health than on a holiday for us. Of course, as a child you haven't a clue as to what really goes on with your parents. Even when they fight aloud, which ours only sometimes did, you don't know what the rows are really about. And Brian and I hadn't a notion about Ma's health yet, as she only fell apart the following year.

Sister Úna got up to make us a cup of tea, it being a miserable rainy afternoon. It's odd enough I'm seeing a nun for counselling, never mind a nun who makes us tea! But I wasn't thinking about that just then. Rather about what had felt like an insight—unlike most of our sessions in which whatever counselling takes place pretty much escapes me. Instead I seem to do most of the talking—about Boston, the Home, Katy or lately Donegal. With Sister Úna occasionally asking what some memory might mean, or whether I worry about this or that. At least she never goes religious on me—there's no talk about God or Sin or Heaven, though sometimes she speaks of spirit or love. And sometimes she suggests an exercise—like writing down a few lines about what I might find if I were to walk into the Lost Property Office of My Life? That last was a bit far out, I thought, nor did I try it out, either. But for the most part it's simply me talking, while she sits and listens.

Nor do I necessarily feel the better for it either. It's one thing to write about a long-ago, sometimes sunny Donegal summer, and another to be getting out of bed to yet another cold, grey Dublin morning. OK, March is never great, here or in Boston, but it seems this year more miserable than ever. Waking up remains the worst, returning to that same dark emptiness even as a new day dawns. That said, I'm generally more able for life once I'm up and about, and even have a bit of energy most evenings after work. Enough to put on a big fire in the sitting room, and curl up with Margaret Atwood's 'Cat's Eye' which Alice May has lent me, while Katy does her History or Biology at the other end of the couch. Whereas it was the winter nights—not mornings—that Chrissie and Hughdy complained about, even in summertime. 'Nothing worse than the long winter nights,' poor Hughdy used to say. 'No harder work than lying in bed, unable to sleep.' So maybe it was the long March nights that got the better of him, before April, the cruellest month, finally took him down.

I do enjoy writing about Donegal though. I even told K something of that first summer—though she knows Glenmore well, as we've gone up every year. Both when Chrissie was alive, and in the seven years since she passed away, leaving us the cottage. Katy loves hearing about it, too, though maybe it's as much hearing about my childhood. Whereas I can't recall Ma telling us much of anything about growing up in that cottage. K being K, however, wastes no time in correcting my facts. 'There're weasels in England,' she informed me last night, 'but only stoats in Ireland. So it must've been a stoat you and Brian saw.'

I realised something else this afternoon, after Sister Úna came back with a cup of tea and a few fig rolls. How not only had Ma seemingly benefited from our absence, but how I came back from Ireland a bit more able for life myself. Not in any hugely conscious way, for what are you conscious of at age ten? But I do believe I came back more able for my differences. To be sure, Donegal quickly seemed like a strange dream once we were back in downtown Boston. All of it—the cottage, Chrissie, Hughdy, Granny, the sheep in the park, the mountains and the sea. Plus the harshness too, the bleak hills when it rained, making everything cold and damp, nothing like summer in Boston. Or the sharp edges on Chrissie when she wasn't in good form, or always missing Pops and Ma. All of it was so different to shiny, up-to-date Boston, too different to explain to Vivian or the few other friends I had. Far too different to describe, yet I see now how for once it wasn't a troubling <u>difference</u>—not like my parents' Irish accents in the heart of Brahmin Boston, or my mother's odd and awkward ways. Or how we lived downtown instead of in a proper neighbourhood. But my Donegal summer wasn't that kind of different—rather more like a quiet secret that helped buoy me up.

'What'd you do over the summer?' somebody would ask at school.

'My brother and I went to Ireland.'

'What was that like?'

'It was OK,' I'd say. Or 'Cool' if it were a pal like Vivian.

But that was all. I didn't have to say anything more—nor could have I. Rather Glenmore remained a secret, like buried treasure, to which I alone possessed the map.

CHAPTER 20

DATE: 17 March 1988

WEATHER: Showers

ACTIVITY: Widespread Paddywhackery

It might have been buried treasure Nora Doorstop was after this morning in the front day-room. Nora who rarely settles at the best of times. 'Are you sitting on something of mine?' she kept asking the other residents. And visitors too, of whom we had a good number, given the holiday. 'Are you sitting on something of mine?' before moving on with her short methodical steps, shoulders stooped, working her way in and out and behind the chairs.

'It's green,' she informed Tom the Teacher's son, both times he got up to show her he wasn't. 'Green,' she repeated, as if in honour of Paddy's Day.

'The Boody Women might have it,' Cassie Boyle told Nora as she shuttled by. 'Take care the Boody Women don't get you too.'

'Are you sitting on something?' Nora asked Kitty the Conductor for the third time.

'I haven't your fecking money!' Kitty shouted. 'Feck off!'

That outburst brought young Clodagh Corcoran into the front room, where she finally got Nora seated. Only Nora popped up a few minutes later, taking the doorstop with her. And so we spent the next fifteen minutes playing Hide & Seek, the day-room door propped open with a paperback, until Clodagh found it under Nora's pillow in her bedroom, a new hidey-hole. 'Remind me to have Leo pick up a couple of spares,' I told Mary O'Mara, not for the first time.

It was corned beef & cabbage for dinner, given the day that was in it. After which three musicians from the local comhaltas came in to play a few tunes in the dining room. We broke out the sherry then, for those who take a drink and wanted to drown the shamrock. Pat the Pope even had an actual sprig of shamrock pinned to his cardigan, given him by a nephew up from Wexford. A moment of panic then followed as Polish Petra hunted for the Lucozade bottle for Happy-As—who's not so far gone he can't see other people having a drink, though, God love him, he thinks he is too, as he knocks back his Lucozade.

Pops took Brian and me to the Paddy's Day parade once in South Boston when I was nine. It was bitterly cold, same as it often is over here, and a lot of the crowd were drinking bottles of beer on the street. Brian kept finding hats on the sidewalk, three or four of them. 'Cooties' were what you got from other people's hats, but that didn't bother Brian who tried them all on, till we got home and Ma promptly threw them out. I don't recall much else about the parade, nor did we ever go again. 'Paddywhackery' was Pops' word for anything overtly Irish in Boston, and he'd likely only taken us that once out of some vague sense of ethnic duty.

Still, I loved taking Katy to the parade here when she was little. Even if it wasn't up to much— a fleet of Post &

Telegraph vans, the Gardaí and Army bands, followed by supermarket floats full of huge papier-mâché apples and bananas teetering on flatbed trailers. Of course all that has changed markedly in the last few years. Massive floats with West Indian steel-drum bands, followed by fire-breathing dragons and troops of fairies. But K's too grown-up now to go to the new & improved parade with her Ma—which is pretty much how life works, no? Instead she went downtown last night with a few of her pals to a huge fireworks display on the Liffey. We'd a row first, after I told her I didn't want her going in. Well, not a row exactly—just Katy bursting into tears and saying I was unreasonable. While in my other ear I could hear Sister Úna suggesting that I practise letting go of K even while holding on, like paying out rope on a skiff as you stand on the shore. So I make K promise to stay glued to her pals, and hop the 20B bus home the moment the skies clear. 'Get da bus!' I want to jest as she goes out, but don't.

I don't want to turn into a crank, but at the same time part of me prefers the old St Patrick's Day. Not the sole South Boston parade I saw, which didn't seem like a particularly happy affair, but the Paddy's Day I imagine Pat the Pope had growing up down the country, foraging along the road for a bit of actual shamrock. Or those K and I enjoyed, bundling up against the cold before catching the bus into the city centre. Tacky as the old parade was, there was something endearing about it. As if it were hand-made, I suppose. Which means, Good God, maybe I'm not turning into a crank so much as into my own mother?

CHAPTER 21

DATE: 18 March 1988
MEMORY FOR THE DAY: Amsterdam
WORD FOR THE DAY: Strippenkaart

I lay in bed last night thinking about how I wasn't in Dublin two St Patrick's Days ago. Seán and I had broken it off just before Christmas, and Orla shortly after suggested we spend Paddy's weekend in Amsterdam, hoping no doubt to get me out of the doldrums. Seán had already departed Dublin, packing in his job as an air-traffic controller at Dublin Airport for a three-year contract at King Abdul Aziz Airport in Saudi. Nor was the irony lost on me: Orla and I flying off together, after Seán of the Free Flights had spent three years trying to arrange a holiday abroad. Only I wouldn't leave Katy, nor bring her along on a dirty weekend, though I actually detest that phrase.

I'd already told Seán that summer how I couldn't see us following him Down Under, after he let on how he was being headhunted by Sydney Airport. Seán said he understood, but I'm not sure he really did. Still, it wasn't my being a single mother—or that I wouldn't go away without Katy, or let Seán sleep over at our house, or emigrate to Australia—that finished us. For had I truly thought Seán was the one, I'd have chanced those changes, trusted K would adapt to having him around, and so gradually come round to seeing us together as a family. Seán had been previously married, but it had broken up, childless, a few years before I met him. Or do only unmarried, non-cohabiting couples like him and me break up, whereas actual marriages break down? Either way, my "lack of commitment" was what ended us according to Seán, and he was right. But I'd have made that commitment—enlisted Katy and myself, I think—had I been absolutely sure about Seán. Or so I tell myself—rather than think I might have a problem with 'committing'.

Still, I do myself no favours by saying 'had I thought Seán was the one'—by still believing there's just one fella out there for me. No doubt it's everything I read as a kid—from 'Ivanhoe' to 'Gone With the Wind'—which has me still thinking at age thirty-seven that we're all somehow fated to meet a soul-mate. The Yang to our Yin, the One True Love who'll do us, and do for us, forever. All those books, plus being reared a Catholic? I might ask Sister Úna that—'Is it what we heard in Sunday School, after the nine o'clock Mass at Holy Cross, Sister, that has me hanging on yet, hoping for a Mr. Right?'

I'm not saying Seán wasn't a lovely guy, and I wasn't in some kind of low-grade love with him. He liked his jar a lot, which gave me pause, and I sometimes feared for whoever was flying out of Dublin Airport Monday mornings after our Sunday nights out. But Seán was a gentle guy, and drink only made him mellower. He didn't read much, but was mad about traditional music—though he didn't play himself, unless you count occasionally banging on a borrowed bodhrán. Nor could he carry a note in a bucket, though that didn't stop him from trying, whenever a session at Hughes or The Cobblestone ended up in a sing-song.

It was in Toners on Baggot St, however, that Seán dropped his bombshell about Saudi. We never went to Toners, which made me wonder after whether he'd chosen it so as not to plant a painful memory in one of our good-times pubs, or worse yet Gaffney's, just around the corner. Imagine going into your local and feeling this pang every time you saw the corner table where you lost yet another little piece of your heart? At least that's how my mind works, matching locale to memory, so I'm thankful it was Toners—even if I was only thankful after the fact.

Nor did I say what I was thinking, either. 'Jesus, Seán,' I said instead, 'you're not even allowed to drink in Saudi?' Whereas what I was thinking ran more like 'Am I that dreary, Seán? So little fun that you'd sooner skive off to a fecking sandpit?' But I didn't say anything like that, as I was already trying not to cry.

A few weeks later Orla, during yet another teary Friday post-work drink in Gaffney's, announced we were going to Amsterdam for Paddy's Day.

'Only if we go Dutch,' I managed to smile before I saw she was serious.

'You're gonna wash that Séan right outa your hair,' Orla lilted. 'We're going to Amsterdam, Amsterdam here we come!'—like a medley gone wrong.

'You mean Kansas City.'

'Kan-sass, my ass,' Orla grinned. 'It's time you stopped moping over Seán Boy.'

'I can't afford it.'

'I've the cheap-flight tickets from Tesco's already.'

'What about my Katy?'

'My cousin Maria's coming up from Waterford for the Parade,' Orla smiled again. 'And I've told her she's staying at your place with Katy.'

'But you were saving those Tesco stamps,' I reminded her, 'for you and Jack to go to Rome?'

'Jack couldn't get the time off work.'

I didn't believe that—as you can <u>always</u> get time off work in Ireland. But I did believe Orla was that kind of friend. And so when the appointed Thursday came, the pair of us flew out to Schiphol, where we caught the train to Centraal Station. I couldn't get over the beautiful Dutch trains all yellow and blue, with padded seats like you'd find on the flight deck of the Starship Enterprise. Nor could I believe the sea of bicycles parked outside Centraal Station, rows upon rows, all patiently awaiting their owners.

Orla, who knows Amsterdam, bundled us onto a tram in jig time, handing a strippenkaart to a woman of colour seated at a tiny counter at the back. 'This don't look like Kansas, Toto?' I marvelled, staring out the window. Nor did it feel like Kansas—or Dublin either—when a roller-skater nearly ran us down as we got off the tram. A tall, tanned roller-skater, mind you, all bulging biceps and shaven head, wearing just sunglasses and a one-piece, black-thonged singlet. Orla and I just gasped, while a group of drunken English lads exiting a bar hollered abuse at his bare bottom as it disappeared up the avenue.

Our hotel was one of those tall narrow townhouses with gorgeous gables, overlooking the Prinsengracht about a mile south of Centraal Station. We took it easy that afternoon, walking back up towards An Lár, and quickly working out the boundaries of the Red Light district, as we weren't interested in that kind of window shopping. I was enchanted by it all, not quite believing I was in fabled Amsterdam, even if there were no Hans Brinker flashing along frozen canals.

We spent Friday morning at the Van Gogh Museum, and took in Anne Frank's house that afternoon. I'd been keen to see the latter, having read her diary in Boston as a child, but I wasn't prepared for the emptiness of it all, never mind my tears at Anne's own bedroom, decorated just like Katy's back in Dublin, only all of Ann's faded postcards and pictures of film stars were covered by Plexiglass.

'Will we do the Rijksmuseum, Toto?' Orla suggested Saturday at breakfast.

'The Rijksmuseum it is,' I nodded, thumbing through our 'Rough Guide' at the table. Only to suddenly find myself back inside Apt 3C, transfixed by yet another of Mrs. Lunenberg's pictures. A small reproduction of another Dutch scene, a townscape this time, tiny foreground figures, light-washed buildings across a river, and overhead the most incredible sky.

'It's called "View of Delft",' Mrs. L said, upon finding me frozen before it. 'By an artist called Vermeer.' Only I thought she had called him 'The Mirror'—which made perfect sense somehow, the whole scene shimmering like something caught in a looking glass. She also mentioned how some character in a novel had thought that painting reason enough—perhaps the only reason there was—to go on living. She named the novel too, only I didn't hold onto that, and occasionally wonder what it was. But I remembered Vermeer's painting all right—which per our 'Rough Guide' hung just a yellow-and-blue train-ride away in the Mauritshuis Museum in The Hague.

'Would we go there instead?' I asked Orla, after telling her of Mrs. L's print.

'Why not?' said Orla, always up for something new.

Two hours later we reached the museum, where after a cursory look at the ground floor, we found the upstairs room we wanted—only for me to promptly burst into tears, while Orla went over to a white card stuck on the wall where the Vermeer should have hung. A white card explaining in four languages how 'View of Delft' had been removed for cleaning.

'I don't know why I'm crying,' I told Orla, who just put her arms around me as a German couple gave us a curious look.

'Well, I do, Sweetie,' said Orla. 'C'mon, let's go get some lunch.'

Sunday morning we did the bloemenmarkt on the Singel Canal, as I'd promised Mary O'Mara amaryllis bulbs, and Mrs. Sheedy next door some tulips. We then looked for some live music before our train back to the airport, but had to finally settle for a bar with taped jazz. It had a nice mix of young and older folk, mostly Dutch, plus a smell of marijuana from the back. We'd already peered into a few smoke shops, all garish neon like the bars in Boston's Combat Zone, but I hadn't smoked grass since college, and wasn't going to take it up again in a Dutch drugs den, reggae music blasting, even if it was Paddy's weekend!

Anyhow, I started to tell Orla a story about Seán—which makes sense, seeing he was my excuse for a foreign holiday. A story Seán had told me when we first met, and which probably played some part in my falling for him. Of how he'd grabbed the elbow of some guy he'd recognised in Waterstones. 'Don't tell me your name—it'll come to me! We started work together at Dublin airport in 1974?' 'I don't think so,' the guy says. 'My name's Tom Hanks.'

'Trust Seán!' Orla laughed, just as the music changed in

the bar. Perhaps the barman had placed our accent, or possibly just because it was Paddy's weekend. But suddenly the jazz is gone, and Paul Brady is singing 'Paddy's Green Shamrock Shore'—which just happened to be Seán's party piece. It didn't take long for my tears to start again, though I dreaded making a show of myself at the bar. But Orla just pressed my hand, and handed me a tissue.

'It's not Seán,' I said, blowing my nose. 'I'm only crying to think the song could be sung so well!'

We had a good laugh then—laughter, not loss, being more how I wanted our Amsterdam weekend away to end.

CHAPTER 22

DATE: 21 March 1988

THOUGHT FOR THE DAY: What Can You Have of a Cat But Her Skin?

Calico Cat was on Veronica Egan's bed this morning when I went in to take her blood pressure. I wasn't thrilled as Veronica's only over her ordeal in the lift, and doesn't need anything upsetting her. But she was delighted with her visitor, same as my Katy who still tries to sneak Nibbles up to her room at bedtime. Luckily Calico hadn't chosen to call on Cassie Boyle who can't abide cats. Or some other resident who wouldn't be slow to point out a cat has no business being in a nursing home. They'd be right too, so I left a note for the night shift to make sure Calico doesn't get upstairs again if they let her in for a nap on a kitchen chair in the wee hours.

'Will I bring in my Calico?' Fiona Flynn had offered, after the poison Leo the Porter laid down failed to do for the rats out back.

'We can't keep a cat!' I'd protested, but Fiona said Calico wasn't an indoors cat. Well, no farther indoors than the kitchen at night anyhow. Besides, she had enough bodies to look after—from Muttly the dog to her eighty-five-year-old mother Nelly, who lives with her in a granny flat.

Pops too bent the rules the same way back in Boston. Turning a blind eye on Jackson, Miss Chauncy's huge grey cat, who slept in her bathroom hand-basin. Jackson too roamed further afield, when he could slip past Miss Chauncy, occasionally making it as far as the front lobby. And deaf Mrs. Getchell on the fifth floor also kept a cat, though I never saw it. According to Pops, it would nudge Mrs. G with its paw whenever her buzzer sounded.

'Will your kids not miss Calico?' I asked Fiona after she brought her in.

'The twins haven't looked at the cat since they discovered puberty,' Fiona said. 'And my mother thinks the short-haired Manx next door is Calico. "Some hooligan's shaved the cat!"' she announces any time she sees him. Her sixteen-year-old twins, Tommy and Tricia, plus thirteen-year old Heather, are some of what keep Fiona in overdrive, along with her Derek. 'All men are idiots, and I married their King!' she declared the other day, giving both Mary O'Mara and me a laugh. I've met Derek a few times, who admittedly doesn't look like much of a prize. Which is puzzling, for Fiona not only has a huge heart but she's beautiful too. Looks years younger than fifty, her fair hair just going to grey, finely chiselled features and bright blue eyes.

Anyhow, that's how we got Calico. Cats were 'a package of poison' according to Ma, so we'd've not had one no matter where we lived. But I've loved them always, not least that half-wild Donegal pair whom I christened Lancelot and Guinevere, which Aunt Chrissie of course thought daft. I got my first proper cat the year after I moved out of Park St with Katy. I say 'got' but in fact Nya-Nya chose us, turning up one August morning at our brown-shingled tenement just off Union Square in Somerville, a scrawny scrap of orange & white fur mewing piteously outside our kitchen door. Feed him once, I told myself, and you'll be feeding him forever. But I gave him some milk anyhow, puzzling how his tiny legs had managed the back steps to our second-storey porch—where he slept on an old jumper, as I wouldn't let a stray cat indoors with Katy. 'Nya-Nya!' Katy named him upon sight, her rendering of 'Meow, Meow'. I got him shots at a vet's, plus worm pills, so K could play with him. And I eventually let him indoors too, where he'd sit by the kitchen sink at night, waiting for a cockroach to run across the white porcelain.

Nya-Nya was K's first cat too, though she doesn't remember him. Nor the morning she looked out the window and saw him sleeping by the kerb, shortly before we were to leave for Ireland. 'Sleeping' was K's word, but I knew it wasn't a cat-nap. Mrs. Lynch next door had already agreed to take him, but poor N^2 hadn't lived long enough for the change of guard. After distracting K, I nipped downstairs and lifted him out of the gutter. I must have told K a white lie after—how Mrs. Lynch had sent him down the country for a holiday. But I occasionally still think of how he came up our back stairs and into our lives for a spell.

CHAPTER 23

DATE: 22 March 1988

THOUGHT FOR THE DAY: Smoking Can Damage
Your Drawers

Sometimes it seems more a loony bin I'm running than a
nursing home. And I'm not talking about the residents
either—rather Lillian O'Leary our cleaner. Lil who came to
us a few sandwiches short of a picnic, but who I'm
beginning to doubt has anything at all in her Thermos.
'She'd get lost in a brainstorm,' I can hear Pops saying. 'If
that one was any dumber, you'd have to water her daily.'

None of this is fair to Lil, I know. It's just when you
figure she's not so swift, she does something to convince
you she's more dotty than slow. Or just deaf, not daft. Like
last week when Nurse Ethel mentioned a new grandson.
'Oh, lovely!' says Lil. 'Was it a boy or a girl?' She's also a
near-relation of Mrs. Malaprop, telling us of the Centurion
section her daughter had, or her sister who went into
hospital for a hysterical rectum.

But my main gripe with Lil is her smoking, how she
lights up everywhere. Of course she shouldn't be smoking

anywhere, given her health. Overweight and bulgy eyes, which suggest a thyroid condition. Plus plagued by her bowels, whose condition she reports on as regularly as Met Éireann. Anyhow, I ask the staff to smoke in the small alcove just off the dining hall that visitors use, though most visitors simply plonk down beside their grandmother, old friend, or former neighbour, and forgo a smoke altogether. Lil however tries to sneak a smoke everywhere. You'd laugh to hear some of the girls tell it—Lil puffing away inside a toilet, door ajar so she can keep an eye out 'for Matron'—a finger to her lips in warning, like she were starring in her own pantomime. Which in a way, I suppose, she was this afternoon.

I laugh now, but only for Clodagh Corcoran flinging a pan of water between her knees, I swear I'd have swung for Lil—and for Nurse Powers too who'd given Lil a suppository earlier for her constipation. So that after lighting up in the laundry, Lil suddenly felt the urge—and had to hot-foot it, fag in hand, through the dining room and down the hall into a toilet. All was well then, until she looked down and saw her lowered knickers all aflame.

I went over to Sister Úna after work, having left Katy a snack and a note saying we'd have dinner when I got home. I don't bother Sister Úna with my workday, but I thought she might get a laugh out of Lil today, which she did. She asked then how I felt I was doing—the melancholy she meant—which I said seemed that bit better. I didn't want to disappoint her, I guess, same as I've spent much of my life trying not to disappoint somebody or other. Though I'm a good bit harder now—else I wouldn't be able to run the Home. But I still find myself fudging sometimes: like this evening with Sister Úna, in order not to let her down. Fact is, I don't feel I'm coping any better, mornings most of all.

I remind myself today's the equinox, the balance now tipped in favour of the sun, but it doesn't feel like that within . . .

CHAPTER 24

DATE: 23 MARCH 1988
WORDS FOR THE DAY: Ghost, Wraith, Spirit, Phantom, Fetch

I told Sister Úna yesterday more about how Ma went into hospital the year after our Donegal summer. How the greater happiness we had witnessed upon our return didn't hold up as far as Christmas. How Uncle Dinny's death in Chicago around Thanksgiving was the start of it. And how his death had me scared to leave our apartment for days after, never mind look at the lobby stairs just outside our door.

'There was a wee girl on the stairs this afternoon, Jim,' Ma told Pops that November evening when he came in from a painting job. 'Seated on the bottom step.'

'Hush, Rose,' Pops said as he glanced at me.

But I hadn't understood what Ma was saying, and probably just asked who the little girl was? I always hoped another girl would come to live at No. 23, somebody other than Brian to try to pal around with. Nor did I understand the stricken look on Ma's face when the phone rang an

149

hour later—as if she'd been waiting all along for it. She was still crying in the kitchen when I went to bed, after asking that my bedroom door be left ajar. 'Dinny died the hour I saw that child,' I could hear her say. 'I knew there was a death in it.' And then my father telling her to hush again.

I didn't wake from a bad dream that night, nor did I feel truly sad about Uncle Dinny, whom Brian and I had never met. But I lived in dread for weeks after of that little girl on the stairs. Ma who took a train out to her brother's funeral never mentioned her again after she came back—on Pops' insistence, I suspect. Still I hated being by myself anywhere in our apartment, in case she might materialise like Our Lady had for Bernadette. Even if I hadn't a word like 'materialise' at age ten. Brian claimed Ma only imagined it, but the description she gave Pops, her mass of dark curls and nut-brown eyes, seemed all too real, like the detail in Uncle Hughdy's stories the summer before. Only this was even more frightening—for this had happened in Boston. In our very building even, as if a bolt of Irish lightning had flashed across the Atlantic and cut across our lives here.

CHAPTER 25

DATE: 27 March 1988

ACTIVITY FOR THE DAY: Taxidermy

PROVERB FOR THE DAY: What the Daughter Does,
the Mother Did

The power a few words can wield. How something as innocuous as Mary O'Mara's 'I've a crow to pluck with you!'—over an error I'd made in next week's roster—could bring it back so vividly: all that bright pink flesh and coal-black feathers. Certainly nothing I told Sister Úna last week about Ma's first breakdown comes near to what flashed back this morning—when Mary O'Mara came up with her crow to pluck.

It was in early April that year when Ma finally flew apart, after battling a major depression through the winter that followed Uncle Dinny's death. Though you don't know as a child to call it that, nor chart the changes the same way Pops undoubtedly had. We saw Ma don the same pea-green sweater day after day, but unlike Pops we didn't know what that signified. How she couldn't be bothered to put on something else, same as she couldn't stir herself to take down our Christmas tree, though that always bothered me.

151

That March however, her energy returned tenfold and she began tidying with a vengeance. "Spring-cleaning," she called it, and both Brian and I were enlisted. Literally so, both of us given a list of chores off the clipboard she now carried everywhere. I unsuccessfully tried to swap the 'venetian blinds' scribbled on mine one day with Brian, as I hated cleaning them, the way the dust just streaks if you wipe it with a damp cloth, and I haven't lived anywhere with those blinds since. On the other hand, I make lists all the time, and can't imagine running either home or Home without that management technique.

All this activity suggested Ma wasn't well, but I didn't really understand until the Saturday morning I returned from skipping rope outside and found her in the kitchen. She had been out shopping early, and must have come back across the Common herself. Or that's where I've always assumed she found the crow after it fell out of the sky. A crow that lay now splayed open on our kitchen table, all gaping pink and glossy black, as Ma struggled to stuff its hollow innards with yellow Indian meal. 'Come here, Maeve, I've a crow to pluck with you!' said Mary O'Mara this morning, and suddenly there it was—as if those colours had fixed the memory so, all black, pink, and yellow against the white enamel. 'Are you mad?' is what you'd say to somebody frantically stuffing a dead crow on their kitchen table, like a loony-tune taxidermist. And so my mother was—mad, barking mad. Except at ten you don't understand that—you just sense something's terribly wrong. I don't remember Ma saying why she wanted to cook a crow, but I can see her frustration yet at the way the cornmeal kept leaking out as she tried to stitch its belly up. And how she finally threw down needle & thread and began tearing at the feathers.

'It's not the one way we all go,' Pops used to say, but that's the manner in which my mother went mad that April. I tried to toss it off last week—describing Ma's hospitalisation to Sister Úna like I was talking of an appendicitis. Until her first psychotic break came flashing back this morning, all Technicolor & Kodachrome. Her madness which has always shadowed me, if I dare own it— the very thing that brought me to Sister Úna after I fell to pieces last Christmas. Telling myself I wasn't going to lose it, as poor Katy clasped that silver ball beside our tree. Telling myself I wasn't going over the edge like my own mother had. And telling myself that yet.

CHAPTER 26

DATE: 28 March 1988
PROVERB FOR THE DAY: Crows Are Black The World Over

A few days after the crow Ma went into hospital. Entering our living room that morning, I saw the coffee table by the couch full of cups and plates. Not a truly remarkable sight, but I can see the clutter like a photograph yet, both parents having sat there all night, as Ma was utterly beyond sleep by then. I went into the kitchen next, where Brian told how Pops had woken him at six to say he was taking Ma to hospital, and for us to get ourselves off to school.

Brian and I had no clear idea what kind of hospital, of course. Not understanding, until our first visit, that you didn't go to Metropolitan State in Waltham to have your tonsils out or a broken arm set. We never owned a car, living downtown where Pops mostly worked at home. So one of his poker pals, Frank McCann or Mike Sullivan, drove us out when we visited, else Pops went alone by bus. Ma had been admitted first into Boston State Hospital on Columbia Ave, which would've made visiting easier, but

Pops managed to get her transferred a week later to Metropolitan State. 'Like out of "The Snake Pit"!' I overheard him describing Boston State to Frank, which had me in tears at bedtime, saying I didn't want Ma anywhere near snakes.

'There aren't any snakes, Pet,' Pops said as he tucked me in. 'That's just a movie about a hospital that's not as nice as where your Ma is now.'

Once her mania ebbed, Ma sank back into depression. Brian & I visited once a month, but Pops went in every Sunday. One rainy afternoon we took her out to the nearby Beaver Brook Reservation. It was too wet for the picnic tables, so we ate the sandwiches Pops had packed sheltering inside the gazebo. Back at the hospital Ma gave Brian a small green pillow she'd made in Occupational Therapy, and myself a stuffed blue horse with a mane of yellow yarn.

Brian and I missed her terribly, but we got used to making our school sandwiches, and eventually used to Pops' cooking also. Pops was almost always in the apartment when we arrived back from school, and he kept an eye on us through the summer till Ma came home in August. Unlike Ma, however, Pops didn't mind me visiting Vivian or another classmate, Marsha Baker on Marlboro St, so long as he knew where I was.

I also played that summer with a new pal, Princetta. Gorgeous coffee-coloured skin and big brown eyes that grew even bigger just as the straight pin she occasionally liked to sneak up and stick you with went in. Whatever about my own shortfall of Personality, Princetta had plenty, plus a name to match—Princetta Ivory. She was terribly bright too, I think, but not much interested in what Miss Delaney had to teach us.

Like Vivian Henry, Princetta hadn't many close friends,

which is probably why I ended up playing with them. Princetta's tenement was towards the South End, not far from Juanita Cruz whom I also sometimes visited, and no great distance from Park St. Summertime also meant it was bright enough for me to walk home in plenty of time for supper. I can't imagine letting a child walk that way nowadays, but this was back in the sixties, before crack cocaine and all, and I never had a problem.

Like Juanita, Princetta too had a grandmother at home. A thin, old black lady with a Southern accent and upswept silver-framed eyeglasses that looked like a shiny metal butterfly had just alighted on her face. She was always in a long dress and looked terribly genteel, everything Princetta was not. I liked talking to her, hearing how her father had worked as gardener at a big house in New Orleans, and raised his family in what had formerly been slave quarters, where her own bedroom had opened onto a lovely patio with a fountain and potted plants. It sounded a far nicer set-up than a Super's apartment, but of course I said no such thing.

We also played at No. 23 where Princetta adored the elevator. But we were getting too old to play the department store game for very long, so after a few trips up and down, we'd take out Monopoly or just listen to the radio in my room. One afternoon we got into this slapping fight, striking each other in turn on the cheek with an open hand. We only exchanged two or three slaps before deciding to make sugar sandwiches, but I still remember how much it stung!

Princetta was a different child around her Grandma, polite and mild-spoken. But she still took a quarter from her purse one afternoon when I was over. The following day we looked high and low for the purse to replace the coin, but her Grandma must have noticed the theft and hidden it. Eventually Princetta gave up and began menacing me with her cat Cuddles, a spooky-looking Siamese who always paid you too much attention when you entered a room, not ignoring you the way most cats do. Another afternoon Princetta cut off half of Cuddle's whiskers with her Grandma's pinking shears, which had her Grandma lifting her butterfly glasses to stare intently at the cat each time it came into the room.

Whatever hold her Grandma had over her, Princetta didn't tiptoe around anybody else. Not even our principal, Mr. Cremins, whom she called an asshole at the end of eighth grade. Informed she'd be suspended unless she apologised—in which case she'd only get a detention—Princetta met him halfway with 'OK, I'm sorry, asshole.'

'You can see his gold fillings when he hollers,' she told me after she was allowed back to school.

I puzzle how Maeve Maguire, Good Girl, was able to pal with Princetta Ivory, unmistakably Bad. Not the least bit 'ladyish' as my Katy used to say. But there wasn't anything genuinely bad about Princetta, whose occasional forays with a straight pin were more than offset by a generous heart. She had a soft side too, for all her mettle.

'How's your Grandma?' I asked her, freshman year at Boston High School, by which time we'd begun to drift apart.

'She died at Easter,' Princetta said, which I was sorry to hear. 'But hold on, Maeve,' she added as she shut her locker. 'You remember the two bits I swiped from her purse?'

I just grinned, which made Princetta smile too.

'Well, I slipped a quarter into her coffin when nobody was looking, and I swear Grandma smiled back.'

I sensed Ma didn't approve of Princetta, the few times she came over to us. But I don't think it was especially because she was black—or 'Negro' as we said back then. Nor did I ever hear my parents use 'nigger', which was common coinage among many of the Boston Irish. But we lived on a little island of gentility at No. 23 Park St, surrounded by gentry, even if none of the residents were filthy rich. Had we lived in an Irish neighbourhood like Southie, it might have been different. Southie where things erupted a few years later over the school bussing of blacks. Got truly vicious, the way I sometimes worry it might here, where we're seeing more so-called non-Irish all the time, like the Asian doing his Tai Chi every morning in Fairview Park as I walk to work.

Ma finally got out of hospital that August, less anxious, but no less abstracted. Plus she had these holes in her memory where electroshock had erased certain events. Like my birthday the previous year when Pops had taken us bowling, or even our June picnic in the rain at Beaver Dam. But she went back to work part-time that October at Jordan's, which meant she usually wasn't around if Princetta or Vivian came over. But she'd give out to me for cracking my knuckles at supper, a trick I learned from Vivian who called it finger farts, claiming it got rid of the gas in your joints and helped prevent arthritis.

CHAPTER 27

DATE: 29 March 1988

FACT FOR THE DAY: There Are More Ways of a Killing a Cat Than Choking Her With Cream

Calico Cat was on Cassie Boyle's bed this afternoon, putting her in a tizzy. You'd swear cats have a kind of radar for people who can't abide them. Like Cassie who was only five when some sadist of a neighbour gave her a box of new-born kittens. 'I hid them in the shed,' Cass told me, 'as I knew I wouldn't be allowed keep them.' What she didn't know was how she'd find them dead the next morning, after sneaking them a saucer of milk from the kitchen.

We don't often hear Cass reminisce, so it's a pity Calico didn't prompt a happier memory. When she first came to us, she kept talking of her only time in hospital as a child down in Tipperary. How white everything was, and how scared she felt, afraid she'd be forgotten. 'But this isn't a hospital,' we reassured her, and after a few weeks she settled in. Sometimes she resists her bath, but even that contrariness is easily managed, more childlike than challenging. And she's like a child with her Boody Women warnings too.

161

'And who, pray tell, are the Boody Women?' I ask, just to see her smile and crow, 'Oh that would be telling!'

Her tale of the kittens brought back a story Manny told one trash day as he emptied the rubbish outside each apartment into an old-fashioned wheelie-bin. It wasn't a story to tell Cassie, however, nor Katy at supper tonight, whose eyes begin to fill up if she's only recounting a sad film. So here I am saddled with it, which is probably why I'm writing it down. How Manny was another who couldn't stand cats, and always made Miss Chauncy put her Jackson inside a closet before he'd enter Apt 5D to fix a leaky tap or unclog a sink. Who knows, maybe just the mere thought of Jackson behind the door as he lifted Miss Chauncy's trash that day is what prompted him to tell of the Sunday his father handed him their cat. In a burlap bag with a couple of bricks, saying it was too old to mouse anymore.

'I cried all the way home from the canal,' Manny told me. 'But the cat had beat me there, and was seated on the stoop, lickin' herself dry.'

'What did your Dad do?' I asked.

'Oh, he gave the cat a wide berth after that,' Manny said. 'But it was *me* the cat wouldn't come near again till the day she died.'

I don't recall what Massachusetts mill town with its canal was Manny's. But it's funny how much of Manny I remember since beginning this reclamation project. Like the evening I came back from college to find Pops distraught at the kitchen table, telling Ma how he'd known something was up with Manny that morning.

I wasn't really paying attention, though I heard him ask Ma, 'You know how he never ate anything sweet?' as I made myself a sandwich. 'Never took a cookie or a bit of cake? Well, he asks me twice this morning do I know where you could get a chocolate éclair? "Did you not bring your sandwiches, Manny?" I asked. "I did," he said, "but I'd love an éclair." So I got him an éclair at Brighams before lunch. Though I made him eat half a sandwich first. You know how picky Manny is—well, he just scoffed down the éclair,' Pops shook his head, 'pushing the filling in with his fingers.'

I smiled at that, for there was indeed something dainty in the way Manny, for all his talk of rats & roaches, ate his sandwich or an apple. Or the fastidious way he always washed his hands with Lava soap, towelling them dry before locking the utility closet and heading home. But Pops who hadn't seen me smile just got up and left the kitchen. I looked over at Ma then, who told me how Pops had got a call just before I came in—from a neighbour who'd found Manny, slumped dead, just outside his door.

I don't remember anything else from that evening. Whether I cried, or how I tried to comfort Pops. But Pops mentioned the éclair again the following day. Said Manny must have sensed something imminent, something that called out for one last treat.

CHAPTER 28

DATE: 30 March 1988
WEATHER: Grey, Grey, Grey

The St John's Wort's doing f-all, as I still wake feeling miserable. Weary enough some mornings I wish I could sleep forever—the Eighth of Uncle Hughdy's Seven Sleepers. It's like all confidence for life has gone off on holiday, not even bothering to send a postcard home. I hate myself for waking like that, as I know from college it's not what my body's actually feeling. The way your blood flocculation index suddenly increases just before sunrise, as if the very planets are summoning you from your bed. Or the fact your pulse rate halves the moment you splash water on your face and shake your head awake. All of which makes me feel a fraud for waking as despondent as I do. 'Count your blessings' as Ma always said whenever I was moaning about something. So I lie in bed and tally them up:

1. Katy
2. Good health

3. A roof over our heads

4. A tolerable job

5. I'm still a size twelve

Or I lie in bed and think of those who truly are up against it—mothers with children sick from hunger, or refugees having to flee their homes. But that only makes me feel worse for not feeling truly blessed. So I switch from feeling fraudulent to envious, coveting the upbeat outlook of, say, Fiona Flynn, who hasn't it all that easy—her Derek constantly out of work, her twins far more challenging than my Katy, and her mother Nelly driving her slowly round the bend. Yet Fiona only makes you laugh, telling how she'd had Derek start to convert their garage into a granny flat the day after she rang Nelly, her mother, in Stoneybatter for a telephone number. Nelly put the phone down to look for it, only to lose track of what she was at. Fiona could hear her mother walking around, when suddenly the footsteps got louder. "Mam, Mam!!" she screamed down the phone, only to hear a click as Nelly hung up.

'Mam?' she rang back. 'What about that number?'

'Number? What number?' Nelly said, winning a trip to a brand-new granny flat.

It was great to have a laugh, but I was in tears again before I got home. Stopping off at Tesco's to get spuds for supper, and breaking down as I passed a bin of Brussels sprouts. 'Fairy cabbages,' Pops used to call them, coaxing me to finish mine at Christmas dinner, the only time Ma served them.

CHAPTER 29

DATE: 31 March 1988
WEATHER: Gales & Heavy Showers
ACTIVITY: Packing
THOUGHT FOR THE DAY: Out Like a Lion

Katy flies off to France tomorrow for four weeks, part of her school Transition Year, designed to improve her parlez-vous. I've been trying not to think about it—never mind mention it here. And don't ask how I'm going to fare without her, seeing I can't watch her go off to school some mornings without feeling my eyes fill up. We spent the evening packing her case, double-checking ticket, passport, and travellers' cheques. Plus her international phonecard, so she can ring me twice a week. She's gone off twice before—to Boston at age eight and again at ten. Staying two weeks each time—one week with Brian and Cheryl, and one at Park St with Pops in Apt 1A. But this trip feels harder, even if she's older and more able to look after herself. Or is it in part harder because she is older? As if this is a kind of a dry run for when she actually does fly the nest—which isn't that far off if I allow myself think about it.

She'll be a month in France, staying with Isabelle, her exchange partner, and her family in La Rochelle. After which Isabelle comes to us next year. I'm dreading her going off, but determined not to make a show of her at the airport tomorrow, honking into my hanky. She's been so sweet this past week—like she's momentarily parked her moodiness, knowing she's going away. 'I'll miss you, Ma,' she told me tonight, her own eyes tearing up, better able to apprehend her emotions than I was at sixteen. And less confused by life, I think, though she still suffers like we all do from that Great Confusion called adolescence. I sometimes worry she's too open, too vulnerable, but I also know she has far more confidence than I had at her age.

I'd like to think of this as a Transition Year for me too, even if I'm not getting a month in France. But it feels more like I'm utterly stuck, unable to shift the weight that settled on me last September. Spring's nearly here, but *I'm* not moving—still mired in what some poet whose name I disremember calls our 'interior winter'. Which pretty much says it all?

CHAPTER 30

DATE: 2 April 1988
ACTIVITY: Laying Out the Dead
WORD FOR THE DAY: Thanatography

Well, April proved the cruellest month for Carmen Cassidy, who died in her sleep yesterday. She took a bad turn on Thursday, and I was surprised she lasted the weekend. As if she were hanging on till April so as to exit in the same month as all her siblings, with whom I hope she's now cavorting. Or gambolling, frolicking—whatever one does on the other side, if one does anything at all. Or has life no flip side—just its negation once the heart stops beating? An infinite black hole, like the darker dark inside that Frigidaire I dreamt of years ago.

Polish Petra went to wake Carmen just before breakfast, only to draw the curtain around her bed. I was in the kitchen, showing Leo how the new dishwasher cuts out in mid-cycle, when Petra found me. I then went upstairs and left a message for Dr Hogan, hoping poor Carmen wouldn't be left waiting for him to come and sign the death cert, which needs to happen before the undertaker can take delivery of her remains. I rang Carmen's next of kin then, a niece in Raheny, and finally Father O'Reilly at Our Lady's, who administered her the Last Rites on Friday.

I might have chosen to look after Carmen myself, had it not been the busy breakfast hour, as there's something almost sacramental about that task. OK, sacramental is not exactly right, seeing it's Fr O'Reilly who has the Holy H_2O & sacred oils. But there's something about laying out a body that absolutely centres you. We used to shut our eyes at the end of those Zen sessions in Boston, as our teacher Alan recited The Six Cemetery Contemplations, which list the various stages of decomposition—from swollen blue and festering to bleached bones and ultimately dust. As if envisioning our own bodies rotting might teach us to cling to nothing in this world. But laying out somebody else, their actual remains, maybe also helps bring that Zen lesson home, helps you to see a body for what it truly is— a vehicle for a life that comes and goes, a penny-candle for the flame.

What we learned about the biology of death at college wasn't unlike the Buddha's Six Contemplations. Stuff like how body tissue first softens and liquefies via bacterial fermentation. Fairly explicit, if less ghoulish than envisioning, eyes shut in a Boylston St loft, a dead body lying in the charnel ground, half-eaten by crows, vultures, jackals and worms, as Alan requested we do. Whereas our pathology Prof only asked that we master the vocabulary of the initial post-mortem stage, death's first blush so to speak. I found such memorisation easy, mostly because I loved the language. Not just rigor mortis which sets in 2 to 4 hours after death as the muscles begin to contract, but algor mortis, the reduction in body temperature—'Literally the chill of death!' chuckled our Prof. Plus livor mortis, the purple discoloration that occurs as red blood cells break down, which was likely the 'blue' Aunt Chrissie spoke of when I finally heard the story of their finding poor Hughdy's body.

I did look in on Carmen however before her niece arrived, as Petra had not done a laying out for us before. I wasn't worried she might introduce some particular Polish twist—like the coin Mr. Barry said the Greeks used to put in the deceased's mouth for Charon the Boatman on the River Styx—but death like mud has its trade too, and I wanted to double-check Petra had elevated the head, tied the big toes together, that sort of thing.

As it happened Petra had poor Carmen in proper order—eyes shut, hair brushed, dentures in, and a peaceful expression on her never-before-so-familiar face. Petra had tidied everything away too, bar those photographs of the Cassidy clan, keeping watch over their youngest sister while a sleet-laced April shower lashed the window.

CHAPTER 31

DATE: 3 April 1988

FACT FOR THE DAY: The Dead Outnumber the Living
by Over 30 to 1

I lay awake again last night, trying not to think of Katy whom I already sorely miss. So I thought instead of poor Carmen, and then of that second Donegal summer without Brian this time—when I first encountered the remains of the dead. In mid-August, towards the end of my visit, when our neighbour, old Annie Gillespie, took to her bed. Her son Francey wasn't much of a housekeeper, so Aunt Chrissie who always made Annie her dinner sent me over with a plate covered by a tea towel to their cottage next to ours. 'Leave it on the chair, will ye?' Annie would say, propped on pillows in her bedroom which smelled of cats. I was thirteen that summer, awkward with adolescence, and no less shy than I'd been three years before. So I did as I was bid, pausing only to ask did Annie need anything else before scurrying out.

A few days later Annie stopped eating altogether, and the doctor was called out. He stopped by our cottage afterwards to say Annie, who was anaemic, needed to go into hospital for a transfusion. Francey then called in after the doctor left, saying his mother was 'for death', to which Chrissie said something like 'poor cratythur'. I was taking it all in— not unlike Germany Gemma does now at the Home— watching everybody and hanging on every word. But only now do I see how an older wisdom was at work. How Francey and Chrissie clearly knew Annie's hour was at hand, for all the doctor's talk of hospital and transfusions. Annie seemed of similar mind too, for she took a bad turn only hours after the doctor departed, which brought Francey over again to report his mother was struggling to get out of bed.

'A bad sign, that,' Chrissie said as she left with Francey, which left me wondering, "A bad sign of what, and how did she know?"

When Annie died early the next morning, Chrissie went into overdrive. Hughdy was dispatched to the post office to phone priest and doctor, and I was told to put a pot of water on to boil as she headed over to the Gillespies. I was terrified of seeing Annie when I brought the water over, but Aunt Chrissie just shouted from the upper bedroom to leave it in on the range which was stone cold. 'I'm sorry about your mother,' I managed to whisper at Francey, who looked just awful, his face streaked with dirt and cap tilted to what Pops used call 'the Kildare side'. I don't think he heard me though, for Chrissie came out of the bedroom and snapped, 'Will you leave off snivelling, and come help before she goes stiff on me?' Which was enough to send me out the door, where I nearly ran into Hughdy coming in with two long planks.

A few minutes later I heard shouting and looked across to see Hughdy coming out of the Gillespie's turf shed. I ducked back quickly, wondering had he taken old Annie in there, and if so, why? 'Did you ever see the like?' Hughdy laughed after he and Chrissie came back for their dinner, washing their hands first at the scullery sink. Chrissie smiled too, and I eventually heard how poor Francey had fainted onto Chrissie as they struggled to get Annie into the shroud, sandwiching her between his dead mother and himself. And how it had been Francey, still dead to the world, whom Hughdy had turfed into the shed!

In bed that night I kept thinking of Auntie Chrissie stretched upon Annie, and whether Chrissie had felt the cold of her—what I didn't know yet we call algor mortis. 'Your hands are like Death!' Ma used to chide if ever I touched her, say, after coming in from sledding on the Common. There's little doubt death is apprehended more intimately in rural Ireland, not cordoned off nor sanitised as it is in America. Like the Glen woman Chrissie told me of years later, who abruptly dismissed the neighbours who'd planned to sit up till morning with her husband's remains, as is the custom down the country. "You 'uns can go home now," the widow announced as she slipped two planks under the mattress, "for I want to sleep with Packy one last time."

'The remains sink down otherwise,' Chrissie explained about the planks, 'even if it's an Odearest.' It's true too, the dead weight you feel, literally so, the first time you go to shift a corpse and encounter its avoirdupois.

'Did his wife actually get into bed with him?' I asked.

'Oh aye,' Chrissie laughed. 'And wasn't it cold comfort she got?'

I had lain awake that long-ago night for Chrissie to return, unaware that she, Hughdy, and Francey would sit up with Annie till morning. And I'd been over at the wake earlier, helped to pass cups of tea, plates of sandwiches, and plates of cigarettes to most of the village, while Francey cut up plug tobacco for the pipe-smokers. More a kind of party than anything you'd encounter in an American funeral parlour.

Not that we were part of any community when Ma died twelve years ago, just a lone downtown Irish-Super's family. Ma's wake was at Waterman's on Beacon St, where I arrived directly from Logan in a taxi. The only Boston funeral I'd previously attended was for an aunt of Eddie's, just before we parted company. Seated there beside Pops and Brian, I thought how the LoPresti family had been far more open about their sorrow, and far more demonstrative too. Eddie's mother weeping for her sister in a manner I simply couldn't manage for my mother. I don't believe grief is any less raw among the Irish—but tears are quieter, body language tighter, and the entire occasion less operatic.

'I want a closed coffin,' Ma had often told Pops. But after the few mourners had departed—Pops' poker-mates and a goodly number of apartment residents including Mrs. Lunenberg—I asked Mr. Waterman to lift the casket cover so I might have one last look at Ma. He or Pops must have anticipated me—for the cover wasn't screwed down—and there lay my mother whom I'd left behind for Ireland some nine months before. And whom, if I'm honest, I'd set out to leave behind. Though I didn't tell myself as much that day, nor did I see it quite so clearly. Indeed I don't know what I allowed myself to see or feel—beyond how my mother now lay there, lifeless. And thinking, much as it shames me now, how she'd never in life have let Waterman part her hair to the Kildare side, before I touched her hand and whispered 'Safe home'.

It was Chrissie who'd combed Annie Gillespie's hair for

the final time, making her look like she was merely asleep—or so I thought when I'd finally braved her remains earlier that evening, nudged by Chrissie to kneel and say a prayer at the bed in the upper room. And it was back in our upper bedroom that I lay awake hours later, a bedroom I now shared with Chrissie, for Granny had died earlier that year, and I was anyhow too old to be sharing a room with Hughdy. Of course, had it occurred to me that night how Granny had likely died in my very bed, I'd have sat awaiting Chrissie in the kitchen.

Instead I eventually I fell asleep, for next thing I knew Aunt Chrissie was shaking me to get dressed for Annie's funeral. As we walked into the village, Hughdy remarked how the wind had gone round to the northwest, and a succession of sharp showers came on us as we huddled around the gaping hole for the graveside prayers after Mass. Following which the coffin and Annie were lowered on two straps held by Francey, Hughdy and two others, after which poor Francey took a shovelful of dirt and flung it into the grave.

Chrissie and I went from the churchyard to the pub, packed out with the funeral crowd, where Chrissie bought me a mineral. Once Hughdy came, however, we headed off home, sheltering for a few minutes in the lee of Scriggmore as a heavy shower blew in off the sea. I was always nervous passing that huge overhanging rock, but it wasn't until we got back to Boston that first summer that Brian informed me how Scriggmore would fall some day on a red-headed woman. And how Uncle Hughdy had told him never to tell his sister that.

There was a lot of talk on the way home about grave-digging—how hateful it was to have a grave too shallow or wild deep. And nothing more hateful than the sound of rocks striking a coffin. 'Aye, you want to take care with the first spadeful,' Hughdy said, recalling a funeral in which a large stone had rebounded off the coffin. 'Making an almighty clap,' he said, shaking his head as if it reverberated therein yet.

'Hurry up, Maeve!' Chrissie chided as our cottage came into view. 'You want to get out of those damp clothes.'

'Ach, you never get a cold from a graveyard wetting,' Hughdy said, showing me his shy smile.

'We'll all fit into a smaller place yet,' Chrissie often said, making room for myself or Katy beside her on the bench in her kitchen whenever we visited. Before she, too, slotted into that smaller space, the summer Katy turned ten. 'May you be as quick into my coffin,' she used also tell Hughdy if ever he chanced sitting in her chair by the range. It took me a few moments to work that one out, and I literally shivered when I did. Being more like my mother, I suppose, for Ma wasn't anyways as offhand about matters of mortality as her sister. Indeed, Ma took to sprinkling our shoes with Holy Water at night after we got word of Hughdy's death, until Pops found her at it and spoke sharply, a rare enough event. Luckily I was in high school by then, too old to get utterly spooked, whereas it might have finished me altogether at age ten.

CHAPTER 32

DATE: 4th April 1988

I woke lower than low not an hour ago. Wishing I could be whatever snail it is can sleep for up to three years without needing to eat. Like a Tom-the-Teacher fact, that, only I heard it from Manny years ago. Plus having Katy away makes it even harder to get kick-started. Miserable enough too that I'm not bothering to cook when I get home. Truth is I don't really enjoy cooking—which undoubtedly makes me an even bigger failure as a mother. Wishing instead Katy and I belonged to whatever Himalayan tribe it is that doesn't bother with regular mealtimes—just cooks up this big pot of gruel to eat any old time they're feeling peckish. Maybe it stems from those mealtimes at 23 Park Street when Ma was seriously depressed—like a low-pressure weather-front had socked in—till Brian and I had our plates cleared and could excuse ourselves, leaving Pops to sit and engage Ma in some kind of chat.

Still I've always managed to put dinner on the table,

apart from the odd evening when K and I order a Chinese or Indian take-away. Or that evening shortly after we moved here to Fairview from our gardener's cottage up in Meath, where I'd left another lover behind, and so was fighting tears much of the time. Anyhow the cupboards were bare that night, so we went out shopping—only I ended up just driving us around.

'We'll have to eat sweets for supper,' I told four-year-old Katy back at the house. 'That's all we have, Pet.'

'Oh, Mama, that's great!' crowed K. 'Don't ever go shopping!'

Or does my lack of interest in cooking come from my having failed as a daughter too? As if those mealtimes where you could almost cut the grey & gloom with a knife were my fault somehow, Ma doing her best just to hold on, while Pops asked what Brian and I had learned at school that day. Pushing the peas around on my plate, or pushing the liver aside. I don't think Ma much liked cooking either, yet she too managed to put a dinner on that white-enamel kitchen table every evening at half-five. Hamburger, tuna casserole, macaroni & cheese, an occasional cheap cut of beef called a cubed steak, and fish always of a Friday.

Jesus . . . !! Has this notebook come to this—a repository for old menus—a fucking dustpan for memories and old pain? The same old pain ... same as it ever was? Fuck, fuck, *fuck* ... Oh sweet Jesus, am I going under ...?

PART II

PART II

CHAPTER 33

DATE: 6th April 1988

SONG FOR THE DAY: 'Have You Seen Your Mother, Baby, Standing in the Shadow?'

Well, I don't think I'm going under yet … even if I left off here terrified two days ago. Terrified I could no longer cope—terrified the darker dark I've run from forever was about to wash over me, like a massive black wave. It sounds mad now, but for a moment or two I was afraid to open my eyes in case I saw it. A monstrous wave, a tsunami—which I always rhymed with Mommy, a mnemonic trick from way back when. Yet all I saw upon opening my eyes was a shard of sunlight on the refrigerator door. And myself on my knees, trapped like a rat in my very own kitchen, heart pounding, whimpering like a child, 'Oh, Sweet Jesus, is this it?'

Of course I knew about panic attacks from nursing school, the shortness of breath and palpitations, only there seemed nothing clinical about the outsized fear I felt was sweeping me under—as if I were witness and casualty both. It eased off after twenty minutes, however, which allowed me take a glass of water, then phone Sister Úna who told me to come in that afternoon.

'Do you think I'm cracking up?' I asked in her study, after describing what I'd felt, the same pitch-black fear as that long-ago nightmare pitch-black garden plot, all its cogs & wheels come rolling home at last.

'No, Maeve,' she replied. 'I think this is more about loss than lunacy.'

I admired that, of course. Lunacy being about as psychoanalytical as Sister Úna gets in her old-fashioned way.

We talked a while longer then. About how Katy's going off has likely touched some place inside me that's hurting yet from Ma's vanishing off to hospital for months on end. And whether in some way I've been running away all these years from my own fear of going under. And why had I felt so trapped in my own kitchen? Only I couldn't begin to give her an answer for that.

CHAPTER 34

DATE: 8 April 1988

GRAFFITO FOR THE DAY: I Can't Believe I'm Getting Away
With Thi ...

I'm more or less back to myself again, I think, if a bit shaky
yet—like after a fever breaks. But the dreadful panic hasn't
come back—and I'm trying not to overly worry it will.
Getting out of the empty house last night also helped.
Down to the IFC to see a French flick with Orla, a low-key
time. But good just to get out and talk to somebody else
about normal stuff—like work, books, and guys—rather
than stay in and talk to yourself about going mad.

"Chacun Cherche Su Chat" was the film—about a
young Frenchwoman, unlucky in love, who loses her cat.
Or the cat she's minding for somebody else. All's well that
ends well, however—cat turns up and she meets a nice fella
too. OK, she's ten years younger than I, plus beautiful, but
at least I've the cat already? 'Cats currently outnumber
dogs by two-to-one in Ireland,' Tom the Teacher recently
told me, still doling out his facts like sweets. And I've
always gone for cats, or rather cats have always chosen me.

185

Like Nibbles, who also just turned up at our door one August morning when Katy was ten. 'Can we keep him, Mama?' K begged—though she hardly need have. Not after Nya-Nya who had come calling too that long-ago Massachusetts August.

I told Orla over a drink afterwards how Jim the Boss had asked me out again that afternoon.

'You don't sound thrilled,' Orla said.

'Even if I were, you don't just start seeing the boss.' But thrilled I wasn't—more like unsettled.

'And what's his day job?' Orla asked, after I explained how Jim only calls to the Home a couple of times a week.

'Another bloody accountant!' I laughed. 'Like your old beau Silvio.'

'At least he's not an actuary.'

'And what's an actuary exactly?'

'Someone with even less personality than an accountant!' Orla grinned.

But that's not fair to Jim, who drives a new VW Beetle, not a BMW. And while the Home is obviously a business venture, I think he really cares about it. He's good with the residents too, taking the time to stop and chat, all except Germany Gemma to whom he understandably gives a wide berth. A decent fella, in short, but nobody I could ever see myself waxing indecent with.

'What did you tell him?'

'I couldn't use Katy as an excuse again. So I said I was doing a Zen class for six weeks.'

'You know why Zen's like sex?' Orla asked, though I wasn't really in the mood. 'Cuz it's considered bad form to fall asleep!' which made me laugh all the same.

'I figured a white lie was OK,' I said, 'seeing the Buddha doesn't believe in sin. But I don't know what I'll tell him in six weeks.'

'What's he look like?' Orla asked, ordering us a second G&T.

'Not bad-looking. Kind of hefty, like an ex-rugby player.'

'Tall?'

'Average,' I said. 'The average Irish male being just over 5' 9".' That last fact courtesy of Tom the Teacher too.

'The average Irish male doesn't measure up!' Orla grinned, fishing the lemon from her drink.

I looked up actuary when I got home—one who calculates insurance risks, esp. natural disasters, etc. Someone so, who sits at a desk figuring the odds on the next tsunami or hurricane. Whereas I'm hoping for someone a bit more windswept himself?

CHAPTER 35

DATE: 10 April 1988

ACTIVITY: Placing One Foot in Front of the Other

Carmen Cassidy, only a week gone, is already a big miss. No longer anchoring her corner of the War Room across from Germany Gemma, who stopped quoting what sounded like Winston Churchill this morning long enough to ask 'Where's the Spanish lady?'

It's just over a week too since Katy left, but I'm doing a bit better. She was downright homesick on her first phone call, but sounded better last night, like she's beginning to enjoy it. School is the hardest part, listening to quadratic equations in French, but she finds Isabelle and her younger sisters great fun. She can't stop talking about the grub either, so I'm not worried about her eating. The house sounds lovely, in the country with a big field at the back, and two dogs, one a Dalmatian. Katy loves the country and always has. Mad for Donegal when we visited Aunt Chrissie, where she'd play for hours outside the cottage. She's mad about dogs too, and undoubtedly will hound me again about getting one when she gets home. Though a dog's far more work than a cat, nor is it fair to leave them alone all day.

Still I was feeling guilty after last night's call—not being able to give Katy a younger sister, a country life, not even a dog. Not to mention a paterfamilias as Mr. Barry used to say. In fact, Katy has never met her father. Nor Eddie her, as he enlisted in the Army shortly after I broke it off with him. I was only seven weeks gone with Katy when I told Eddie we wouldn't marry. Feeling huge guilt then—like I'd sent him off to Vietnam to die—and praying nightly he'd come through unscathed. He did too, for the war ended shortly after he went over, but K and I had already left for Ireland by the time he was discharged. K has said little so far about wanting to meet him, though I expect that'll change someday soon. Meantime I worry how she's never had a father figure, nor even got to really know Pops, who she only ever saw on those two visits to Boston, plus the single trip Pops made back here, to take Ma's ashes up to Donegal the year after she died.

'Guilt's almost always wasted energy,' counsels Sister Úna whenever I mention the word, so I tried thinking last night of what I <u>have</u> given Katy, apart from having to grow up in Catholic Ireland as the daughter of an unwed mother. If no dog, two cats, and at least a love of rural living, via our holidays in Glenmore. And now a month on the Continent, eating chocolate rolls for breakfast, and chips with mayonnaise. There's something wonderful about travel at that age—getting to spread your wings despite the inevitable homesickness and confusions. I wasn't even K's age my second Donegal summer, awkward and shy, but still able for what seemed almost as big an adventure as our first visit. What's more, this time Brian had stayed behind, working that summer at an Army & Navy store on Washington St, too old at sixteen to be knocking around his uncle and aunt's farm in Ireland.

My plane ticket must have stretched Pops financially, though I suspect he booked it because I was so miserable at home. Fighting with Ma, or more often sulking, since I was too much the Good Girl for sustained hostilities. Instead I waged war with my moodiness, spraying my unhappiness around the apartment like mustard gas. Yet I somehow managed to say yes, when Pops asked did I fancy another trip to Donegal? And so I spent six weeks of my thirteenth summer there, from mid-July to the end of August. Chrissie seemed easier this visit, possibly unburdened of her own mother's care. Hughdy was as soft-spoken as ever, though looking back I can see how dispirited he also was. Away from the cottage more of the time: out with Lolly after sheep, or footering with the turf up on the bog. He told fewer stories that summer too, but I'd come prepared this time—with a bagful of paperbacks from a second-hand bookshop on Boylston St.

CHAPTER 36

DATE: 11 April 1988
WEATHER: Sunny for Once

I found Alice May in the front day-room this morning at half-seven, fully dressed. 'I felt like rising early,' she explained—like she were still at home with that autonomy we take for granted until it's gone. I've grown hugely fond of her since she came to us, and was delighted to find her freelancing like that this morning. I often drop by her room—and not just to see might I borrow something from her bookcase. I've also lent her some Alice Munro stories, though she's not reading as much now as she initially did. She's also on meds for congestive heart failure, though nearly fifty per cent of the elderly get five years or more with that.

Anyhow, I brought her a cup of tea in the day-room, where we chatted a bit about my Katy in France, after which Alice May told of a French boyfriend she'd visited at age nineteen in Brittany. Describing his small stone cottage with its large fireplace where they broiled sausages and roasted potatoes, followed by crêpes and a kind of Breton poitín made from apples.

'Is there no place you didn't live?' I asked, knowing she was years in St Louis, before coming back to care for her mother in Dublin.

'Oh, I didn't live in Brittany,' Alice laughed. 'I only used to visit him there.'

'Tell us about the boyfriend?' I chanced.

'He was a marionettist,' she smiled, 'and I was just too practical to think we could make a go of it. Travelling from village to village, putting on puppet shows. So I ended up going over to America instead.'

I didn't ask any more questions, nor did she volunteer anything more. But it was a lovely start to the workday, which seemed to colour the hours that followed. Which is to say, Constance for once forgot about her mother, Polish Petra elected to report for work, Lil the Mop didn't go afire, and Eamon Kerr's new T-shirt— FILTHY, STINKING RICH —WELL, TWO OUT OF THREE AIN'T BAD—made me laugh aloud. Plus Sister Úna rang to reschedule our appointment, which enabled me to meet Orla at Gaffney's for a coffee after work, as I hadn't to put on the dinner for Katy.

CHAPTER 37

DATE: 13 April 1988

WEATHER: Snow!

MOOD: Nostalgic

THOUGHT FOR THE DAY: 'Où sont les neiges d'antan?'

What joy! Waking this morning to two inches of snow on the back gardens. Enough to trim hedges, trees and erase the dark circle of soil around Mrs. Sheedy's missing apple tree. There was even a proper leaden sky like you got in Boston afterwards, making you hope that there was more snow on the way, even as you bundled up and raced out to play in it. I only wish Katy had been here to see it.

I try never to act the know-it-all Yank, but watching Dublin deal with a few inches of snow is a challenge, and traffic will probably come to a standstill again. The Midlands sometimes get snow, but we rarely see any in Dublin, which made opening the curtain onto a winter wonderland this April morning only delightful. New England is as unseasonable—except you can get ten inches there, not two, in a freak spring storm. Like the snow that fell our last April in Somerville, making Katy, just two, screech with delight as Nya-Nya gingerly picked his way from one boot-print to another, before William our Chinese neighbour shovelled us out. I once offered William a hand shovelling, seeing as how the Irish and Chinese had between them laid the Central Pacific Railroad. But William resisted so vigorously I decided it must be some kind of guy-thing, not to be seen working with a woman.

Of course the sidewalk at 23 Park St was the first thing Pops shovelled when it snowed, sprinkling the path and front steps after with sand and rock salt. Brian would help Pops once he was old enough, before going off with a schoolmate to ring doorbells on Beacon Hill. He made good money too, which seemed totally unfair, seeing I wasn't allowed to go door to door shovelling with Vivian or Princetta.

The snow also delighted many of the clientele at the Home. But the sun was shining on the last daffs in Fairview Park by the time I was walking home, not a trace of this morning's snowfall anywhere, as if this were suddenly another country. Not unlike the country we find ourselves in once childhood's left behind.

CHAPTER 38

DATE: 14 April 1988
SONG FOR THE DAY: 'The Last Rose of Summer'
ACTIVITY: Ice-Skating

With Katy away, I was able to reschedule Sister Úna for half-seven last evening. After hearing again of how much I missed my daughter, Sister Úna asked how my own parents had met. I don't know what prompted her query, but it promptly summoned up another winter scene.

'Ice-skating, would you believe. On the Boston Common.'

'The same Common you talk about?'

'The very one,' I said. 'Just across from where they would someday live, though they hadn't a notion yet of that.'

The story I told Sister Úna is also one of the few my mother ever told me. At age eleven, I reckon, before adolescence made it untenable to think of my parents in love. 'How did you and Pops meet?' was one of a zillion questions I'd have asked Ma. But one that elicited an actual story in lieu of her customary abridged response.

197

'Ice-skating.'

'You were skating, Ma?'

'No, your father was. I was just watching with a girlfriend.'

'Where?'

'On the Common, where you and Brian skate.'

'On the Frog Pond?'

'Yes, Maeve,' my name an indication that question-time was nearly up.

'Was Pops already Super here?'

'No, he was living in West Roxbury.'

And thus it was that Róisín O'Byrne of Glenmore, Co Donegal first spoke with James Maguire of Foxford, Co Mayo. On the Boston Common one Sunday afternoon in January, 1945. Not as star-crossed, say, as meeting on a frozen lake at the stroke of midnight, but sufficient unto my romantic, pre-teen needs.

'How'd you meet,' I prompted, 'if you weren't skating?'

'Oh, Maeve,' Ma bridled with her habitual impatience, 'how do you expect me to remember that!' But then—as if relenting for both our sakes—she wrinkled her brow. 'He stopped to tie a skate-lace, I think, near where Ellen and I were standing.'

'He'd probably spotted you already, Ma!' I speculated, which made her laugh.

'I doubt he'd noticed me. But he must've heard me talking to Ellen, for he said something foolish, like "It's a long, long way to Donegal".'

Whatever spell Ma had cast for us kept her talking— how Pops had treated her and Ellen to a hot chocolate at Bailey's Ice Cream Shop on West St, and taken just herself to the pictures the following Friday. He never managed to coax her onto ice skates, but they used go roller-skating at a rink in Dorchester, where the lights would dim whenever the organist announced 'Couples Only'. And they married two years later in 1947, moving into 23 Park St the next year, just before Brian was born.

I told Sister Úna all this yesterday, yet am only thinking now how much our lives hang on mere happenstance. The fact Brian and I wouldn't exist but for a skate-lace having come undone? And how Katy wouldn't be here but for her father Eddie having asked for the loan of a pen? Imagine if you could chart a family tree that honoured all these acts of fate—a wrong turn, a train missed, a cigarette which needed a match—all the inconsequential consequentials that first brought our forebears into each other's ken?

That same night I asked Pops to tell me <u>his</u> version of how they'd met. But he just laughed and recited a ditty he used to tease Ma with whenever things were going OK:
'It was not in winter,
Our loving lot was cast!
It was the time of Roses,
I plucked one as I passed!'
I tried other times to get more of Ma's story from her. Her first two years in Boston before she met Pops, working as a chambermaid in the Parker House on Tremont St, another stone's throw into the future from 23 Park St. Rooming with Ellen from Sligo Town, and a couple of other Irish girls, in a three-storey Dorchester tenement. But that's pretty much all I got, and so much less than I'd like to have. Like what was Ellen like, Ma? And where did she end up? Or how did you, Ma, who seemed to lack nerve and verve for so much in life, steel yourself to leave Donegal at age twenty-two for the faraway lights of Boston? Or had growing up in Glenmore been so hard you simply had to get away? There's so much I don't know, but

it seems almost enough tonight—knowing how she and Pops met and fell in love. For there *was* love there, I believe, unhappy as Ma so often was.

Or at least a memory of love that allowed her tell that afternoon how it all began. Even if her recounting begs other questions—like what kind of coat and hat had she worn that winter afternoon in 1945? Or however had that slim, brown-eyed, handsome man from the bogs of Mayo learned to skate?

Of course those questions are pretty much a nonsense. But maybe I'm beginning to better understand something Sister Úna said when we began—after I had hesitated at the idea of keeping a notebook. 'When we're young, Maeve, we think all the answers lie somewhere out ahead of us. But as we grow older, we begin to see how some of them lie behind—from whence and where we've come.'

And I wonder now might not that help explain some of Ma's own unhappiness too? Ma who resolutely refused to look back, refused to entertain—never mind take the measure of—her memories. When Granny died that February, my mother flew over for the funeral—her first visit back in twenty years, though of course many Irish of her generation never went back. But what puzzled me, even at age twelve, was how little Ma talked about Donegal, of Chrissie and Hughdy, when she got back to Boston. As if having left all those years before she was unable to take up her family or Ireland again.

CHAPTER 39

DATE: 15 April 1988

THOUGHT FOR THE DAY: Death, Taxes and Sun Holidays!

As I write the date, a memory flashes, clear as a film clip. Of Pops at the small desk in our living room, a few nights before the mid-April IRS tax deadline, muttering to himself as he labours over his returns. So many of his ways were Irish—as I see better since coming here—but Pops was far more like a Yank when it came to paying his taxes, scrupulous down to the last decimal place.

What's more, the care he took with his finances explains the lump sum Brian and I found in his bankbook the afternoon we sorted his effects. Last month Brian sent me my share, a cheque for around £2,600. I planned to put it into an account for Katy—a surprise for her 21st—but when I told Sister Úna how sorely I miss her, she suggested something else.

'Would you two not go away this summer? Before she's too old to want to go on holiday with her mother?'

It bothers me sometimes how much I still need

permission to do what I'm entitled to. Like taking K to Greece in July which, thanks to Sister, I'll now do! I'd a few bob set aside for Donegal again, but I'll borrow another £500 from Katy's legacy to take her 'out foreign' as Hughdy used to say. Even if Hughdy was only talking of those who ended up on building sites in Manchester or Mannheim, not the thousands of Irish who fly out now for sun holidays.

Greece I've always longed to see, ever since I encountered the Cyclops and Medusa in a leather-bound volume of Greek myths on Mrs. L's bookcase. Later, in high school, Mr. Barry had us translate passages from Ovid, promising us racier bits if we signed up for Latin III. But I'd my sights already set on nursing, and gave up Latin for Chemistry. Still, Greece has always beckoned, and Pops would be pleased, I know, to think he'd helped send us there.

CHAPTER 40

DATE: 21 April 1988

WORDS FOR THE DAY: Haboob and Alopecia

Orla and I went to an Amnesty International table quiz at the Mansion House last night. I was happy to get out, being a bit jittery still after my morning melt-down a few weeks back. Besides, the house is like a tomb without Katy. Even Nibbles misses her, I think, as he won't settle evenings, though he's a bit more himself since I decided to let him sleep on my bed till K comes home.

Two lads from Orla's work, Matt and Joe, rounded out our team, and while we neither won nor placed, we had a laugh and a few drinks. Nor was my head too bad this morning either, the high ceilings in the Mansion House helping with the cigarette smoke. 'Matt's good crack,' Orla said when she collected me, by way of marking my card for me. And Matt seemed a nice guy all right, only I'm not doing guys at the moment. Even if I could see he was impressed I had the answer for 'haboob'.

Arabic for 'sandstorm', doncha know, though don't ask

how I knew that. Possibly from Pops' 'New York Times' crosswords, as haboob doesn't sound like one of Miss Dewey's 'Word for the Day'. 'Incognito' or 'snafu' were more her style (though it was brother Brian who gave me the etymology of the latter) and I can see those words yet on the corner of her blackboard. I can see Miss Dewey too as she recites a passage from Dickens, her free hand fluttering across her lacy bosom, as Arthur Levin behind me whispers: 'She must think it's called "A Tale of Two Titties"!' Our English teachers were all unmarried ladies— Miss Marr, Miss Woods, Miss Wetmore—but Miss Dewey Senior Year was the best of a good lot. Passionate about what she called 'the classics', she assigned us everything from 'Silas Marner' to 'School for Scandal', which is how I recognised Mrs. Malaprop in our Lil the Mop—who just last week told of her neighbour who got 'Al Pacino' after her husband left her, and she ended up having to get a wig!

Sex too was in its way as much a high-school subject as English or math. Of course I was scared of it as so much else—and certainly in no great hurry to discover it first-hand. Nor was there, even in the Swinging Sixties, half the pressure kids feel nowadays to be sexually active. But sex was in the air, and not always as sub-textual as Miss Dewey's declamations. Certainly not with Miss Rossi, our biology teacher who, when the boys were at an assembly, told us girls how the thumb roughly indicates the relative size of the male penis. Nor was there much subtlety in how my pal Vivian stretched her turquoise leotard tight across her chest to show Mr. Stamp, whom we all fancied, a stain she'd incurred in Earth Science.

'Close your legs, girls,' Miss Rossi, who was in her sixties, repeatedly intoned from behind a huge glass jar of sheep-eyes on her desk. Who knows, maybe sex is why they become biology teachers—since Katy claims her Ms Harney is sex-crazed too: 'Now, girls,' she said, pointing to an earthworm's genitalia, 'this is how they do it!' Miss Rossi's stricture always reminded me of Sister Evangelista in sixth-grade Sunday School, who warned us not to wear patent leather shoes because the boys could see our knickers in them. Only Sister, being American, said 'panties' instead. And what she made of the mini-skirt which appeared a few years later doesn't bear thinking about.

'Close your own legs, Miss Rossi,' Vivian would whisper back, as we bent over a splayed rat pinned to the black wax of our dissection tray. Vivian who always left the slicing and splicing to me, a task tagging along after Manny with all his chat about vermin had no doubt prepared me for. 'That formaldehyde's gonna make me puke,' she also constantly threatened, which might've made for a spectacular stain on her turquoise top, only she never followed through.

CHAPTER 41

DATE: 25 April 1988

SONG FOR THE DAY: 'There's a Rat in Mi Kitchen!'

'We've good news and bad news both,' Mary O'Mara greeted me this morning. 'Which first?'

'Oh Christ, the bad,' I said, 'seeing I already know Polish Petra's out.'

'I've just heard the Home's being sold.'

'What?' I stared at Mary.

'For a lodging house. Although those who can afford it can stay on.'

'Where'd you hear this?' I asked, beginning to relax.

'Yes, that's the good news!' grinned Mary. 'Got it straight from Germany Calling, who says she got it straight from Jim herself.'

'Feck you, O' Mara,' I said. 'And feck Gemma too. Plus the tank she rode in on.'

'I believe you were talking to Jim,' I smile at Gemma later.

'Oh, we're on a first-name basis,' Gemma assures me.

'And I hope to kill him if I get the chance!'

That sounded more like our Gemma, who would only grow bored covering a real-estate beat. 'I'm still looking for the gun I lost somewhere,' she informed me after lunch. 'And she'd better find it before I do,' Nurse Ethel informed told me in turn, having failed to persuade Gemma to shed her shoes before getting into bed last night.

'Are you going somewhere?' I ask Gemma those nights she tries that on with me.

'You never know, I might!'

Leaving the shoes on her chair usually does the trick. But other nights I too give up and let her wear them into bed.

You can't help laughing at such antics, which often works best with someone like Gemma. To say 'Yes, how exciting it is, drinking with the enemy!' Or 'Yes, you'll keep an eye out for any Huns in the lift, or dead bodies in the bathroom!' But my heart breaks for Gemma when terror is truly playing on her—those days when she gives in to the Apocalypse. 'Welcome to the Funeral Feast!' she whispered to me last Tuesday, her hands trembling. 'I've been ducking the axe all day!' There's nothing risible in that level of paranoia, nothing as benign, say, as Cassie Boyle's 'Boody Women'. And how awful it must feel to be so besieged at the age of eighty? Yet all you can do is take her hand and try reassure her, like a child afraid of the dark.

A not dissimilar paranoia preceded my mother's second breakdown, as I told Sister Úna earlier this week. Spring of my freshman year in high school, and once again only a few months after she'd lost a brother, Hughdy this time. It was a more florid psychotic break too, though she took ill in much the same way, disappearing into a deep depression at Christmas. Once April arrived, however, Ma stopped sleeping and started spring-cleaning like mad. Literally mad, insisting among other things that we take out all our woollens and spray them with a naphtha solution for moths, before she packed them in an old trunk filled with mothballs.

One morning Ma sat smiling in the kitchen, describing the rat she'd seen the previous night. We might possibly have believed in the rat too—had Ma not claimed to have been chatting with it, like some city cousin of Templeton in 'Charlotte's Web'. There was something almost playful in her madness that morning, like Gemma sometimes gets at the Home, showing you the button on her wrist that renders her invisible. But then, two days later, Pops saw an actual rat scuttle behind the fridge, where he discovered a hole in the skirting board. And Brian who discovered the large trap Pops had baited with peanut butter sprung the next morning, his blood splashed all along the wall and floor the sole sign of Templeton II.

The final thirty-six hours before she went back into hospital were the worst. Convinced our phone was bugged, Ma blasted the kitchen radio as a countermeasure, pacing the floor and talking to herself. Pops tried to calm her, but she flung a coffee cup at him, then threatened him with a kitchen knife, before finally consenting to go see Dr Cohen at Metropolitan State. Pops was phoning a cab when she took out both our living room windows with two swings of her sweeping brush. 'Keep your noise down, Ma!' I wanted to scream as Pops wrested the brush from her. 'Do you want Pops to lose his job?'—same as she'd warned us down the years. Instead, I fled sobbing to my room as Pops and Brian carried Ma, now hyperventilating, down the front steps to the cab. Crying still, I swept up the broken glass and took it out to the bins, where I discovered Templeton II lying dead in the alley, his face torn nearly in two.

'How long was your mother in hospital that time?' Sister Úna asked.

'About five months,' I said, telling how I took over the cooking and the big fuss Pops made over my first meatloaf, which had way too many cornflakes in it and crumbled as he cut it. 'I prefer my flakes straight from the box,' Brian remarked—which upset me, and so Pops, who told Brian to eat what he was given. I kept cooking even after Pops got me a summer job in the Parker House laundry room, leaving pork chops or chicken legs out to defrost before walking around the corner to the hotel where Ma had first worked upon arriving in Boston.

Ma was no longer manic when she came home late that September. Just more withdrawn, with holes in her memory again from electroshock. Pops told me years later how he would quiz Ma at night as they lay in bed, ask her about this name and that event, as she struggled to rebuild her database. Yet I only wonder now had he needed to tell her all over again of the phone call from Auntie Chrissie with saddest news of Uncle Hughdy? Strange, too, how you can so clearly picture something you actually never saw—like Chrissie at the Post Office as she made that call, cranking the handle on the outsized black phone with its A and B buttons.

I wasn't privy to the details of that phone call, nor do I imagine Chrissie gave many either, as there was little privacy in the Post Office which doubled as a shop. All Brian and I were told was that Hughdy had drowned in a lake. Most likely Ma got the full story later in a letter from Chrissie, who told me it the year Katy and I came over. But after Ma had hung up that night, I found myself wondering whether Hughdy had tried in the end to unearth that O'Byrne treasure, hoping to somehow side-step the Curse of the Evil Fairies? I'd asked Ma about that treasure a few years before, but she brushed it off as with most things Donegal, telling me not to repeat stupid stories. So I said nothing, and later lay crying in bed, where I could overhear Pops tell Ma in the kitchen she should go over for the funeral, whatever the cost. And Ma saying we hadn't money enough to be going over for every death.

Tears ending, I began to play a kind of home movie of Hughdy in my head—only the silent images were crystal-clear, no jerky hand-held camera or flickering film spooling noisily off a reel. I can't of course replay it now, but I can see two clear bits yet. First is towards the end of our initial visit, an August evening when Hughdy stood beside the cottage gable, an old horsewhip in hand, trying to snare a dark shadow that darted every so often through the gap between house and byre. Of course Brian then had to try, while I watched and of course worried for the bats who were only chasing their buggy supper. Hughdy never got one, nor had he ever seen a bat other than flying. 'The bat is one of the Seven Sleepers,' he informed us that evening. 'Along with the bee, the butterfly, the cuckoo ...' and whatever else he named.

The other image of Hughdy is from that second summer and just as vivid. He was more withdrawn that visit, though had Brian come over it might have been easier for him to engage with a nephew than a decidedly awkward thirteen-year-old niece. Still, one afternoon shortly before I left, Hughdy asked did I want to come fishing, and so we climbed up to a tiny bog lake a mile east of the cottage. The sunny afternoon was too bright for fishing—what you want, Hughdy said, is damp and breezy, even a bit of rain. The few trout he caught weren't half the size of his huge hands, but what I best remember is coming home along the hill, when suddenly Hughdy stopped, pointing below. 'There, Maeve,' he said, and suddenly I saw it: a fox darting away some distance below us, sunlight playing tag with its red coat as it bounded through the bracken. And the image of that fox, running free, is how I prefer to remember Hughdy, rather than number him among Seven Sleepers slumbering in some cave.

CHAPTER 42

DATE: 30 April 1988

SONG FOR THE DAY: 'Maxwell's Silver Hammer'

I told Sister Úna this afternoon how Ma never was in hospital again after Dr Cohen put her on lithium, which heretofore had only been available in Europe. Lithium seemed to even her out and, if she still slumped in winter, her mania never returned. Not to her anyhow, though it came in years later through the bathroom window after Brian.

I told how Brian had tried to join the Marines after high school. While keen about his toy soldiers as a kid, there hadn't been anything truly gung-ho about Brian, and his enlisting caught my parents by surprise. He failed his physical however, after the Marine Corps doctor discovered his hammer toes—or 'permanent flexion deformity of his interphalangeal joints' as I learned at college. Inherited from Pops it turned out, who had simply thought his own shoes had never fit comfortably across the toe cap.

Brian got a job then laying cable with the phone company, but what he really wanted was to become a cop. He began to skip dinner then, studying in his room for the police exam, which he easily passed—only to fail another physical on account of his feet. The following year he got a job as a bus driver with the MBTA and moved out of No. 23. A move he had wanted to make for a long time, I think—as if you can ever truly leave family behind.

His hammer toes were not all he inherited, however, even if my only brother has never told me about his breakdown. About the month he spent on a psychiatric ward at McClean's Hospital in Arlington in 1984. I only heard about it three years later from his Cheryl, when I flew over first to see Pops after his tumour was diagnosed. How Brian had been unable to sleep for weeks, claiming at breakfast a whip-poor-will in the woods out back was keeping him awake. At first Cheryl suggested sleeping pills, only to arrive home one evening to find the living-room blinds drawn, 'Born in the USA' blaring, and Brian crouched at a window, assuring her a copter was coming in any minute to fly them out.

'Had you known our mother was bi-polar?' I asked.

'I knew nothing,' Cheryl said. 'You know how Brian is—about anything too personal.'

'Pre-purchase inspections should be obligatory for husbands as well as used cars,' I smiled.

'You won't tell Brian I told?'

'No,' I reassured her. 'That skeleton goes straight back into the family closet. Nor will I give him "Springsteen's Greatest Hits" this Christmas either'—at which thankfully she laughed.

I didn't tell Sister Úna that last bit, as I doubt she was ever into the Boss in a big way. Though she surprises me all

214

the time—like answering the door last week in jeans and a sweatshirt, what she calls her gardening clothes.

'And your own melancholy, Maeve?' she inquired before we finished.

The fact she seldom asks me outright how I am is a lot of the reason I'm still seeing her. And when she does, the fact she rarely says 'depression' makes it easier for me to say 'Just ducky, thanks!' Though today I just said I'm doing better.

'And any idea why that might be, Maeve?' Sister pursued.

I hadn't an answer to that. Maybe it's the change of season, or the chance to simply talk it out? Or is some of what I write down here helping to unsnag me? I still miss Pops terribly, and can easily find myself in tears. But the sorrow that had me paralysed last Christmas seems most days to have eased a little. And the fright I gave myself in the kitchen a few weeks ago seems to have passed on too.

And, strangely, the fact I'm aware, at least, of how I never cried for Ma seems like progress also.

CHAPTER 43

DATE: 1 May 1988

ACTIVITY: Flower Arranging

No cut flowers outside my door this morning, though Katy did make me a May basket once when she was eight or nine. Just my Amsterdam tulips showing their goblet-like heads either side of the front step. It was Mrs. Lunenberg who told me of that tradition, how she and her sisters in that other Dublin always rose early this day to gather a bouquet of New Hampshire wildflowers to place in a makeshift basket at the front door for their mother. It must have been a May Eve too she told me that, for I promptly went across to the Common to cut a few hyacinths and tulips which I hid under my bed. 'Just a project for school,' I told Ma later at the kitchen table, as I pasted pink construction paper around an egg carton. And it was outside Apt 3C that I left my May basket the next morning on my way to school. No, not outside Apt 1A—it being far from May baskets Róisín O'Byrne was reared. Besides, Ma would've only given out to me for having robbed the flowers in the first place.

Nor had I May baskets in mind this morn by the time I reached the Home, where for all I knew Gemma Dunne might be awaiting that traditional May Day show of strength—a parade of Soviet tanks and missile carriers—to roll past the Home on its way to Red Square.

Gemma however was quietly seated in her usual corner, with nary a word of Molotov nor Kalashnikov. I keep waiting for Wang Wei, the Chinese nursing assistant we hired last month, to set Gemma spouting off about Sino troops massing along the border. Not very PC of me to think that, I know, nor does Gemma's imagination need any prompts, seeing she managed to conjure up a thieving Pakistani out of thin air, even if we've not recently heard of him. Still, it's as much mashed-up geopolitics and military history as any homespun racism with Gemma, who, like all of our clientele, grew up in a lily-white Ireland where you rarely saw anyone of colour. But all that's changed utterly these past few years, and I don't doubt we'll have African as well as Asian care staff here soon.

Meantime Wang Wei has not only slotted in nicely, but is also willing to work any shift, which is a God-send on weeks we're short-handed. Yesterday at break she told Fiona of having worked at a Beijing night-club, starting off as a barmaid but eventually working up to DJ. It seems she hardly saw the sun for six years—until she quit the club and China, getting herself to London before she came over here.

Clubbing and DJs don't entirely square with my impressions of China: like those Yanks who think Ireland is all thatched cottages yet, with a pig in the kitchen. But what intrigues me is the thought of Wang Wei swapping that routine for a Dublin nursing home. To go from spinning records in a Beijing disco to spooning porridge into Pat the Pope seems a quantum leap, and I marvel at how someone like Wang Wei, not yet thirty, can juggle such disparate worlds.

Once again 'it's not the one way we all go'. I used wonder what exactly Pops meant by that. That not everybody cut through the Common to get to Deluca's Market on Charles St, where Ma sometimes sent me for a quart of milk? Or not everybody took the same route to the Arch St Chapel? But it obviously wasn't anything that literal—rather just how one life differs from another. Like Aunt Chrissie who spent hers in a single cottage, doing the same daily tasks year in, year out. Because there are <u>those</u> lives too, all those folk who never get to experience anything as disparate as Beijing and Dublin both, or Alice May's Breton boyfriend and a brother Johnny on an Arizona ranch.

CHAPTER 44

DATE: 5 May 1988
SONG FOR THE DAY: 'Soldier Boy, Oh My Little Soldier Boy'
GRAFFITO FOR THE DAY: Don't Drink and Park – Accidents
Cause People!

Katy's home again, hooray! We sat up late like schoolgirls Wednesday night—well, like I too were a schoolgirl—as K described her Continental adventure. Café au lait et pain au chocolat for breakfast, and how French subtitles make 'Psycho' even scarier and 'Forrest Gump' almost credible. And how she cut class a few times to have coffee with other students at a nearby café. And once or twice a glass of beer. 'Don't worry, Mama!' she reassured me. 'I'd only have one and I didn't always finish it!'

I'm not worried either, as I feel Katy has great sense—yet without needing either to be always the Good Girl, which was how I navigated my childhood, never playing hooky or mitching as it's called over here. And I've only to hear Fiona worry over her thirteen-year-old Heather, who goes off to her Saturday afternoon disco in a tiny belly-top and a slip of a skirt to know the easy time Katy's giving me so far. Even if I was a bit anxious about leaving her in the house last Saturday afternoon, to watch a video with Chris from her jiu-jitsu class, who she says is just a pal. I only nipped out to do the shopping, but I must've looked anxious upon my return, cuz Katy smiled, 'Don't worry, Mama—the video ended, and I'm still a virgin!'

I just laughed aloud—marvelling at the light years between K and myself at that age. And delighted my daughter can be that cheeky with her mother. Certainly sex was not for joking—never mind discussion—'twixt Ma and me. Which meant I couldn't speak my mortification when it eventually dawned on me what a construction worker on a scaffold had meant by shouting down, 'Hey, Carrot Top, are you red all over?' as I walked to school one morning my sophomore year.

Nor spoken my unease about Stanley at The Parker House, my fifteenth summer, even if Ma had not been in hospital. Pops had got me that job via his poker pal, Walter Murphy, who operated the hotel freight elevator. Stanley meantime was a dining-room waiter, thirty-something and married, who occasionally came into the laundry between shifts if Mrs. Gomes was elsewhere, to sit and talk while I sorted dirty linen. He read a lot and fancied himself for that but, when I made the mistake of saying I too liked to read, Stanley turned into a kind of quizmaster.

'Who wrote "The Caine Mutiny"?' he might demand, running his fingers through his thinning black hair. 'Name a novel by Norman Mailer?' Most of the time I hadn't a clue, but it only seemed to bother Stanley if I knew the answer. He was also always recommending books—on Tibetan monks who meditated naked beside frozen lakes, or Hindu mystics who fasted for days, before swallowing a towel to absorb the remaining poisons. Stanley never laid a finger on me, but there was definitely a sexual undercurrent there, and I began to dread his visits—fearful, for all his manners, that I'd end up fleeing him round laundry bins piled high with soiled sheets.

Still, by junior year I had—despite myself—a boyfriend of sorts. Tall, skinny Perry Morris, who was even shyer than I. An aspiring ventriloquist, Perry put what confidence he had into his alter ego, Maurice Perri. I'd sat next to Perry in homeroom since freshman year, but he only began to phone me at home in junior year. Or Maurice Perri rang, as Perry would pretend it was the puppet on the line. We went to the pictures a couple of times, but we'd meet up at the Saxon or the Orpheum, as he hadn't the nerve to ring our bell. Afterwards we walked back to No. 23, where he once awkwardly kissed me on the front steps—which was as far as things went with either him or Perri.

My pal Vivian Henry, who went from ugly duckling to swan overnight, had a boyfriend too: Paul Haley, nearly as good-looking as she, but not half as bright. I puzzled why Vivian put up with a 40-watt bulb like Paul, but being gorgeous at sixteen was probably enough to handle—without the added handicap of a clever boyfriend. Which maybe explains why you so often see stunning young girls saddled with dunces. Still, you knew from the way Vivian and Paul slow-danced at record hops that they wouldn't kiss goodnight like Perry Morris and me.

'I ought to be playing shortstop for the Red Sox,' Vivian, who actually played that position in Girls Softball, told me one day in French class.

'Shortstop?' I puzzled, despite knowing a fair bit about baseball from Pops and Brian, who were mad about the Sox.

'You know,' Vivian laughed, 'how I always manage to keep Paul from getting past second base?'

I had my own hands full as a rookie first baseman that next summer, struggling to keep a blind date from getting all the way to second his first time at bat. TJ was his name, a pal of Vivian's Paul, only a year older than us, and already in the Army. Or a weekend soldier anyhow—having joined the National Guard which a lot of guys did to avoid the draft and Vietnam. What's more, he wore his olive-green Army trousers along with a white T-shirt the night the four of us drove out to Revere Beach. TJ wasn't strictly a blind date, as I'd seen him ahead of me in school. But there seemed something slightly exotic about him that night—as if he truly were a soldier—not some boy whose sum total of worldliness was six weeks at Fort Dix in New Jersey, learning to peel potatoes and march in step. Or maybe it was those olive-green trousers, given the soft spot I've always had for a uniform, though I'd hardly confess that to Sister Úna. At any rate, I laughed at his jokes, and dutifully screamed as he rocked our car atop the Ferris Wheel on the Revere Beach midway.

Later, in the back seat of Paul's car on a quiet side street, I stopped him from unbuttoning my blouse, but let him touch my breasts through the thin cotton instead. Up front Vivian was repeatedly feinting to her left, as she endeavoured to hold Paul at second base.

I was a little bit turned on by my Soldier Boy, though his tongue in my mouth had me regretting the onion rings I'd eaten earlier. Along with strawberry pie and a root beer, not what I'd normally order, only I was unused to a boy buying me food, and hadn't factored in what the Ferris Wheel and the Scrambler might make of the mix. In any event, the slow tingle in my tummy began to feel more like nausea, and Lord knows what might've followed, had Vivian not tagged Paul, attempting to steal third, for the final out and we all headed home.

'It's just a tummy bug,' I told Ma who heard me getting sick in the toilet back at No. 23.

I never saw Private TJ again, but I began to date more in my senior year. It's a wonder I ever necked again though, for fear it might make me nauseous. But not till I met Eddie, Katy's father, did I let anybody round third and all the way home to score.

CHAPTER 45

DATE: 9 May 1988

ACTIVITY: Hide & Go Seek

THOUGHT FOR THE DAY: If All Is Not Lost, Where Is It?

It's the doorstop that usually disappears with Nora
Doherty, but Nora herself went missing this afternoon after
dinner, throwing us into a major panic. 'Have you seen the
Doorstop?' Nurse Powers asked as I was doing some
paperwork, but I took her literally and just said no. But
when Wang Wei, who had last seen Nora in her chair, asked
the same, I joined the search straight away, imagining the
look on the Desk Sergeant's face at the Garda Station if I
had to ask for a Missing Persons form. To make matters
worse, Nurse Powers inquired of a few residents had they
seen Nora—which prompted Enda Glynn, God love her, to
join the search, tripping through the Home with her
impossibly light steps, like an eighty-year-old ballerina,
calling 'Here, Nora, Nora!' as if she were a cat. Then Eva
Glynn, in sick bay with a kidney infection, hearing her
sister's voice, began bellowing 'Enda! Enda!' so loudly I
could envision the rest of residents taking up the cry,

227

banging their tin cups on the bars of their cells.

Cassie Boyle meantime had worked herself into a right state in the front day-room. 'The Boody Women have her! Oh the Boody Women have her!' All we lacked was for Germany Calling to wake up and inform Cassie it was the Huns who took Nora prisoner, not her bloody Boody Women—whoever they are when they're at home. But luckily Gemma slept on in her chair, while young Clodagh managed to settle Cassie.

'We've an APB out on Nora Doherty,' I informed Mary O'Mara, who'd been downstairs with Constance Fitzgerald and a few others.

'Apy-bee?' puzzled Mary, who obviously never had an older brother glued to his short-wave radio, and bent on becoming a cop.

'She's gone missing!' I clarified.

'Sure, she has to be around somewhere,' Mary laughed. 'But you're going about it wrong. Let's just look for the doorstop and see if Nora doesn't turn up?'

I doubt Mary knows how to panic—which had helped me calm down a bit until a shout suddenly sounded from the laundry room. 'Something moved in them sheets,' Lil the Mop stammered as we ran in, pointing to where Nora Doherty, wrapped in a large pile of bedlinen on the floor beside the washer, had been sleeping off her Shepherd's Pie. 'I thought it was that cat Calico!'

'Well, there's one bed Diarmuid & Gráinne missed,' Katy quipped at supper tonight, bright spark that she is. Nor had I encountered those fables growing up, as Ma wasn't much interested in anything Irish. But had I ever said anything clever, on any score, I wonder? Or if I had, would Ma have thought it—or me—especially clever? For that's what troubles me—not that I wasn't clever, but that my mother simply couldn't take to me.

CHAPTER 46

DATE: 10 May 1988

ACTIVITY: Insomnia

THOUGHT FOR THE NIGHT: A Freudian Slip Is When
You Say One Thing & Mean Your Mother

I shut this notebook in tears last night, weeping, I suppose, for both my mother and myself. But also feeling this deep-harbour dredging is too fucking much, just bucket-loads of muddied pain that only make me more miserable, and to what avail?

I'd my mind made up not to write any more, but here I am just 24 hours later. Worse yet, it's 2.00 a.m. and I'm teary again, having replayed this afternoon's session with Sister Úna in my head for half an hour in bed. Until I got up, made myself a cup of camomile tea, and opened these pages—only to be reminded how I wasn't going to do this anymore.

It doesn't help either how this afternoon's session dovetailed so neatly with last night's final lines. As if there exists a hidden script here, wherein one night's sorrow merely sets the stage for another afternoon's tidal wave—which if it were true, would unnerve me even more.

And all because I remarked to Sister Úna how often I feel

229

entrapped. Though come to think of it, maybe it was 'entrapped' that suddenly caught her ear—like a tiny bell?? Echoing how 'trapped' I said I'd felt as I fell to my knees in my own kitchen that awful morning just last month? Or maybe it wasn't so sudden at all? Maybe Sister's been patiently waiting all along to make her move? For make her move Sister did, swooping down like a magpie that's spotted a shiny bauble.

'"Entrapped" how, Maeve?'

'Oh, I don't know. Just boxed in …'

'Boxed in?'

'Yes, hemmed in.'

'Your job?'

'Yes, my job. But more than that, too,' I said, not really trying.

'Entrapped?'

'Yes, entrapped. You know, not able to move.' Shifting in my chair and wondering how much longer Sister wanted to hang out in yet another cul-de-sac.

'Trapped like you're tied down? Or more like paralysed?'

'More like caged, I think …'

'And how long have you felt like this, Maeve?'

'Oh, Christ!' I snapped. 'All my fucking life!?'

I still can't believe I actually cursed—all but cursed Sister herself, as this huge wave of anger swept over me.

'I'm so sorry, Sister,' I stammered, feeling my face red as my hair. 'That just came out of nowhere …'

'There's no need, Maeve,' Sister Úna smiled, before getting up and going over to the CD player. She didn't look a bit bothered either—like she hears that kind of language every day. At breakfast, say, from Sister Alphonsus: 'Well, fuck me if we're not out of porridge oats!'

'There's no need to apologise,' she repeated, seated now

again. 'But there's no such place as "nowhere" either.'

'Sorry, Sister?' I said, not following.

'You said your anger came out of "nowhere" … '

I tried cutting her off, but Sister was too quick. 'Think back, Maeve. Go back to the first time you felt "entrapped"?'

I simply shook my head, though I sensed now Sister wasn't chasing me up any dead end. And sensed too that wherever "nowhere" was—I didn't want to go there. But Sister Úna was as determined as a magpie too—not to be shifted.

'Try to remember, Maeve. Close your eyes and think back.'

Only after I closed my eyes did I really hear the CD she had put on. I'm not great with classical music, but I'm open to persuasion. I even hum 'Are You the O'Grady Who Runs the Hotel?' aloud sometimes as I listen, a ditty that seemingly helps you to distinguish Mozart from Beethoven. But I was far too shaken this afternoon for such foolishness, and merely took the music in. A cello concerto, I think, sounding like all the sorrows of the world had been captured for four strings.

'Good woman, Maeve,' Sister Úna encouraged, but I was already underway, following the music, until I suddenly found myself somewhere else. Found myself back in the kitchen at Apt 1A: only I'm in my wooden playpen in the corner, beside the white-enamel table where my mother will someday disembowel a crow. Yet Ma has her hands full even now—even if she's only holding a sweeping brush. Though not so much holding as wielding it. Wielding it furiously. For that's what I see from my crib: Ma sweeping the kitchen floor like one of The Furies. That's what I see, but what I feel—even if I hadn't words for it back then—is her implacable anger as she sweeps. I must've been standing, for I'm not watching her through any playpen bars. But bars or no—here's the answer to Sister's query—here's where and from whence I have always felt entrapped ...

And here's also where I possibly first felt I needed to be the Good Girl, as Sister and I tease out over the next half-hour. Always and forever the Best Girl, by way of placating my mother's implacable anger. I couldn't stop crying, nor did Sister Úna encourage me to. 'Let it go, Maeve,' she counselled instead. 'Lay it down, my dear.' She didn't push me to talk either, just mostly listened, same as ever, letting me ask the questions.

'How old was I?' was the first I managed.

'How old do you think?'

'I couldn't've been in my playpen much after eighteen months?'

'Well, that's how old you likely were.'

'Is that possible, Sister?'

Sister Úna smiled, lifting her hands slightly as she sometimes does. Like a bird taking flight, only slowly, more gull than magpie. 'Who knows how much we remember, Maeve? But did you see what you saw?'

'Oh, I saw all right,' I said, wiping my eyes.

Sister Úna left the room then, returning shortly with a cup of tea, and I rang home to tell Katy I'd be late, after which Sister and I talked on.

I gradually stopped crying, but what didn't cease was the extraordinary energy I felt—like a current through my body, radiating from my chest and down my arms. The same energy that has me unable to sleep now, though I believe the camomile tea may do its trick. Along with a few deep-breathing exercises before I go back upstairs. And, why not admit it, setting down these lines has probably helped to settle me somewhat too.

PART III

CHAPTER 47

DATE: 12 May 1988

THOUGHT FOR THE DAY: Old Age Ain't for Sissies

Today was Mother's Day all over again—only other people's mothers for a change. First was Cassie Boyle, who wouldn't let Polish Petra bathe her this morning. 'Go on away out of that now!' she kept telling Petra. 'My mother already gave me a good wash.' I don't recall Cassie talking about her mother much, unless she was one of the Boody Women? But there was no persuading her, so I told Petra to forget the bath and try again tomorrow. Meantime Constance Fitzgerald wouldn't touch her breakfast. 'My mother's after giving me a massive fry,' she informed Fiona Flynn. There's no keeping up with Constance—who's either looking after her mother or being served up breakfast by her.

'I'm mothered out myself,' Fiona announced after she persuaded Constance to eat a few spoonfuls of porridge. Telling us how her Nelly is hearing a mysterious beep ever since she returned home from her bowel operation.

'What's it sound like?' asked Nurse Ethel.

'A high-pitched beeping she says.'

'It's not tinnitus so,' Mary O'Mara offered.

'"Do you think that surgeon left something up me hole?" she asks my Derek. "Like his alarm clock?" he says. So now Nelly's not talking to him.'

Had I been able to care for my mother—like Fiona, or Aunt Chrissie, or even poor Constance did for theirs—might it have done me some good? Helped to temper some of the anguish that spilled out Tuesday with Sister Úna? Had Rose Maguire not died, of course, the year after I came to Ireland. Keeping a parent out of a Home as Fiona is doing—even for a time—is a wonderful thing. I like hearing about her Nelly too—even if I seldom speak of Ma. Not at tea break in the Home anyhow, though I sometimes chat a bit about her with Mary, whom I'm meeting this evening after work.

Meantime I still wince when I think of having cursed with Sister Úna. 'Don't worry, Maeve,' she reassured me after I apologised again on my way out. 'It's only language—and not the first I've heard.' Then, standing at the door, she told of the secondary school in Botswana where she taught English years ago, whose Headmaster, an elegant African in an impeccable blue blazer, invariably announced at every Assembly how either the boys' toilet or the mimeo machine was 'fucked'!

'I couldn't believe my ears,' Sister Úna smiled.

To be honest, neither could I—which was her intent, I suppose, Sister's way of taking the sting out of my own foul mouth. And suddenly I wanted to tell her of Vivian's sketched 'fuck', or Sister Amadeus's scented mimeo sheets, or my own English teacher Miss Dewey—all of it retrieved via the very notebook she suggested. But I just touched her arm and thanked her once again.

CHAPTER 48

DATE: 14 May 1988

ACTIVITY: Sun-Bathing

VERSE FOR THE DAY: 'Gather ye rosebuds while ye may,
Old Time is still a-flying.'

This afternoon was warm enough to take several of the
ladies out of the dining room into the garden, where Lil had
sheets drying on the line. Constance Fitzgerald and Nora
Cricket insisted on sitting squarely in the sun, so we
outfitted them with the straw bonnets we keep for such
occasions. Real T-shirt weather, so it was, even if I'd had to
ask Clodagh earlier to get Eamon Kerr out of his, with its
reminder how LIFE IS SEXUALLY TRANSMITTED & ALWAYS
FATAL. Had Eamon a sense of humour once, or are the T-
shirts his son sends over from Florida just his revenge on a
dour daddy? Either way Eamon just grunts if somebody
laughs at one of them. Like WE'RE BORN NAKED, WET AND
HUNGRY—THEN THINGS GET WORSE! which had Alice May
chuckling, whereas Germany Gemma just stares at Eamon's
chest like she's solving a word puzzle. Or knowing Gemma,
more likely trying to decipher a coded message from Axis
HQ.

Speaking of puzzles, Fiona told today how Nelly had them all over in her granny flat again, searching for her mysterious beep. Nobody heard anything, including Nelly, who said it mostly happened whenever she lifted her right arm. 'I felt like asking God to either strike her deaf,' Fiona said, 'or me dead!'

'So what did God do?' Leo the Porter asked.

'He sent Mr. Clancy round,' Fiona laughed, 'to collect her Church envelope. He always takes a cup of tea with her—only this morning he looks up and says, "Sounds like your smoke alarm needs a new battery?"'

The garden is my favourite part of the Home, though I only get to go out and draw an occasional deep breath in it. There's a good expanse of lawn, bounded on three sides by an old, ivy-overgrown stone wall with an ancient apple tree in the corner. Above the back wall is the embankment for the DART line between Clontarf and Killester, whose trains you hear from inside the Home, and sometimes see rattling by from a window.

Last weekend I managed to dig a bit in my own flower border out back, preparing it for some delphiniums Orla's giving me. Each year I promise myself I'll get stuck into the garden, inspired by Mrs. Sheedy next door who's always out, even in winter, bundled up against the cold and poking a fork into the ground. She looked far more feeble last Saturday, however, pottering around her perennials, and I wonder how much longer she'll manage on her own? Harry her son says she's already fallen twice indoors, but won't hear of coming out to him in Lucan. Which doesn't surprise me, as I can't imagine her shutting the kitchen door for the last time on her beloved garden.

Alice May spoke of her own garden as I brought her indoors this afternoon. Telling how she used to dig rusty nails into the soil beneath her hydrangeas to turn the flowers a deeper shade of blue. 'Had you a garden growing up?' she asked, once we reached her room with its easy chair and reading lamp.

'Yes—if I can count the Boston Public Gardens!'

'Were they lovely, Maeve?'

'Absolutely,' I said. 'Not unlike Stephen's Green—lots of flowerbeds and ducks on a pond.'

I've talked a fair bit about Boston with Alice May, who lived all those years in St Louis—before turning her back on the Mississippi to come back and look after her mother and those blue hydrangeas in Killester. And I certainly always thought of the Public Gardens as mine, crossing it daily en route to high school and university, even after I'd outgrown playing there. But they weren't a garden like Mrs. Sheedy or Alice May had had. Or, for that matter, like the garden Mrs. L once told me of. Only that was more about a single rosebush her grandfather had given her grandmother on their Maine salt-water farm. 'My mother went back there once,' Mrs. L told me, 'just after I was born. The farmhouse had burned down, but she dug up the bush, roots and all, and brought it back to New Hampshire where it still blooms.'

I remember envying Mrs. L that rosebush. Or was it her sense of place I really coveted, her own roots in New Hampshire and Massachusetts both? Or was it the love that rosebush represented? Not that there wasn't love between my parents—for love there had been surely, if not of a variety that bloomed as vigorously as those roses had for Mrs. L—and in my childish imagination. One grows up, however, and now I'd just like to think her rosebush flourishes yet, together with those peonies and marigolds either end of the footbridge in the Maguire Public Gardens.

Better that than thinking thoughts which—like rusted nails dug into soil—can turn the past into an even deeper shade of blue.

CHAPTER 49

DATE: 16 May 1988

ACTIVITY: Shopping

'Second Floor: Ladies' Wear,' I joked with Alice May and Cassie Boyle today, taking a page from that childhood Park St game. 'First Floor: Kitchenware'—like we were in Arnotts, not going down to dinner at the Fairview Home for the Elderly. 'Ground Floor: Hats & Handbags,' I announced, taking their arms as we stepped out.

Ladies' Wear being what sparked the row Katy and I had yesterday morning. A sharp exchange over my reluctance to buy her a new top to wear into the National School on Dorset St where she's working with refugee kids, mostly from Nigeria and Romania. Especially as she has only a week left of her school-year Community Service there, and a press already full of perfectly good tops. Still, a row I see now was mostly my fault. Our negotiating—OK, arguing—over new clothes happens, but it doesn't usually end in tears and the front door slamming. Nor do I often feel that angry either, which suggests something else at work behind my refusal to compromise. OK, give in—as I'm far too soft with K, no matter how determined I am not to spoil her.

But I don't like admitting what I was really feeling, either. Resentment, that is. Resentment at Katy having a Transition Year, with options like work experience or learning a language abroad. Options I never had back in Boston High School, where our guidance counsellor, Mr. Shaw, an ex-gym teacher, would administer multiple-choice vocational tests he probably never bothered to score. Not that it mattered, as I'd already decided on nursing. A career that would keep me employed, and one I probably chose out of the same fear of poverty that had shadowed my emigrant parents all the way from Ireland. And a career choice I've never since reconsidered, given the economics which govern single motherhood.

Which, if I follow my reasoning through, suggests I might at heart resent Katy too, for limiting my choices? Whereas truth is I love her more than life itself—and only want her to have each & every option to find herself. Every option—plus the new top I'm going to get her to make up for my meanness. And for my resentments. Maternal ambivalence the textbooks call it, and wasn't I foolish to think I'd be totally immune to it myself?

CHAPTER 50

DATE: 20 May 1988
WEATHER: Italia! Oh Italia!

This afternoon I told Sister Úna about college, where I met Eddie. Fact is, this lovely weather already had me thinking of that time—as if those memories come wrapped in springtime sunshine. I was certainly happier much of the time: out of Apt 1A more, and less trammelled within. More impervious to my mother's moods, and less the prisoner of my own.

I told Pops my last year of high school that I'd do a hospital-nursing course if I didn't get into, or get enough financial aid for, the Bachelor in Nursing programme at Boston University. But my lack of a Personality—all those hours spent reading—finally paid off, and I was offered a full scholarship.

I continued to study hard at college, devouring anatomy & physiology texts like I had thick novels at age thirteen. What's more, I loved it. Not just the written comp and English lit, but my science subjects too. Chem, psych and microbiology, my favourite, the colonisation of cholera outbreaks coming so easily my Prof suggested I think about doing a straight science degree, followed by a doctorate. I declined, but had I it to do over, I'd opt for medicine. There's no way, though, I'd have had the confidence back then—as if growing up the Super's daughter automatically precluded that kind of aspiration.

Instead I kept my head down, justifying my scholarship by making the Dean's List every marking-quarter except my last, when I was already pregnant with Katy, and struggling just to see the term out and graduate. I wasn't a total swot though, the early Seventies being too carnival-like to see out entirely from a carrel in Mugar Library. But I still picked my way cautiously through those turbulent times, same as I'd traversed my first two decades.

'Were you ever a hippie, Mama?' Katy asked when she first heard of flower children.

'Was I ever a hippie-potamus?' I replied, just to tease her.

'Did you ever smoke pot, Mama?' she asked a year or two later.

'No, Pet,' I lied—something I hate doing with her. But I didn't want to admit I'd done drugs—given how Dublin's now awash in them. When she asks again however, I'll tell the truth. How I only smoked grass, mostly with a nursing pal Laurie Scott, who would then make up these awful jokes, like the Italian orthopaedic surgeon who thought the fibula was a tiny lie. 'Good girls go to Heaven,' Laurie told me the night we crashed a party at the top of the Parker House, twelve floors up from the laundry of my fifteenth summer. 'Bad girls go everywhere!' But I was still too much the Good Girl—never mind too cautious—to sample anything like acid or cocaine.

'Were you at Woodstock, Mama?' K likewise asked after

seeing the movie on TV. I wasn't, but I told her how I'd heard Richie Havens play in Boston. Again, it's the afternoon sunlight at that free concert on the Common I remember best. Or the sun on the Charles, a slight breeze off the river teasing the leaves on the trees by the cycle-path, as Laurie and I lay on a blanket after a late lab. Or the early evening sun in that loft above a pizza joint on Boylston St where I did a Zen meditation class my junior year. Twenty of us, two evenings a week, sitting eyes closed in the lotus position, while shouts and sirens sounded from the street, and a gorgeous smell of pizza wafted up.

I looked anxiously about that first class, half-afraid I might see Stanley the Waiter from the Parker House, wearing but a towel, and beckoning me towards a bed of nails in the corner. But I recognised only Steven, whom I'd fancied from afar in Chem 101 the previous fall. Nor did our instructor Alan, a small man in his forties, chat up the prettiest girls afterwards as my yoga teacher had done the year before. In fact, Alan's quietness is what I remember best. How little he said, apart from illustrating some precept he wanted us to consider: about Being Mindful or Letting Go. What's more, his was a <u>quiet</u> quietness—without the tension that sometimes crackled like static behind Ma's frequent silences. Or the preoccupation you could all but hear humming when Pops' mind was elsewhere, and he wouldn't even hear the question you'd asked. Whereas Alan's silence didn't emit any such signals; rather simply was—like a tiny forest pool.

Come to think of it, the silences in the O'Byrne kitchen that first Donegal summer weren't a million miles from a kind of Zen-centred stillness either. Even if I was fairly unnerved at first—the way the talk could suddenly lapse and Auntie Chrissie would simply sit there, feeling no compulsion to take it up again. I was even more anxious when the chat died with Hughdy—who said little enough inside the cottage to begin with. But it wouldn't go absolutely quiet either, for there was always the fire muttering in the range, rain on the window, Hughdy sucking on his pipe, or the clock ticking on the mantel beside the china cats.

It's funny how often a silence is anything but. When Katy's fighting with me, say, yet won't talk—even if she's beside me chopping onions for our supper. We don't speak for what seems ages, yet it's like Wagner's blaring—all thunderheads and kettledrum—until the silence grows too deafening, and I have to ask Katy is she annoyed with me?

Steven, from Chem 101 and Zen, was another quiet fellow, but in his case it turned out still waters also run dull, his Personality nearly as wooden as my old puppet pal, Maurice Perri. It wasn't until I told him a joke after class, however, that I finally copped that. 'Where's my change?' the Zen monk asks the hot dog vendor, who has just pocketed his five-dollar bill. 'Oh, Master,' says the vendor, 'change must come from within!'

I told it OK too, but Steven just looked at me like I had two heads. 'Make Love, Not War!' was the battle cry of those years, but 'Make Jokes, Not Love!' seemed more my line. Not that I was looking for sex so much as a fella—the story of my life. And who knows, perhaps I'd have ended up a secular nun—had I not met Eddie later that spring? But Eddie's another chapter so to speak, and morning already comes early enough.

CHAPTER 51

DATE: 25 May 1988

WEATHER: Wet Again

THOUGHT FOR THE DAY: Non c'è rosa senza spine!

I was secretly delighted the weather broke yesterday, as it was looking like I'd maybe chosen one of those rare but wondrous sunny Irish summers in which to take ourselves out foreign. Katy and I spent last week looking at brochures—tiny Mediterranean fishing villages beneath impossibly blue skies—before settling on Crete for the last fortnight in July. K's boss said she can have those weeks off from her summer job waitressing at a café on Duke St, so I'll book our flights tomorrow, and pick up a phrasebook so we can order something more than moussaka off the menu.

'Will there be bugs there, Mama?' K asks, making me feel I've failed her in that department. The way she goes into hysterics if she discovers a single clothes moth—like she inherited that particular thread of her Granny's madness. Sending me all over Dublin last month after mothballs, which are impossible to find. 'You know how to find moth balls?' Manny asked Brian once. 'Easy! Just lift their wings!' But maybe it takes a Manny to keep you from growing up skittish of creepy-crawlies. Telling us how the Chinese use maggots to cleanse a wound, because maggots only eat dead flesh.

Tom the Teacher is like Manny in that regard, a great man for a fact. Only Tom's too polite to describe how cat piss glows under black light—as Manny likewise informed Brian. Or how Italians feed ripe olives to turkeys, since the pits will germinate more rapidly after a turkey passes them. That an ostrich egg constitutes the largest single cell is more Tom's kind of fact. 'You can't fatten thoroughbreds,' he told me today, refusing a second biscuit at tea. Each day he dons a shirt and tie: all dressed up & nowhere to go. 'Nothing to do & all day in which to do it!' as he says himself. There should be medals for the likes of him, Nora Cricket or Veronica Egan, who sit with such equanimity through the boundless hours of what looks to us like their diminished lives. Or Alice May who has pretty much stopped reading altogether. Again, I think it's hardest in a Home on the compos mentis, whereas the witless can be anywhere. Like Happy-As Ferguson knocking back his Lucozade, or Kitty the Conductor who came up to me today, all abother:

'I've the two lads coming in for their dinner!'

'Have you anything in, Kitty?' I ask.

'Chops!'

'I'll put two on,' I tell her. 'And how about some peas and spuds?'

'Oh, would you do that?' Kitty says, going off as happy as Happy-As.

'Will you throw a chop on for me too?' jokes Tom, whose smile reminds me of Pops.

Pops who loved a laugh, and told Ma of the good one he got on yet another nixer he had, collecting rents in East Boston for the same crowd who owned our building. 'I knocked at the last apartment,' he told Ma in the kitchen one night, as he made himself toast. '"Whadda ya want?" this guy shouts. "I'm looking for two months' rent," I shout back. "Come in, come in," your man says, '"and we'll all look for it!"'

But Pops wasn't a debt collector at heart, and so eventually gave it up. He seemed to always have a part-time gig, though: night watchman, painter, or a couple of months on the evening shift at a car-battery factory, which made him constipated despite the milk the workers were advised to drink. Evening shifts were dodgy anyhow, because technically Pops had to be on call at No. 23—in case something like a water pipe burst. Nor did Ma like him out at night, even though she often watched TV those evenings he was home. It's hard gauging exactly what their marriage was like, nor have I ever had a live-in relationship against which to measure theirs. They didn't bicker much, but I'm not clear to what extent they really interacted? 'No Rose without a thorn!' Pops liked to tease Ma when we were little, but even something like teasing only happened now and again.

I still miss Pops like crazy, which will never change. And I could still cry at the drop of a fedora—like the one someone was sporting in an old black & white movie on the telly last Saturday night. A beat-up one just like Pops wore, grey with a black satin band. No tweed cap for James Anthony Maguire—son of Mayo—once he hit the streets of Boston. Or inside Apt 1A for that matter, where he often wore his hat, except at suppertime to oblige Ma. Maybe that was the Irish in him, for Uncle Hughdy wore his cap indoors too. I love the fact Pops affected a fedora, but wonder how he thought it made him look? If not entirely like Elliot Ness, at least every inch a Super, and certainly nothing like a Paddy. Not that I think Pops cared about being spotted for immigrant Irish. More likely he just took a fancy to things, like ice-skating or fedoras, which weren't par for the course in Co. Mayo.

It's nearly nine months since he went, and the grief which had me frozen last winter seems to have shifted a bit. Nor am I so scared about losing it altogether—that sorry moment with Katy beside the Christmas tree that brought me to Sister Úna. Or finding myself on my knees by the kitchen fridge two months ago, terrified my own talking rat might scuttle out from behind. Born in the USA, but determined not to go doolah in Dublin, c'est moi. Plus Sister Úna thinks we can finish up soon, and while she doesn't charge much, it'll be handy to have a few dollars more for Crete.

CHAPTER 52

DATE: 28 May 1988
Verse for the Day: 'Hundreds of bees in the purple clover,
But just one mother the wide world over.'

It was a bit awkward with Jim O'Connor for a while after he last asked me out. But he hasn't bothered again, and things seem alright now. Meantime he told me this morning his own mother may be coming in to us.

'Is she not managing at home?' I asked.

'She still gets about OK,' Jim said, 'but her memory's shot.' Telling me how his sister got a cake for their mother's birthday with a big 85 in red icing. And how the next day his mother told a neighbour of the lovely cake they had for her daughter's 58th! Not unlike Nora the Cricket who blew her candles out last week, then inquired: 'What is it we're celebrating?'

'Is she willing to come in?' I asked.

'She was yesterday,' Jim said, 'but what she says one day doesn't necessarily stretch to the next.' Then he took care to add, 'But I wouldn't want her singled out for special treatment.'

'I don't see that as a problem,' I told him. 'Unless she's used to a second sherry Sundays.'

'She doesn't drink,' Jim laughed. 'But she's driving me to it.'

Speaking of which, I believe Nurse Powers had drink taken yesterday, a 'smell of etho' as we were instructed to jot down in our clinical notes if we got a whiff of alcohol off a patient while doing an assessment. Anyhow, I called her into the office and said I'd have to take action the next time I felt we had this situation. 'I've gum trouble,' she told me. 'It's this antiseptic mouthwash the dentist gave me that smells like drink.'

And denial ain't just a river in North Africa, I wanted to respond—but didn't. I hate that part of being Matron, but I can't take the risk with the residents. Imagine being Matron of that Copenhagen Home where a male nurse murdered a dozen patients a few years back? 'For making too much noise,' he said! Please God I'd smell something that rotten in the state of Denmark as readily as Jameson's or Paddy's off Nurse Powers. Meanwhile there's Polish Petra to worry about. Not her attendance which has been grand, but her well-being—for Mary O'Mara has twice found her in tears downstairs before her shift, though she won't tell Mary why.

'Your mother could go in with Veronica?' I told Jim, who maybe has delayed filling Carmen Cassidy's bed for that very reason.

'My mother could finish me altogether. Before I ever get her this far.'

In fact my own mother is actually why I sat down here tonight. To record a dream I had last night—not my work woes. Though it's often easier to stop worrying about work once I've written a few words about it here. 'Lay them

252

down,' Alan the Yogi used to say of our cares, telling us to empty our minds in that Bolyston St loft. I still wonder, though, if Zen isn't primarily for men who are wired so differently to women? The way Zen asks you to simply ignore your emotions and get on with your practice. And that's whether you're menstruating or not! Which is probably why I've never been especially good at it, even if I'm managing to <u>sit</u> for fifteen minutes some evenings now.

There's simply no time to try meditating mornings. Though I did lie on in bed for a minute this morning, replaying last night's dream before it faded altogether. Katy and I were on a bus—in America, I think—for it looked like a Greyhound terminal, rows of plastic chairs and that dreadful neon lighting which always looks like the middle of the night, whatever the hour. Anyhow, I had to get off the bus, after telling K to just sit tight. Our Psych Prof said one function of dreams is to preserve sleep—which is why we dream we're in a toilet if we're bursting for a pee. But I wasn't searching for the Ladies' in last night's dream— instead I go through a door into a room full of shelves, where my mother stands behind a counter. We don't speak, but there's something I desperately want to ask. And my mother is smiling. A quiet smile, sad, yet something more. But a real smile—and one I'd dearly love to believe was for me.

CHAPTER 53

Nurse Ethel had difficulty getting a catheter into Kitty the Conductor this morning, not that it's easy getting even just a bit of dinner into Kitty. Never mind keeping her blouse buttoned up, those days she decides to dance around topless. Last Sunday however she stayed in her bedroom, fighting with one of her two daughters who are both married out in Australia. 'What time did you get in last night, ye hussy?' Kitty kept shouting. 'Out hoorin' till all hours!' Tending her doesn't help much either, especially if Kitty takes you for a daughter, as happened to young Clodagh. But Kitty knew me for Matron this morning when I stuck my head in.

'Keep that Cheeky Chink away from me,' she shouted, gesturing at Wang Wei who was helping Nurse Ethel with the catheter.

'That's lovely talk,' I told Kitty, like I was remonstrating with a five-year-old. But W^2 just grinned as if she'd heard far worse in her disco DJ days.

We learned the catheter procedure at BU our junior year, when Laurie Scott fainted into the arms of fellow student Dan Oliver, just as her turn came for insertion. Half our class fancied Dan, I think, even if I never went beyond trying to sit near him in the library. Nor had I thought of him since, till this creepy short story I read last year, where this guy keeps staring at a girl asleep in a library, only to discover when he finally approaches that she's dead—not dozing! I might have envied Laurie in Dan's arms, only I'd fallen for Eddie LoPresti a few months earlier, after meeting him one lunchtime in the BU student union where he'd borrowed a pen—nothing so romantic as Ma and Pops at twilight by the frozen-over Frog Pond.

Eddie was about to drop out of college, but he didn't start to chat me up by revealing that. Instead he told me a joke. It sounds dubious, falling for somebody because they make you laugh, but there you have it. And Eddie was great fun, always laughing, an easy-going charmer. Still, there's no escaping the banality of how we began.

'What's your major?' he asked, after returning the pen.

'Nursing,' I said, thinking I liked the brown eyes.

'This fella wakes up after a car crash,' Eddie replied—which lost me for a second. 'Sees a cop peering down at him. "Don't worry!" the cop says. "There's a Red Cross Nurse on the way!" "Ah, no," the guy says. "Can't I have a blond, friendly one instead?"'

I laughed and blushed both. Beet-red, the way I might as a child when some adult remarked on my hair. But I also saw Eddie looking like he maybe cared more about having embarrassed me than whether I liked his joke. Not a totally insensitive guy, in other words.

He asked me out for that Saturday and I accepted. Had

he suggested the pictures or a party, I might've only gone out with him once or twice, as I'd done with a handful of fellows since high school. As if I preferred fancying the likes of Dan Oliver in the library or Steven in Chem 101, from afar.

But Eddie suggested we go for something to eat in the North End, just off Haymarket Square where Pops used to take us shopping. And seeing Eddie on his own turf touched some kind of chord. You don't fall in love out of envy, but Eddie clearly possessed something I hadn't— namely, a proper neighbourhood. Not proper as in 'proper Bostonian'—that smell of old money and old manners which, wafting the few blocks over from Back Bay and Beacon Hill, invested No. 23 Park St with a faint whiff of Brahmin respectability to which the Super's family could never measure up.

Instead, a proper neighbourhood as in narrow, cobblestoned streets, family shops, small brick townhouses, and neighbours on all sides. And neighbours that actually interacted, not just wordlessly walked their dogs, straight-laced & poker-faced, down Marlboro or Dartmouth St. For here were old women leaning out of windows everywhere, looking down on streets crowded with men chatting in twos and threes, while kids darted to and fro between parked cars.

Eddie suggested going for a beer and a pizza, but I was comfortable enough to say I'd like to stroll around some more first. So stroll we did, peering into cafés, grocery stores, and countless bakeries, the smell of warm bread mixing with that of espresso, plus a slight hint of the salty harbour that you don't get by the Common. Too little travelled at age twenty to recognise what was in ways a translocated corner of Europe, I fell hard for the North End straight away. I didn't meet la famiglia until we'd been going out a while, but it wasn't a big deal either when Eddie finally brought me home. Not a big deal for him at least. Like many Italians, he saw family as an extension of self— more the sea in which you swim than a minefield to traverse. Plus his mother had an ease about her my Ma could never manage, not least meeting somebody for the first time. Even if she insisted that I eat more than I possibly could. And yes, there actually *was* a big pot of tomato sauce simmering on the stove, like you see in every Italian film.

If Eddie and I took sex slowly, his world seduced me straight away. Unfamiliar as it was, I surprised myself by slotting in—never my strong suit. It took a few Sundays before I said much, but that hardly mattered, given the laughter and bickering which flooded the kitchen, two if not three simultaneous conversations in which everybody talked more than they listened. Everybody except Mr. LoPresti who seldom opened his mouth, except for another forkful. Eddie's was a large family, two sisters, three brothers, plus Nonna, his grandmother, who it seemed never left the apartment except for weddings or funerals. Nonna didn't join us in the kitchen either, preferring to poke at a plate in her corner of the living room. But she'd always throw up her hands whenever I arrived, exclaiming 'Bella la mia Rosa!' and stroking my head as if she'd never seen red hair before. And I quickly grew so fond of her I could even forgive her that!

I never quite figured out how they all fit into that third-floor tenement. Doubling up in bed, I suppose, same as the Irish had. And it says something too, I suppose, how what I write about Eddie speaks mostly of his neighbourhood. Or his family. But I couldn't help feeling had I grown up a Super's daughter in the North End, I might've fit in easier too, no different to the greengrocer's or baker's daughter down the block.

CHAPTER 54

DATE: 5 June 1988
THOUGHT FOR THE DAY: Motherhood Is Not a Sin

Another of our residents, Margaret Walsh, passed away yesterday, leaving her doll behind on her bedside locker. Jim only told me her story last year, having assumed I already knew. How Margaret had been one of the Magdalenes, handed over by her parents, pregnant at nineteen, to the Sisters of Charity. And how after her baby was given up for adoption, Margaret stayed on with the nuns for fifty years, working in the convent laundry. A few Magdalenes are still in a Home run by the Order, but an older sister, who moved back from England after her husband died, tracked Margaret down, and took her in until she herself passed away a few years later, at which point Margaret came to us.

I'm as happy I hadn't heard her story earlier, for knowing what her doll represents is just too too painful. Poor Margaret who never gave us a moment's bother—just ghosted from room to room, carrying her baby tucked under her arm. I too was an unwed mother, but the gap between our experiences is too great to even imagine myself in her shoes: Margaret stripped of her baby, then indentured for life, while I was able to carry on with my daughter.

I hadn't thought Margaret was for death last week, though she was down with a bad chest infection. But Sunday afternoon Mary O'Mara suggested Margaret might not make it through the night. Once again, the vital signs weren't too alarming, but hadn't I thought that with Mildred Lacey too, the first time Mary made such a call? I wasn't about to ask Mary if she could smell the death again, but I had Wang Wei wheel Margaret's bed into the infirmary to spare Nora Cricket any distress, should Mary have it right. And right she was, for Margaret crossed over yesterday morning around five o'clock.

Fact is, I was entirely unsettled when Mary foretold Mildred Lacey's death two years ago. Scorpios are intuitive, I know, but that's pushing it. We didn't really talk about it either, as Mary isn't that comfortable with her gift. Like a ham radio operator reluctant to tune in to the other side. Though she did tell me last summer of having asked her Ciaran one evening had he heard from his father – and how their phone had rung before Ciaran could reply, his sister on to say their Dad had just passed away.

There's apparently also some business to do with mirrors, but I didn't press Mary on it. Christ knows I'm jumpy enough without having to look away each time I pass a mirror at night. But I did tell her of what my mother had seen on the stairs outside our apartment the night Uncle Dinny died: a wee girl with chestnut curls, not unlike her childhood self.

I had hesitated yesterday over Margaret's doll, before

placing it atop the pile of her clothes which Wang Wei had taken from the wardrobe. I went off duty then before Lanigan the undertaker arrived, so when it wasn't there this morning, I asked Mary about it.

'It's not lost,' Mary smiled—like we were back in school.

'You didn't!' I exclaimed, but Mary only smiled again.

'How?'

'Lanigan was in a hurry, so he decided to coffin Margaret here.'

'But *how*?'

'I just said I wanted to slip in her missal and some holy water wrapped in the scarf her sister had brought her from Lourdes.'

'Do you think we're daft?'

'No,' laughed Mary. 'Just latter-day Egyptians.'

'Or Iroquois,' I said, who we learned in primary school had buried beads and pottery along with their dead.

Meantime we've a second empty bed for Mrs. O'Connor, should Jim decide to bring his mother in from the cold. Moreover, Nora Cricket should get on great with Mrs. O'Connor, seeing both their memories are shot.

'Those are lovely cards, Nora,' I told her last week, pointing to her bedside table.

'What are they for?' Nora asked as if she'd only noticed them.

'Your birthday, Pet,' I smiled.

'Oh?' said Nora. 'I wonder how old I am?'

CHAPTER 55

DATE: 9 June 1988

GRAFITTO FOR THE DAY: God is Alive & Well & Working
on Another Project

Today was my last Sister Úna session. She said to call her
in a few weeks—plus any time I'm struggling. But the long
haul seems over—for the moment anyhow. I've cut back on
the St John's Wort too, down from three to two to one a
day. If not out of the woods entirely, at least on a
signposted trail, and not the psychopath which Brian told
me was what lunatics cycle along through the woods. A
woods of Christmas trees, no doubt, all trimmed with
bloody crows and rats.

Today was lovely, and Sister had her study window
open, the scent of lilacs filling the room. We'd a cup of tea
first, after which Sister asked had I any last questions?

'I don't think so,' I said—only I had. A last question
about my memory—if memory it was—of Ma sweeping
furiously as I watch from my playpen. I'd not wanted to
revisit it, afraid of the tidal wave of tears it had unloosed.
But last evening just before bed I found myself back there,

like a criminal to the proverbial scene. Or more like a cop maybe, looking for further clues.

'What could've I done,' I asked, 'to anger her so?'

'How old were you again?' Sister asked in turn.

'Not even two?'

'Does that answer your question?'

'I suppose it does,' I let out a deep breath.

'We are not responsible as children for angering our mothers,' Sister Úna smiled. 'Surely you know that from raising your Katy?'

'I do,' I conceded.

'Nor are we capable of provoking the depth of anger you described.'

'It wasn't me then?'

'It wasn't you, Maeve,' Sister Úna said. 'It was never you.'

A few tears started up again, but I also felt something else—like a proverbial weight lift palpably off my shoulders. Not unlike that lightness of body & being you felt as you skipped out of Confession on a Saturday afternoon, your sins whispered at the priest—how you spoke back to your parents, or swore at your brother. Only Sister Úna's words were more absolution than any priest had ever offered, muttering the Sign of the Cross in the half-dark and assigning five Hail Marys for your penance. For hers was absolution for the sin never committed—forgiveness for not having failed Ma as a daughter before I'd even outgrown my playpen.

Neither of us spoke then for a few moments. Instead, seated in that lilac-scented silence, I thought of a story Aunt Chrissie had told, the sole time I ever mentioned her sister's psychiatric history. I could see the subject discomforted Chrissie—as if the shadow of Hughdy's suicide still ghosted about the kitchen. 'There was always plenty of that going,' she said—meaning with the O'Byrnes – and I thought the subject closed until she began to tell of another relation. An uncle of hers & Ma's who lost the run of himself one morning at age twenty-two, as he helped his brother, their father, to clear a drain below the cottage. Digging like mad, Chrissie said, the sods flying in the air, each shovelful followed by a gigantic bellow, before he came roaring up to the house and cleared the entire family.

And what I still see so clearly is what Chrissie next described. How after the Guards arrived, his mother, Chrissie's grandmother, came out with needle and thread, and knelt in the road, with a Guard on either side, to mend a tear in the seat of her son's trousers. 'After which they took him away to the mental,' Chrissie finished, 'where he died the year.'

And that image of my great-grandmother kneeling in the road suddenly illuminated that other tableau, the one wherein my fit-to-be-tied mother furiously sweeps—as if trying to banish misfortune itself. As if the anger spilling out of her—like grain from a burst sack—was more than she could ever hope to sweep from her kitchen floor. Nor was it necessarily hers alone, rather more like a far older fury—at being dirt-poor and oppressed perhaps, or having such madness come and carry off your own—a rage that went back generations, however such things carry on down the years.

I might've ended our session by telling Chrissie's story— one last tale in my extended story time with Sister—and Auntie Chrissie among the several voices that have helped me to tell my story—as I'm only beginning to see. But I don't tell it. Instead I simply thank Sister and take my leave —knowing I'll write it down later for myself.

'Might you keep up the notebook?' Sister Úna asked at the door.

'I might,' I laughed, ambivalent as always. But if Sister Úna has done her part, I'm not sure I'm yet finished here.

CHAPTER 56

DATE: 11 June 1988

BENEFITS OF AGING: Things You Buy Now Won't Wear Out!

K and I saw a play last night—about a Nantucket whaling ship that sails to Australia in 1875 to rescue a Fenian prisoner. A one-man show, whose actor played everybody & everything—wind, whale and boat—up on a table, flapping his arms like a gull, like he might actually take flight. The kind of magic that makes me wish I got out to the theatre more often.

It also reminded me how much I'd wanted to join the Drama Club back in Boston High. Vivian encouraged me too, but lacking confidence I settled for the vicarious, listening as she recounted all the gossip, rivalries and romances. After graduation Vivian went on to do theatre studies at NYU, so we only saw each other on holidays. Last time was summer of my junior year, when I was doing my geriatric clinical placement at the Cambridge Home for Aged People. We met for a drink in Harvard Square, where Vivian told how she'd changed her major to marketing.

She'd also swapped her habitual black Bohemian gear for a Laura Ashley top and smartly tailored khaki shorts. A few years later I heard she was working as a realtor, a role I'd never in a million years have cast her in.

CHAP was a long, three-storey redbrick building on the Charles, catering to the genteel elderly, its clientele not unlike the tenants at No. 23 across the river, older versions of Mrs. Lunenberg say, or Captain Evarts. Most of them hailed from Cambridge, and while not all had been born to money, they clearly had enough to end their days in comfort. Each bedroom like a plushly furnished mini-apartment compared to our more utilitarian rooms here in Fairview, except for one or two like Alice May's with her pictures, bookcase and floor lamp.

But the best part of being a nursing assistant was having a role other than that of the Super's daughter, which meant class and background didn't really come into it. My placement lasted some three months, yet the only faces I can name now are Mr. McKay and Miss Litchfield, plus Bob the cook. Mr. McKay whom I used to take out for a daily stroll. 'Walking is vital,' he informed me every time. 'I can't understand those like Miss Litchfield who never walk!' For her part, Miss Litchfield was mad for shuffleboard. 'Do you know shuffling?' she'd ask, leaning on her long cue like a cane, and describing how years ago in Florida she had shuffled morning, noon and night.

Those summers at CHAP were my first look at the land of 'the long-living'—what the Chinese call the elderly. A territory I understand better now, and a country most of us with luck will hopefully inhabit. At twenty, however, old age struck me like a separate reality—or at least one whose angle of approach differed radically to my own. Like the way Mr. McKay carefully negotiated the broken bricks on a sidewalk. Or something as simple as lettuce. Romaine lettuce, which Bob the cook discovered had been delivered one day instead of iceberg.

'Do they not like the taste?' I asked, as Bob swore a blue streak.

'It's the texture, not taste,' Bob replied. 'Romaine's far too slippery for dentures.'

CHAPTER 57

DATE: 13 June 1988
SONG FOR THE DAY: 'Welcome to the Hotel California!'

Katy hit it on the head some years back, telling a pal how her Mama worked in a Home for the Bewildered. And bewilderment likely awaits most of us too, like a train-stop down the line. I hope to jump off the train myself, still cognitively intact, a few stops this side of Befuddlement Junction, but who knows what wits we'll have left at the end of the day? Never mind a day like today, with Constance Fitzgerald yet again repeatedly asking to be let out to see her mother. Luckily Dr Hogan was due in, otherwise I might have opened the door for her and walked out too. 'You're staying with us today, Constance,' I told her instead. 'The Doctor wants to see you.' And that finally settled Constance who, like most of the residents, has great time for The Doctor. Even if all The Doctor mostly does is take a pulse, peer down a throat, then prescribe another course of Xanax or Tryptizol.

No sooner was Constance sorted, however, than Wang

Wei reported Veronica Egan wouldn't come out of her room to dinner.

'What?'

'She thinks she's under arrest.'

'Under arrest?' I puzzled as W^2's English is generally quite good.

'Under arrest,' Veronica subsequently confirmed herself, though at first she wouldn't say for what. But it came out eventually—how the Guards had lifted her for shoplifting.

'You've been with us all morning, Veronica,' I reassured her. 'The Guards aren't interested in you.'

Veronica smiled weakly, like she wanted to believe me. Whereas Germany Gemma bristles if you so much as question whether the IRA Army Council is actually convening in her bathroom. I sat with Veronica for a few minutes, while W^2 brought up her dinner on a tray. It puzzled me, her losing the plot to that degree, but Mary O'Mara cracked the case this afternoon. 'It's all in here,' holding up Veronica's copy of 'Woman's Own'. 'A story about a girl who steals a leather skirt, assaults the security guard, and gets arrested.'

Getting lost in a good book got me through a lot of my childhood, and many a night since, but poor Veronica went well astray to end up incarcerated. 'We'd better monitor what she reads,' I told the girls, as if you can just re-route a mind that wants to go its own way-ward. Like Ma receiving transmissions from our kitchen radio, personal messages to her alone from the police, or fearing her every word was being recorded by the black phone on our kitchen wall.

An instance of paranoia at the Home occasionally brings back my mother's own. Like last week when I passed through the empty back day-room and found the TV on low. I hate the sound of anything playing in an empty room, having described for Sister Úna how Ma always sat with radio or telly on, as if trying to counter her own silence. And how empty the kitchen or sitting room felt as I retreated to my bedroom, passing Brian hunched over his ham radio, listening to a conversation between two deep-sea trawlers off George's Banks, and no doubt waiting, like all three of us, for Pops to come home.

Except the back day-room wasn't empty after all, for there was Gemma Dunne in the corner, staring up at the TV.

'Would I higher the sound for you, Gemma?' I asked.

'It's turned down,' Gemma whispered.

'Well, it's higher now,' I said, pushing a button.

'I mean it's turned down at the station,' Gemma glared. 'They don't want to broadcast what's happening!'

For a moment it felt like a switch had been thrown—and here was my mother again: muttering about the FBI as she scribbled some madness on an envelope at the kitchen table. But Gemma isn't my mother, nor am I any longer a frightened daughter clueless as to how I might help.

'Shall we turn it off so?' I asked.

'No!' Gemma shot me a look. 'We need to know when they're lining us up.'

'Lining us up?' I asked—though I knew better.

'To be weighed.'

'Weighed?'

'Yes, weighed! Didn't they line us up already this morning to be weighed?'

'Whatever for?' I couldn't resist.

'To see what we're carrying!' Gemma snarled, as if she were talking to a half-wit.

'And what might you be carrying?'

'Rocks!' Gemma smiled triumphantly. 'Rocks, if not bombs!'

Get da boat! I want to echo Katy.

'Did you get your tea?' I chance instead.

CHAPTER 58

DATE: 17 June 1988

FACTS OF LIFE: Motherhood Is For Life

Orla and I went for a walk Sunday along the Boyne in Slane, heading out east from the bridge below the village, and keeping the river to our left. I don't know the Boyne Valley, but I know my co-ordinates, thanks to the compass Pops gave me one Christmas. I took it outdoors daily—to verify the State House still lay due north and Tremont St southeast. I had it lost by the summer Brian and I went to Donegal, but Hughdy himself was a walking compass, always remarking from what quarter the wind blew. Nor could you miss where the sun rose up the glen, or the tiny swath of sea that occasionally turned crimson when it set at the other end. True north lay over the hill behind the cottage, the same hill that held the O'Byrne treasure, but I'd have wanted my compass to pinpoint that precisely.

Last Sunday was lovely, making me wish Katy had come along. But she'd pals to meet in town, and I'm slowly learning not to press too hard. In any event, Orla and I had the path to ourselves, apart from a few cows and a single heron poised like a fencepost in the shallows. And I forget as always how the countryside differs so from a city: the way a vista suddenly changes, a path bending to reveal a flowering whitethorn or a clump of yellow flag, whereas you generally have to walk a fair bit, often at right angles, before a cityscape shifts.

On the way back we paused to look across the river at the rolling hills, their dark hedgerows like thick brushstrokes, while overhead big cottony clouds sailed the blue.

'What's that?' Orla asked, hearing it first.

I heard it then—a loud, astonished hammering in the air—as five swans flew past, following the river downstream like a causeway. Standing there amid the meadowsweet, Orla and I beamed our delight at one another.

Then, as if the swans had turned a page, Orla began to talk about her love life.

'Jack wants us to marry.'

'That's great!' I offered, only Orla pulled a face.

'That's not great?' I backtracked.

'I'm not sure.'

'Well, what do you want?'

'A child, for sure.'

'Folks have been known to marry first,' I teased. 'Though not all of us, of course.'

'I'm just scared, I think.'

'Not unreasonable,' I said. 'Especially for Pisceans who always learn the hard way about love.'

'I'm not so worried about love,' Orla rejoined, 'as about what marriage does to it.'

'Monogamy's another word for monotony!' I offered

from another of Eamon Kerr's T-shirts. And lots of marriages do end up like double solitaire—like my parents' had in its final innings. Though it's baseball or cricket, not card games, that have innings. 'No mixed metaphors, Maeve!' as Miss Dewey constantly chided. Anyhow, I mostly listened as Orla poured out her hopes and fears, only putting in the odd comment, not unlike Sister Úna. However I did say what a sound man Jack is, and how many of them do you meet riding your bike around the block? And I made Orla laugh at what Fiona Flynn said last week about her Derek—'I knew I'd married Mr. Right—I just didn't know his first name was Always'.

I used worry about our friendship, should Orla marry, but I don't feel that any more. Even if I'm destined to fly solo, upstream, the rest of my life. And I was relieved to find myself feeling only happiness at her possible news, as I'd hate feeling envy at her good fortune.

It helps too that I haven't been feeling that lonely of late—not even after Seán rang up from Jeddah two nights ago. He must've found an Arabian sheebeen, for I'd say he'd had a couple. We chatted for a bit, exchanging what little news we had. In fairness I think he rang only to say hello, and I thanked him for calling. But I was pleased at not feeling too blue after he rang off—which is what would have happened a month ago. OK, I felt a twinge or two, but more for what we'd shared than anything I wish we had yet. He's a sweet guy, Seán, but I can see ever more clearly how he was becoming more a comfortable habit than a lover the longer we stayed together. Though being together, as he always pointed out, was something we truly never were.

I'd intended telling Orla about Seán's call, but decided to save it after she opened up her heart along the Boyne. A typical Pisces, Orla, needing buckets of emotional support. As it was, I ended up talking about Eddie and me, though not until after we stopped at Francis Ledwidge's house on the way home, a small three-roomed cottage with a lovely, large back garden. I hadn't heard of Ledwidge, but Orla said he was the only poet she liked in school. Plus he had his heart broken by an unhappy love affair before getting blown up in WWI. 'Nothing like a happy ending!' I enthused.

Then, driving home, Orla asked me straight out why I hadn't married Katy's father.

'Because I didn't love him enough.'

'Even pregnant?'

'Especially pregnant. Pregnant made it clearer.'

The late-afternoon sunlight on the fields either side of the road made me think how it was this time of year that I cut Eddie loose. At the very end of June, my life having turned upside down in a matter of weeks. All thanks to a late April evening at Crane's Beach, where we'd dragged our blanket into the dunes for a cuddle. Only to end up making love, chancing nobody would stumble upon us, and Eddie would withdraw in time. Recalling the Saturday six weeks later when I dropped off my urine sample, worried sick with my clockwork period overdue. Afterwards Eddie and I strolled down to Waterfront Park where Eddie lit up a joint and I sat staring out at a tiny plane suspended over Boston Harbour, as motionless as a drawing in a children's picture book.

Two days later I learned I was pregnant. As it happens, Eddie and I had never made love that often—both of us still living at home and Eddie without a car. Not that I'd have liked making love in a back seat, any more than I'd liked it the afternoon we chanced it in his bedroom, with his Nonna in the next room. Or, even more furtively, in a back room at a party on Huntington Ave, on a bed full of coats, and myself terrified somebody would walk in. But any time we did Eddie had used a condom—unlike Crane's Beach where we'd only gone for a swim.

Eddie spoke straight off of our getting married when I told him the news. But it wasn't hard to see his heart wasn't in it—which no doubt helped me see mine wasn't either. But to be honest the choices I made at the time felt more like gut reactions. Certainly that's how I executed them—breaking it off with Eddie a few weeks later. But telling him—yes, I would both have and keep the baby—before he could ask. My classmate Laurie had travelled to NYC that winter for an abortion, but I wasn't prepared to do that. Being pregnant was a disaster, but abortion was somehow not an option. Clearly Catholicism was mixed up in it, even if I no longer regularly went to Mass and considered myself pro-choice. But it seems the only choice for me was to become a mother myself—even if I still don't fully understand how or why I made it.

Eddie didn't handle it especially well when I said I wouldn't marry him. Not that I made it easy for him—though I couldn't see that at the time. I see it better now, after talking with Sister Úna. How my decision to have Katy maybe had as much to do with my relationship with Ma as it did my relationship with Eddie. How motherhood offered me an opportunity to break out or move on—to make a separate peace with Ma and make a new life via my new-born.

Half-hearted or not, Eddie was prepared to help rear our child—even if we didn't marry. But I listened to nothing—only laid down my own plans as if I were going into battle. That I wounded him sorely I can see now. And certainly I wounded his pride. We had countless rows, capped by a shouting match the week I graduated, after I said I wanted to call by to see his mother. I went round too, while Eddie was at work, painting a fire station somewhere in Mattapan.

'We're not doing so well right now,' I told Mrs. LoPresti by way of saying goodbye. And I said even less to Nonna, just gave her a hug as she stroked my hair.

'It takes time,' Mrs. LoPresti said. 'Just give yourselves time.' And whether or when Eddie ever told her I was pregnant is one of a thousand things I'll never know.

Somehow I got through that summer, cramming for the State nursing exam and working full-time at the Cambridge Home for the Aged. I waited until August before telling my parents, trusting Pops would not reprise a favourite joke: it's not the stork that brings the babies—it's the little lark at night!

'Where's Eddie?' he asked instead. 'Why's he not here?'

'Eddie's out of the picture,' I said. 'I'm not marrying Eddie.'

Once Pops saw I was certain he swung in behind, saying he only wanted what was best for me. And if Ma wanted me to marry, she never said it outright. Instead, I sensed what I so often had—her disappointment and that palpable sense of distance between us, even when she tried to close the gap. Which, in fairness, she attempted that night, holding me briefly and smoothing my hair. And who's to say I didn't project some of that disappointment onto her? Good Girls certainly don't come home pregnant, though by twenty-one I had finally begun to tease out some of the difference between that persona and my potential self.

I saw Eddie just once after that last big row. Not in his North End, but for a coffee at Brigham's on Tremont St.

Only it was too hot for coffee, so I ordered a lime rickey instead. After it arrived, Eddie told me he'd been drafted, and was in all likelihood headed for Vietnam.

Guilt-stricken, I blurted, 'What if we were to marry?'

I'd have understood had Eddie lost his head over that. But he just laughed, ending us as we'd begun—with a lame joke.

'You get a 4-F deferment for flat feet, Maeve. Not fatherhood.'

CHAPTER 59

DATE: 18 June 1988

SONG FOR THE DAY: 'What's Love Got to Do With It?'

I lay awake last night thinking what more I might have written here before I turned out the light? To set down thoughts that have already cost me sleep seems daft, but I suppose they belong with the rest of whatever story I'm telling myself. The world's longest bedtime story, surely, as I most often sit down to it before turning in.

Anyhow, what kept me awake last night was feeling I'd told Orla more of <u>how</u> Eddie and I parted than <u>why</u>. Or only the <u>whys</u> as I'd understood them back then. We'd certainly never talked of marriage before I got pregnant; it was far too early, and my first serious relationship besides. What I loved most about Eddie was his happy-go-lucky manner—like a beam of sunshine in a dimly lit room. Yet when push came to pregnancy, I bailed out. And quickly too—as if what I'd loved about Eddie as a boyfriend had somehow promptly turned to negative equity in a prospective life partner. Faced with motherhood, had I

283

suddenly seen easy-going Eddie as altogether too laid-back? He had already put in a year as a painter with the Boston Public Works Dept—not lucrative but secure—probably as permanent & pensionable as the Irish civil service. But did that employment also underscore a casualness in Eddie that scared me off, some kind of race memory, an imprinted fear of hedgerow poverty, which saw me walk away? Or was it having an immigrant mother who went out to work, and an immigrant father who never stopped—in contrast to Eddie's more casual, second-generation take on life, cushioned by a large family and their sunny Mediterranean optimism?

Or, truth be told, was I worried about another kind of laziness in Eddie? We had a row a few months after we started going out, some comment Eddie made about blacks. He wasn't overtly racist, and in fairness had conceded most of what I argued about opportunity and education. Nor had he, growing up in the North End, a chance to sit next to black kids like Princetta Ivory and Salathial Edwards since grade school, which makes all the difference in attitudes. But Eddie was lazy that way too, too prone to parrot the reactionary wisdom of his workmates or the tabloid 'Record-American'. The Massachusetts State Lottery had also just started up—but it hadn't affected the numbers racket, nor the illegal football betting cards—which it happened Eddie also peddled. I didn't learn about his numbers side-line straight away, nor had we ever really fought about it either. But it bothered me—for all Eddie's assurances it was just a harmless way of making easy money.

OK, it risks cliché: the Italian boyfriend grows up to be a Wise Guy too. Only Eddie was no Mafioso, just a part-time numbers runner, and I wasn't worried about getting

Married to the Mob. But his nixer troubled me, ran counter to the probity Pops had bequested us, the way he paid his taxes to the penny every April, and how scrupulous he was in all such things. Not Italian, nor especially Irish either— judging from the corruption that fills the newspapers here. I don't pay much heed to the scandals, but I do remember how differently Pops did things. Entirely up-front and honest—as if he owed America that much.

It happened I brought Eddie back to No. 23 only once— just to meet my parents, not even for a meal. I puzzle over that now, of course. Was it because Ma had fairly flatlined on lithium by then, her days spent largely watching TV or napping in her room when she wasn't working? Or was I reluctant to bring Eddie around in case Pops got the measure of him and found him wanting? Either way, he called by only once, sat and chatted about the Red Sox with Pops, while Ma brought us all iced tea.

Leaving that afternoon, we passed Mrs. L coming in.

'Was that handsome young man a beau?' she asked the following day.

'I suppose you'd call him that,' I laughed, happy for the chance to chat about Eddie in a way I couldn't with Ma or Pops.

Yet for all that, it was probably pretty much as I described it yesterday to Orla. That had I felt Eddie was mad about me, and I mad about him, love might have conquered all—insecurities, economics, and questions of ethics. Only that kind of love wasn't there. We'd been together but eighteen months, yet I could sense already where we were headed. I might've been too young to know how most lovers eventually turn into couples, but the lovers I knew best—Scarlett & Rhett or Heathcliff & Cathy—had never got within a shout of coupledom. Ruined by reading and romance, I knew that kind of fire was missing between Eddie and me.

'We can get married, Maeve,' Eddie said when I told him what had come of our Close Encounter of the Procreative Kind at Crane's Beach. Only he sounded, as I said, more dutiful than passionate. 'Terrified' I'd have understood, but 'dutiful' focused me like an icy draught. Having grown up amid a worn-down marriage, I probably knew enough not to go and make a lukewarm one of my own.

CHAPTER 60

DATE: 23 June 1988

WEATHER: Strictly for the Birds

FACT FOR THE DAY: An Ostrich's Eye Is Bigger Than
Its Brain

'Petra's in absentia,' Mary O'Mara told me first thing this
Monday morning.

'Oh, is that where she's gone off to?' I said. She'd called
in sick Friday too, but grabbing both ends of a weekend
struck me as a bit Irish—or in Petra's case Polish, I suppose.

'What excuse this time?' I asked Mary, after ringing Mrs.
O'Sheehan for an Agency replacement.

'No excuse. No phone call. No show.'

I'll need a word with Jim first, but Petra's as good as
gone. I saw her getting out of Jim's car one afternoon last
month which worried me, but it happened he'd merely
spotted her at her bus stop. What Jim gets up to and with
whom is his business, but fraternising with any of the hired
hands here at the Fairview Ranch for the Elderly would
only complicate my job—same as if I'd started seeing him
myself after-hours. Not that you could blame Jim, had he
taken a fancy to Petra, given her habitual joie de vivre, plus

the way she fills her uniform like a 1950s pin-up.

Later this afternoon Calico brought a robin upstairs to Veronica's room. Luckily Nurse Lyons found it before Veronica did and took it as some kind of omen. 'The special providence in the fall of a sparrow'—which Miss Dewey had us memorise from 'Hamlet'. Or a Willy Wagtail which foretells nothing good, per Mary O'Mara. Telling how her father lay awake for hours in a Tralee ward, listening to a wagtail beat frantically against the skylight, until another patient three beds down finally let out a strangled cry and died. But that's maybe more a Kerry belief, for Uncle Hughdy had great time for wagtails, pointing to a pair at his feet evenings as he coped the spuds.

Then again, Nurse Ethel suggested a few birds are precisely what Veronica needs, given the grasshoppers currently plaguing her.

'Oh Christ, what's she reading now?' I asked.

'Not reading this time,' Ethel said. 'Something she saw on the telly.'

'The National Geographic Channel?' I guessed—but apparently not. Rather Veronica got lost this time in an old sci-fi film, giant grasshoppers soaring over skyscrapers, and has talked of little else since.

'Sounds like a job for the Missouri Robin,' I told Nurse Ethel, after tossing Calico out back with instructions to kill rats, not songbirds. And to stay out of the laundry too, where she's taken to sleeping in the washing machine. Or was it the Mississippi Robin Pops sang of, who kept bob-bob-bobbing along?

Assistant Matron Fiona has offered the Home her dog Muttly too. Plus her mother Nelly, who apparently left her dentures on her coffee table yesterday before heading out with Fiona for a walk. 'We didn't know what the white bits were when we got back,' Fiona said. 'Like somebody had spilt popcorn on the carpet.'

'Her teeth?'

'Chewed to bits,' Fiona shook her head. 'I didn't know who to kill first— Muttly or my mother.'

'A fish tank,' I told Fiona. 'You need a fish tank à la Kitty for Nelly to stash them in!'

CHAPTER 61

DATE: 26 June 1988

THOUGHT FOR THE DAY: 'Daughter Am I in My
Mother's House But Mistress in My Own.'

A 'For Sale' sign up next door greeted me when I came in
this evening. Poor Mrs. Sheedy fell and broke her hip two
weeks ago, and will go directly into care when she comes
out of Cappagh Hospital. I've visited twice and Katy, who
grew up toddling in and out to her, went in too. We knew
the house was going on the market, but I never expected to
see a sign up this quick. She'll get something for it, of
course, but what good will money do her now?

Just before her accident I asked Mrs. S the name of the
large bush with the bright yellow flowers that I admire
from my bedroom every June. 'Hypericum,' she said, same
plant as my St John's Wort, which I've stopped taking
altogether. It might be associated with St Colmcille but
Chrissie never had any luck growing a shrub that big in
Glenmore. But funny what you discover under your nose—
or in next door's garden. The loss you feel when an apple
tree goes AWOL in the dead of winter. Or the lift you get

from a spray of yellow blossoms in early summer.

Anyhow Mrs. S is already a huge miss. You couldn't ask for a better neighbour, and I'm praying we get somebody half as nice moving in. Only last week Orla told how her sister, a teacher, woke up one weekend to a familiar voice. And there, swinging from the 'Just Sold' sign next door, was the Little Horror from last year's classroom! Whereas I've been blessed with a Mrs. Lunenberg or a Mrs. Sheedy, showing me how I too might someday manage my own maturity.

Or blessed with Durca Walinski at No 14 Linden St, Somerville, Massachusetts—if I'm paying tribute to Women I Have Known Next Door. There was no provision for unmarried mothers in the Super's lease at Park Street, and I couldn't have managed both my new-born and my mother for much longer under the same roof. So three months after Katy was born, she and I moved across the Charles River into Durca's brown-shingled, two-storey house. Somehow I managed it all—a new baby, moving out of home, juggling part-time nursing at Somerville Hospital with full-time parenting on Linden St. Katy, of course, was the centre of my world, but those other changes brought their own promise too, and it didn't take me long to feel somewhat at home among the immigrant Portuguese and Latino households on Linden St.

Durca the Landlady, a short, stout Pole in her seventies with close-cropped grey hair, had left Cracow in the 1930s, arriving in America without a word of English, and just in time for the Depression. She found work regardless—in an East Cambridge meatpacking plant, and later at the big NECCO candy factory just off Central Square. And she hadn't stopped working since—even if it was just working around her house by the time I met her—shovelling snow, putting out the bins, and working the soil in the back garden where she put in cabbage and beets each spring.

'Husband, I hope?' she inquired the afternoon I came by to see the apartment.

I shook my head—figuring that was that.

But Durca just muttered something like 'Sorry' or 'Sorrowful' in her still heavily accented English, and took me up to see the apartment. We moved in the following week, and shortly after I arranged with Maria, a young Guatemalan woman downstairs, to take care of Katy when I worked. Durca who had the other upstairs flat kept to herself, though I used to see her about, walking back from Stop & Shop that summer with a string-bag of groceries in the sweltering heat, or knocking icicles off the gutters with a tall bamboo pole once winter came.

Pops was a great support, ringing me almost daily those first months, after which Ma would come on the phone for a few words. He also took the Green Line across the Charles to us for a quick visit every fortnight. Katy and I also tried to visit them weekly, when my shifts permitted. I had a bout of the blues that spring, but nothing as severe as post-natal depression. Nor anything as black as the Slough of Despond through which I've slogged these past months. My college pal Laurie was great too, and called over with a bottle of cheap burgundy every few Friday nights. Plus Maria downstairs became a real pal, full of fantastic tales about growing up the youngest of eight in a small Guatemalan village near the Mexican border.

Some nights I'd hear Walter Wong from Taiwan yelling at his wife in the other apartment below, then muttering to himself as he went up the street. But he eventually moved out altogether, and things quietened down. Later that summer I was reading in bed one night, K asleep in her cot beside me, when suddenly a magnificent spray of red-and-green flowers suddenly burst into bloom beyond the window. A fireworks display along the Charles River, but all I could think of was Eddie, 10,000 miles away, under a far more lethally lit night sky. We were to meet before his basic training began the previous September, but Eddie had cancelled twice. And he hadn't called either when he was briefly back in Boston that December before shipping out. At first I wrote him regularly, but he only replied a couple of times and I eventually stopped, myself.

Were this a Country & Western song, Eddie would have died overseas, but it happens the war ended the following January, and he was re-posted to Germany. It's possible he was back in Boston too before K and I left for Ireland but, if so, he never got in touch. And I knew by then I'd no business knocking on his door, after having slammed mine shut on him. I used to cry in bed sometimes, like that night of the fireworks, over how I'd treated him. But time moves you downstream, and I just trust he's well now with hopefully his share of happiness.

One morning that first Somerville September, I looked out to see Durca being shunted into an ambulance. 'A mild heart attack,' her son Martin said when he called for the rent. Durca was home within a fortnight, but several weeks passed before I saw her outside. 'Don't talk about it!' she snapped when I inquired how she was, so brusque I didn't know what to say. The next day I saw her again by her back stairs. 'Don't talk sickness to me!' she said by way of an apology. 'I just spit it out.' And turning she spat into the garden. We spoke for a minute and Durca asked after Katy. A week later I saw her raking the grass out front, though moving at half her pace. We began to chat regularly after that, even if her staccato delivery took some getting used to.

'Whatever problem, I just spit it out!' was a favourite refrain, though she didn't always spit peasant-style.

The following spring Durca went into hospital again. 'An irregular heartbeat,' her son informed us on rent day. And when she reappeared this time, she had a cane, not hoe, in hand. She'd lost weight too, but that interior spark was there yet, and the same drumbeat delivery that made everything, even a comment on the weather, sound like an imperative. Only by now Katy could toddle after Durca, who for all her gruffness doted on my daughter, fishing out sweets for her from an apron pocket.

The occasional late-night phone calls started that second Somerville summer. A prank caller I first thought, as there was nobody there when I picked up our yellow kitchen phone. Or rather nobody <u>spoke</u>, for I sensed somebody there all right, a sound like muted breathing and a chair or something creaking once. Yet I didn't feel any menace in the silence, oddly enough, given how easily I spooked growing up.

One night, listening hard, I suddenly remembered the ghost back on Park St. Fortunately I was doing my homework when the keening started, not lying half-asleep in the dark, which would have finished me entirely. I tried putting my ear to the wall, then fetched a kitchen glass à la my heroine, 'Nancy Drew, Girl Detective'. Brian was at his short-wave radio, trying to tune in something from farther away than Apt 1B next door, but he knew the glass-tumbler trick from 'The Hardy Boys', and followed me back to my room where we knelt in turn on the bed to listen.

What we heard came and went, a kind of wailing that rose and fell. Like a baby trying to cry itself to sleep, I think now, though I knew nothing of babies at age ten. Nor were there babies in Apt 1B, just ancient Mr. Faustini, a small wizened man with a cane and heavy overcoat, who had a home-help woman in daily to make his dinner, and in good weather take him out for a walk.

I listened at that wall for many nights after. The wailing always seemed to happen around seven, as if the supper his helper left out gave Mr. Faustini sufficient energy for a sing-song. Because that's what I finally decided he was at, after managing to make out the words '*I love you*', repeated like a refrain throughout. So not just singing but love songs!

What I overheard seems at this remove like Memory & Loneliness put to music. And had Mrs. Sheedy next door taken to singing in that key through my bedroom wall this winter, I don't know what I'd have done. But to a child Mr. Faustini's lament sounded more mysterious than plaintive, like radio signals from a distant planet. In any event I forgot all about it after Mr. F died, and another tenant moved into Apt 1B.

Forgot, that is, until one night on Linden St when listening hard, I thought of Mr. F and suddenly felt I knew who my mystery caller might be. And that same night I began to hold up my end of our nonversation, too. At first offering just a few words of reassurance—in case I had it wrong. It seems a bit daft now—answering the phone at those hours, never mind chancing a lullaby. Because that's what I eventually ended up doing—singing to my anonymous caller before ringing off, convinced it was Durca next door unable to make it through the night. Singing a few lines from one of K's bedtime songs like 'On Top of Old Smokey'. Or 'All the Tired Horses' from a Dylan album Vivian Henry played non-stop during her black-turtleneck days. I never said anything to Durca, whom I might see the next day, slowly sweeping the sidewalk, until autumn arrived and the calls ceased altogether.

CHAPTER 62

DATE: 27 June 1988

SONG FOR THE DAY: 'Tears on My Pillow'

I never got to tell Sister Úna about Durca Walinski. But glancing at what I wrote last night, I can all but hear Sister pointing out how I've once again written my mother out of the story. Describing a Polish ex-landlady who doted on my daughter, but scarcely a word about that daughter's Irish Granny. Would it have proved just too painful to describe those same two years between Ma and me—or weigh up whether Katy might have helped bridge the gap, had I given Ma half a chance? Is that why I once again choose to tell it slant?

That said, I'm not sure how able Ma was to act the granny, give how hesitantly she held Katy as an infant, rarely bringing her close up to her own face. Never looking for a family resemblance—a nose like her own, eyes like Auntie Chrissie's, or hands like mine. Nor declaring the baby more of an O'Byrne or a Maguire. Nor did she jolly Katy up, play Peek-a-Boo with her, or Fly Away Peter, Fly

Away Paul. Never bonded as I learned to call it in my introductory psych class at college, wondering if Ma were not herself a text-book study in her inability to consistently engage with yours truly, her only daughter, who so sought her love and approval growing up.

Still I never really gave Ma a true chance with Katy. Rather we pretty much resumed our old roles the day my baby daughter and I returned from hospital. Holding her only grandchild in Apt 1A for the first time, my mother's first words were that Katy was overdressed. 'Far too warm!' she said, or something like that. The effect anyhow was devastating. Rather than reflect fondly on how Ma had once cradled me like that, I promptly took Katy from her. Or was it the thought Ma might have held me <u>precisely</u> like that? Not clasping me to her breast, that is—but holding me tentatively, obliquely angled, from herself.

The truth is even harder—if I truly care to write my mother into this account. The fact that having Katy saw me put the Atlantic Ocean between us some two years later, as if the Charles River itself were not water enough. I can still see Ma on one afternoon visit back to Park St on which we had rousted her from the telly, Pops elsewhere in the building, tending his Superintendancy. Can clearly see Ma at the kitchen table while a year-and-a-half-old Katy jigs up and down, delighted with life and singing some gibberish ditty. As she beams up at her Granny, I see Ma turn and begin to clear our tea things—not so much ignoring Katy as simply failing to tune her in. It's not disapproval—rather distracted abstraction—but I feel it on K's behalf like an all-far-too-familiar stab to the heart. And I resolve then & there to shield my darling daughter from such indifference—should it mean travelling to the ends of the earth. Or merely Ireland, as it happened, a scant six months later.

Small wonder then that I airbrush Ma out of any account of K's toddlerhood. Nor do I usually bother re-reading what I scribble here. But I was looking this evening for clues, after what transpired last night when I turned off the light. How I suddenly wondered had it been Ma instead? Not Durca but Ma who had rung up those nights from across the Charles River? I no sooner thought that than I dismissed it—for Ma hated the phone at all times. But the sudden image of my mother, silent at the other end of an open line, had me crying into my pillow like a child.

CHAPTER 63

DATE: 30 June 1988
ACTIVITY: Stories From the Mouth!

We'd a phone call from the Guards today about Polish Petra, who has vanished altogether. An English-speaking neighbour of her parents rang from Gdansk, saying they'd been trying to contact her for over a week. I told the Guard it's been ten days since we heard from her, and took his number, though I doubt Petra's going to check in here. I only hope she's OK. Ten days is a long time to go astray, even for a free spirit like Petra, and there've been so many women missing of late, you worry if somebody fails to turn up overnight.

A few residents have asked about her. Including the men, which doesn't surprise me, given the full-bodied figure Petra cut about the place. Eamon Kerr was one who inquired after her. Not by name, mind you. 'Where's Blondie?' he asked, holding his cupped hands to his own chest, which encouraged us to HONK IF ANYTHING FALLS OFF! But I didn't honk—only checked to see he wasn't unzipped.

Tom the Teacher inquired after Petra too. By name, not mime, as Tom's always the perfect gentleman.

'She's taking some time off,' I said, not wanting to say she left without a word.

'Back to Germany?'

'Poland,' I said, 'but I'm not sure if she's going home.'

Not like Tom to get a fact wrong, though he was possibly persuaded by Field General Dunne who always insisted Polish Petra was really a German operative. Which prompted Tom in turn to tell one afternoon of a Clare neighbour who answered to the name of 'Paddy Hitler'.

I'm not great at a story myself, which is probably why I occasionally write one down here. I can speak out as Matron, issue orders or give report at hand-over, but telling a story is usually beyond me, same as it was for Ma. Many women tell them wonderfully—and I don't mean just Annie Proulx or Margaret Atwood. Take both my Assistant Matrons Mary O'Mara and Fiona Flynn, for instance. Or Nurse Ethel describing last week how her Roscommon grandmother had flattened a drunken neighbour at a family wedding: 'Hit him a clip and left him sleeping!'

Still, storytelling comes more naturally to men, I think. Along with other stuff—like thinking of sex every seven minutes, or never dusting, or simply taking life easier. We talked about that at a coffee break recently—how the male residents, well-used to being waited on, tend to settle in more readily, while the women resist, reluctant to cede their care-giving roles.

It's not so simple, I know, as women always cooking while men sit around swapping yarns. But growing up male helps you to speak out, I think, and maybe develop a Personality too. For how else do you explain how so many girls fade away in early adolescence, their confidence ebbing, while boys tend to hold sway inside the classroom? Which has me happy my Katy goes to an all-girls school— even if only last week she remarked how her two male teachers are the funniest. As if a sense of humour is something else having a penis helps?

That said, I had no problem spinning yarns of my childhood for K—who used to ask 'Tell me a story, Mama, from the mouth!' Nor is finding your voice such a problem for the elderly, either. All those voices crying out at The Fairview Home—whether talking to their dearly departed or answering the voices in their heads. Like chair-bound Eva Glynn who kept shouting 'Nurse! Nurse! Nurse!' for an hour yesterday after Dr Hogan left. Prompting Nurse Ethel to finally snap: 'Christ—what did he inject her with? A gramophone needle?'

CHAPTER 64

DATE: 3 July 1988

FACT FOR THE DAY: Nature, Red in Tooth and Claw

It's not yet seven, but awake for an hour I decided to get up. Nibbles it was who woke me earlier. Or rather the poor wood pigeon he had snared atop the coal-bunker below my window. Each spring a pair or two wake me with their lovemaking, but this time I woke to wings beating even more frantically and its final, strangled cries. Too late however to chase off Nibbles, who had it carried off by the time I opened the curtains, leaving a fair scattering of feathers below. I got back into bed, only for the sound to play on in my head, like a dirty grey shirt flapping on the line. And I began to worry over Polish Petra then—as if I'd wakened to some ill omen, whatever about lacking Mary O'Mara's gift.

One spring years ago, I heard a noise in Katy's room around 5.00 a.m. and found her at her open window. 'What are you doing, Pet?' I asked in alarm. 'Listening to the dawn chorus, Mama!' K beamed back at me. 'Our teacher told us about it yesterday!' And on another morning later that summer I held her as she sobbed for the sparrow she'd seen a kestrel pluck from the sky in front of Chrissie's cottage up in Donegal. One of those darker notes to the dawn chorus, such as awakened me this morning.

I'd worry for the likes of Petra or any young woman these days. Above all for my Katy, who I hear upstairs now, getting ready for her waitressing shift. Last year I persuaded her to enrol in a jiu-jitsu class, hoping she'd learn enough self-defence to give herself a fighting chance. It took some convincing, but there she was a month later, breaking the hold of a lad her own age as they rolled about the floor—which itself seemed a very healthy thing. As is a good breakfast which I'd better rustle up, as Katy won't bother if she's running late.

CHAPTER 65

DATE: 6 July 1988

TRUISM FOR THE DAY: Every Life's a Story

A Guard came down to the Home this afternoon about Polish Petra. Burly Sgt Breen with a country accent. There was little to tell him—beyond Petra being a good worker when she showed up. Did I know about her social life? Sergeant Breen asked. Very little, I said, and nothing exceptional. Petra was young, pretty, full of life, and no doubt made friends easily. She went clubbing sometimes I offered, but then who her age doesn't?

Did I think she was involved with drugs?

Did I what? I asked back.

Sgt Breen told then how a Schiphol Airport security camera had caught Petra coming off a Dublin-Amsterdam flight two Sundays back, carrying only a small overnight bag. I doubted Petra used drugs, I replied, being just so relieved she'd been seen alive. Nor had she ever shown me a shoe-box as my nursing classmate Sandy once had—half-full of tiny vials with one or two pills in each:

307

amphetamines, Seconal, and Valium. Plus some painkiller a large black woman on a post-surgical ward had inadvertently recommended, telling Sandy 'I don't want no more of those pink pills, Honey. They make me feel like I'm flying!'

I also told Breen I very much doubted Petra was working as a courier, when he finally got to where he'd been heading all along. Or a mule as I think drug smugglers are now called? Maybe she was going to meet a boyfriend? I suggested, after which the Sgt thanked me and left. Without Germany Calling spotting him, thank God.

Petra was a bit scatty alright, but not so fly, I think, as to get mixed up in running drugs. But then what do we really know about other lives? About the man next to us on the bus or the woman in the queue behind? For that matter, who would imagine, watching her carefully pour Alice May her tea, that Wang Wei had once presided over a strobe-lit Beijing disco? Or picture the French puppeteer boyfriend Alice May herself once had? The best you can do is wonder at the story behind, say, the couple not talking in a restaurant, or the young woman in tears that Orla and I passed on a bench in the Bots on Sunday last.

CHAPTER 66

DATE: 8 July 1988

THOUGHT FOR THE DAY: All I Want for First Communion
Is My Two Front Teeth

I got our Irish citizenship sorted ten years ago, but I never
saw a need to have two passports. Like I was some kind of
a spy or secret agent—or mule like I'm pretty sure Polish
Petra's not. But I've decided to get an Irish passport for
Crete, and got the photos taken last week after work. I was
never keen about having my picture taken—even before I
passed the wrong side of thirty. So I simply adjusted the
stool, pressed the button, and hoped for the best.

What dropped into the slot wasn't too bad—a few
crow's feet around my eyes but a good hair day at least.
And my mouth closed as always—which prompted Katy to
ask at supper how come I never smile for the camera?

'You know about my First Communion photo?'

But K didn't, so I told her as we ate. How I'd wanted a
watch, same as Brian got with his Communion money.
Only Ma said I wasn't to waste my money so. And to keep
my mouth shut for the photo, on account of my missing

309

two front teeth. The photographer was somebody Pops knew, otherwise I doubt there'd have been Communion photos in the budget. 'Keep your mouth closed,' Ma cautioned again as we went up the narrow stairs to the tiny studio on Hereford Street.

It reminded me a bit of going to the dentist, sitting in a special chair and having your face adjusted.

'Getting anything nice on the Big Day?' your man asked from behind the camera.

'A watch!' I said.

'You're not,' Ma put in.

'Smile!' he commanded.

So I smiled—a big, broad smile, eyes and mouth wide open. An act of outright rebellion, decidedly out of character for $M^2 G^2$, Maeve Maguire, Good Girl.

Katy was all questions—what had Ma done and had I got a watch? Ma said she wouldn't bother collecting the photo, but she did of course, and hung it next to Brian's with all his teeth. I got less money than he had however, not nearly enough for a watch, as neither Mrs. L nor Pops' pal Buddy Grimes happened to see me in my Communion Dress. But Pops did his best, taking us all to Bailey's afterwards for hot fudge sundaes.

I was surprised Katy hadn't heard of that photo—out of all I've told her of my growing up, as if trying to counter the shutters my mother drew down on her own childhood, and so hand down to K more than Ma had been able to bequeath me. When Sister Úna asked me once to bring in a photo of her, I duly dug from my dresser drawer the snapshot I'd found in Pops' room last September. Of Ma in a short-sleeved blouse & skirt, seated on a bench in the Public Gardens, what Pops liked to call our "Back Forty". Of Ma looking slightly askance at the camera, as if asking herself why did I agree to this?

But showing Sister Úna that photo helped me see something beyond just how camera-shy Ma was. I'd already told of how I came home that second Donegal summer to discover Ma had thrown out a large box of stuff I kept beneath my bed. Old school notebooks, magazines, drawings I'd done, my worn-out Teddy, plus the paper dolls & all their outfits that I'd treasured for years. I was hugely upset and we had a real row, as bad a shouting match as I remember. But as Sister Úna handed me back Ma's photo, something seemed to fall into place, another piece of the puzzle.

'It's like she constantly shed memories,' I said. 'As if there were too much sadness tied up in old things: photos, baby shoes or old letters tucked in a drawer, the kind of stuff she never kept. Like she told herself, "These are memories. They belong to the past. Which I must let go." And once you start shedding memories, maybe you can't stop? The way they're linked, one to another? Was it simply too hard for her, leaving Ireland?' Or did she need to expunge Donegal itself? Had something too hard—or hardscrabble—happened to her growing up? And is that why I hang onto the image of what Aunt Chrissie told me once—of how as little girls she and her sister loved following my grandfather, of whom I know nothing, down to the byre whenever he had a bottle of milk for a lamb he was trying to save? And how the pair of them would take porridge oats down to the stream across the road to feed the robins and long-tailed tits.

Sister Úna said something about how I'll likely never know those things about my mother. But my seeing how Ma herself had dealt with the past was perhaps itself enough. Enough for what I'm not exactly sure, though it's beginning to make a kind of sense—Sister wanting me to talk about Ma amid all my sorrow at losing Pops. And who it was Sister felt truly needed to see that photo of her—which I placed atop my own dresser when I got home.

CHAPTER 67

DATE: 9 July 1988
LYRIC FOR THE DAY: 'April is the cruellest month, breeding
Lilacs out of the dead land ...'

I kept on writing once again in my head after I went to bed. Wondering if Ma's frenzied spring-cleaning had been some desperate effort to sweep the past away, and so keep herself from going under. If so, it seems a terrible way to live your life. Having to centre yourself always on a blank page: minus the context of memory, no margins of a previous life. And how easily you might be knocked off-centre, by whatever knocks life continues to offer you. Like a phone call out of the blue: to say your brother's been found by a mountainy lake, the ground around him torn up in fistfuls. Which is probably why Hughdy's death knocked my mother off the rails again, his demise calling forth a host of memories, more than she could hope to shed or sweep away.

I too have shied away from describing his death here: what I eventually learned from Chrissie. Katy and I had gone up for a Bank Holiday weekend, the weather lovely that June, even in Donegal. K had played for hours below the cottage, like a miniature Demeter, collecting feathery heads of grass in her little upturned dress. But she was fast asleep in the lower bedroom when Chrissie finally told what had happened that April Sunday twelve years before. How Hughdy, after dinner, had tied Lolly up, before setting out to mark some lambs.

'I didn't understand why he wasn't taking the dog,' said Chrissie, who had watched from the scullery door as Hughdy climbed the hill behind. And who left the door on the latch when he hadn't come home by bedtime. The next morning she alerted both Francey Gillespie and Watty the Wire, who in turn alerted the Guards that afternoon. The following morning a search party found Hughdy, lying by a small lake three miles up from the cottage. His body bruised blue along one side, fists still clenching the clumps of heather he'd torn up after dosing himself.

'Wherever did he get it?' I asked.

'Sure, the chemist in Killybegs sells strychnine,' Chrissie said. 'To leave out on the hills for foxes out after lambs.'

Chrissie spared me none of the detail. Nor did she weep in the telling either, though maybe it did her some good simply to recount it. For who knows how much she had ever got to talk about her brother's death—beyond that brief phone call to her sister in Boston?

Later that night I lay in the same bedroom where Hughdy used recite his prayer about laying ourselves down to sleep—only it was Katy I now heard breathing lightly in the dark. That same susurration making me think how others can serve to anchor us in this life, like a rope round our waist holding us back from the edge. That no matter how low I may get, the simple fact of Katy precludes my ever calling it a day. Unlike poor Hughdy who had no such safety line. As a child I'd hoped he hadn't drowned in the lake where we'd gone fishing—the kind of self-centred thought a child has, for it wouldn't have changed a thing. But I think I sensed even back then Hughdy hadn't drowned—that there was more to the story. Even if I'll never know exactly how—having once again managed to weather the long winter nights—Hughdy had lost his way that April.

CHAPTER 68

DATE: 13 July 1988

THOUGHT FOR THE DAY: All's well that ends well.

These pages may yet prove 'A Dublin Book of the Dead'—
though Cassie Boyle's departure last night in her sleep was
a happier death than Hughdy's. And while I don't want to
end up like Brian's sister-in-law who pastes her obits into a
scrapbook, I do owe Cassie a few lines here, given how she
held her own so nicely at the Home right up to the very
end. As well as salute the Boody Women who, like Cassie,
have finally come in from the cold. And who, Lord knows,
might have been buried with her—had her son Dan not
overheard Nurse Ethel as he came into the room.

'God love Cassie,' Ethel was telling Clodagh. 'Do you
think the Boody Women have her at last?'

'Jaysus!' Dan smiled. 'Not the flipping Boody Women
after all these years?'

Nearly fifty years in fact, since Dan had not dared
wander too far from his door in their tiny Tipp village—
never mind venture out at night—for fear of the Boody

Women. One of whom would invariably appear whenever a toddler strayed too far. Pop out from behind a shed or suddenly from a boreen, wearing a smiling mask cut from a cornflakes box. 'There were four mothers at it,' Dan explained, 'not just mine. One at each corner of the village. After it happened once or twice, you simply learned the limits.'

Like the Africans say—it takes a village to raise a child. Or, in Tipperary, to terrorise them! 'Were yous not frightened?' Nurse Ethel asked. 'Oh, Jaysus, we were,' laughed Dan. 'But a benign kind of fright—more like a real-life fairy tale.'

Indeed there seems something almost archetypal in that quartet of unknown women with their painted masks. Or is it only a colourful case of what mothers are always at— endeavouring to keep their children from straying too far, too soon, into the unknown? The constant reassurance, a hand held, the cuddle when they wake from a nightmare. Though my Ma was never able for that late-night duty, leaving it for Pops to comfort us. But she still did her best to keep me safe, paying out her own fears like a string of brightly coloured floats that might keep me at my depth. Nor had Ma herself had the benefit of any Boody Women, growing up in an isolated, stony Donegal townland as she did. Had she come from a Tipperary hamlet like Cassie's— more 'kindly ground' as Hughdy called good soil—might she possibly have better found her way?

To finish on a brighter note, anyhow. Namely today's phone call from Sgt Breen, who reports Polish Petra is alive & well! Moreover it *was* romance—not cloak & dagger stuff— that whisked her away to Amsterdam. The Guards always tell you as little as possible, but Petra and her new Dutch boyfriend are seemingly safe & sound back in Gdansk. Case closed, end of story, and thank God (or Goddess) for that!

PART IV

CHAPTER 69

At breakfast I ask K to look up peacocks in the 'Encyclopaedia of Dreams' I gave her for Christmas. But she can't find it in the midden masquerading as her bedroom.

'I'll look after work, Mama,' she shouts, flying out the door.

And tidy your room too! I want to shout back. But surviving as a single parent means choosing the hills for which you're prepared to die—a bit of battle-speak courtesy of Brian in his toy-soldiering days. And so I've surrendered the hillock of discarded garments and assorted detritus into which Katy burrows at night, only to re-emerge, bright-eyed and bushy-tailed, each morning. Surrendered after years of trench warfare between us, though I never swept everything into a pile in the middle of the floor, Ma's favourite tactic in that same campaign. I hated when Ma did that—the way my stuff got covered in dust. And I'd be nagging K yet—only for what Mary O'Mara said last month. Of how her Ciara won't be at home much longer, and what time remains is too precious to waste squabbling over tidiness.

I'm heading into town to get a new swimsuit for Crete, just five days away. But first I want to note down the peacock in last night's dream. Its tail spread wide, like the peacock which unfurls itself as the snow falls in whatever Italian film that was? Only mine made a stunning show of itself inside a huge empty ballroom instead! Whatever storyline there was vanishing as I awoke, but the image of that bird lingers yet, its tail like a feathered tapestry.

What peacocks bring to mind however is dead easy— even if those at Balkill, Co Meath, never managed to get indoors. Nor was there a ballroom either in the gardener's cottage we rented there our first eighteen months in Ireland. Though that didn't stop the peacocks from trying to gain entry or so it seemed, for they constantly circled the cottage, occasionally hopping up to peer in a kitchen window—which delighted Katy no end!

Our cottage was one of several outbuildings attached to a large Georgian manse hidden by trees at the end of its unmarked drive. Such anonymity suited Peter Wolff, master of Balkill House, who at thirty-four had few airs or graces about him. Apart from a whiff of loneliness, living there on his own, both his parents some years dead.

The only other tenants were an older couple in the gate lodge: Seamus who helped Peter run the dairy farm, and his May who looked after K during my shifts at Our Lady's Hospital in Navan. May like Durca doted on K, who loved her madly back. In fact Balkill itself was like an early idyll for Katy, for we'd the freedom of the entire estate, including the formal gardens behind our cottage, full of robins, chaffinches, and blue tits that followed our progress through it. Or the scores of rooks that K, ecstatic, would call me out evenings to admire as they swirled overhead, loud as a cocktail party, before flying off to roost.

Believing I couldn't have found a better home for Katy is what helped me survive that first year in Ireland. That and the unabashed beauty of Balkill. The damp and cold were brutal, the cottage like an icebox from October to May, despite a fire on all day, the not always seasoned logs Peter supplied sizzling away on the raised kitchen hearth. Terrified that K would catch her death of cold, I kept her swaddled in layers—which maybe explains why she has resisted dressing warmly ever since.

Hardest was the isolation, however. I got on with most of the girls at work, especially Siobhan, another redhead who'd also hated her hair growing up. But there was no time for real friendships, nor a chance in hell of finding another single mother among the nurses. Instead I spent all my off-work hours with Katy, calling into the gate lodge for a cup of tea with May and Seamus most weekends. Keeping us going kept me busy, but the solitude—no matter the fairy-tale setting—made the loneliness near unbearable at times.

Then, towards the end of our first Irish year, Ma's heart gave out as she was making Pops his dinner—and my guilt at having fled her and Boston went off the scale. I told Sister Úna about all that—how I'd flown back with K for the funeral, and told Pops we'd move back home.

'You come back for yourself, Pet,' Pops said. 'Not on my account.'

I don't even now entirely understand why we didn't move back. Had we simply been able to stay on in Boston, we'd probably have done so. Yet when our week ended, I found it a relief to get on the plane again. 'Numbed,' I told Sister Úna when she asked what I'd felt at Ma's death. 'Shell-shocked,' I offered when she asked me to elaborate, 'a kind of amnesia almost.' But 'analgesia' would have been closer to the mark, another of those terms we memorised for our State Exam: 'analgesia: the absence of a normal sense of pain.'

I rang Pops regularly, who'd assure me he was managing fine. I also rang Brian, who also said Pops was doing OK. That life might be easier for Pops without Ma was nothing I could say to my brother—as just thinking it riddled me with guilt. And difficult as I found Ma, Pops had always managed her well. 'He's still playing cards Friday nights,' Brian reported which gladdened me. And had Pops known how hard I was finding Ireland, I don't doubt he'd have urged me to come home. But neither of us was much good on the phone, and by February we'd pretty much gone back to postcards, which we exchanged every week down the years till he died.

Whatever reasons I had, apart from my nursing contract, for returning to Ireland, Peter the Landlord certainly hadn't numbered among them. We only became friends that spring, when the warmer weather took Katy and me outdoors any chance we got, and we began to encounter Peter, helping Seamus to prune an old magnolia in the formal gardens, or down by the lake where he fly-fished evenings. All formality at first, he gradually began to loosen up under Katy's constant barrage of questions, though I blushed bright red the afternoon she demanded, 'Why does he say Hellair and not Hello?'

One June Saturday, Peter invited us to supper in Balkill House. Soup was served by a local woman who came in weekends to cook. Once again Katy's unfettered delight

with everything—from linen napkins to multiple spoons—
helped us through an otherwise awkward time. Worse yet,
the high-ceiling dining room looked enough like the one in
her picture book—where Beauty sups alone—that I half-
expected her to blurt out any minute, 'But Mama, when do
we get to see the Beast?'

A cup of tea at the old deal table in his basement kitchen
would have suited us far better. But Peter, uneasy from the
start about our tenant status, would have never seated us
where the servants once dined. In any event I declined to
dine at Balkill House again, preferring Peter to join us for
a simple meal in our humble cottage after we became an
item. Had I been Irish, I suspect our brief fling would never
have transpired, Peter being far too well-bred to bed one of
his cottiers. But my being a Yank likely blurred those
boundaries, and he gradually relaxed into our company.

At least so it seemed to me—though I'd need another
lifetime here to fathom the ways of the Anglo-Irish. Or fully
fathom, for that matter, how the Catholic-Irish feel about
their lapsed Ascendancy. Even someone as clued-in as Orla
couldn't hear of our romance without casting Peter and me
in a BBC costume drama. Nor did I even try to tell Seán
about my first (Anglo) Irish lover. Still, that Balkill summer
saw Maeve Maguire, the Super's daughter, for the first time
not discomfited by the question of class. No longer a
squatter on the fringes of Brahmin Boston, I found I didn't
give a fig about baggage like accent, breeding or religion
over here.

Equally unshackled by 800 years of Irish history, I saw
Peter merely as landlord, albeit a landlord with a classy
piece of real estate. A landlord who hailed from a long line
of Protestant corn millers, the first of whom had built
Balkill House in the 1760s, just a few miles from their mill

on the Nanny River. After hearing me marvel over a family history that stretched back centuries in a single spot, Peter drove us one Saturday afternoon to see the mill, which had sat idle since the early 1900s. As we walked round it, he spoke of someday hoping to convert into a kind of corn-milling-cum-local-history-museum, one of various schemes he had, from a butterfly farm to a garden centre, that might supplement the dwindling income from his dairy farming and inheritance.

Truth be told, I'd found Peter a dishy landlord from day one. Tall and thin, with a mop of unruly black hair and dark brown eyes whose expression generally alternated between abstracted and amused. A fetching landlord, but I don't think I actually set my cap for him. And even after we became lovers early that summer, I still saw him as a paramour and not a potential partner. OK—I may have fantasised a little, as one does. Picturing us en famille at Balkill House, Katy growing up the young lady of the manor, and myself bringing Pops over to live out his days with us, just as Beauty does with her merchant father after she marries the Beast.

But I knew better. Knew that I couldn't append a fairy-tale ending to what I'd set in motion by walking away from Eddie, family and Boston. And I knew too from too many novels that Peter and I had not so much fallen madly in love as stumbled bedward from our loneliness. Whether or not love ever blooms from such beginnings, I believed I knew better in this instance. Or do I just tell myself that now—rather than consider whether I'm in fact incapable of committing—unable to let love blossom? Always looking for a storybook hero, instead of just falling for someone decent and true. As true as Pops was to Ma through it all. A typical Virgo, Pops, willing to put up with anything.

As for Peter's intentions, who knows? Confounded by our becoming lovers, he fretted so much over charging us rent that I finally threatened to move out if he mentioned it again. As it was, we only slept together every few weeks, and always in the spare bedroom of my cottage, after I'd put Katy down. I didn't mind either if he sometimes stayed over, though I'd always be back in our bedroom before Katy awoke.

That we came from different planets no doubt circumscribed our affair, but there was something else in Peter's nature, I think, that gave me pause. I never told Sister Úna about him, only that Katy and I had at first lived in Co Meath. But if I ask myself <u>why</u> we parted?—the kind of question Sister Úna invariably posed—I think of a habit Peter had of inquiring the hour if ever I turned over, or got up to check on Katy in the middle of the night. 'What time is it please, Maeve?' he'd ask, sounding wide-awake and ever so formal, though I might've taken him in my mouth only hours before.

OK—so I probably wouldn't have said all of that to Sister Úna, had she asked. Nor was it his manners that made me almost shiver in the dark. Rather, there seemed a note of patent anxiety beneath his query that invariably unsettled me. A certain quotient of existential unease, if you like, which I think frightened me off, seeing I had terrors enough of my own.

I gave notice late that October, not able for another Siberian winter in the gardener's cottage. Peter refused the last month's rent, insisting I add it to my small down payment on a tiny terraced house in Dublin near Fairview Park. All thanks to a saintly bank manager who approved my mortgage on the back of a nursing position I'd landed at the Mater. Peter called into us in Fairview twice coming up to Christmas. But only for a cup of tea in the hand, no overnights.

It took Katy, four that January, some time to get over her Paradise Lost. Her cottage, woods and lake replaced overnight by an overgrown back garden. 'Dublin's wonky, Mama!' she informed me each night as I tucked her in at No. 4 Cadogan Rd. I'd point out how Fairview Park looks like a country field from our front door—the way our narrow road foreshortens the view—but Katy wasn't a bit impressed. And when on her birthday a pair of peacocks strutted right up to the café window at Dublin Zoo, she promptly burst into tears.

'Can we go to the zoo, Mama?' she asked for weeks after, until the memory of our former domestic fowl finally faded away. I'm not fond of zoos myself, and was delighted the Sunday she asked instead, 'Can we go to the Dead Zoo, Mama?' By which she meant the Natural History Museum that we'd visited the previous week. Still, it seems unfair she has no memory now of those peacocks which cried like cats outside our cottage, enchanting both our worlds. No memory of mornings when three or four would march slowly abreast towards our door—as if to breakfast, though truth is I sometimes flung a stone to keep them from the food we'd set out for Peter's half-feral cats. Or to keep them from the hollyhock seedlings I set in spring. 'Don't hurt them, Mama!' Katy would wail as we watched them flee up the lane, their tails flowing out behind like tiny, coloured streams. Is it any wonder she missed them so—before forgetting them altogether? Still there's my memory of them here, should I choose someday to show her this storybook.

CHAPTER 70

DATE: 20 July 1988

THOUGHT FOR THE DAY: If You Look Like Your Passport
Picture, You Probably Need the Trip

Katy's been worried about leaving Nibbles ever since Mrs.
Sheedy vacated next door. There's a 'Sale Agreed' sticker
already across the 'For Sale' sign, but no sign yet of the new
neighbours. However Mrs. Mahon across the road is happy
to feed Nibs while we're away. Meantime I hadn't the heart
to tell Katy how Lil the Mop had found Calico Cat
wrapped inside a load of wet sheets from the washer. Poor
Lil was so distraught I let her light a cigarette up right there
in the laundry—where she told of the feline tragedy in <u>her</u>
childhood.

'Are you missing a cat?' the next door neighbour had
asked one day.

'Oh, have you seen my Tippy?' said Lil, delighted.

'Aye, in my coal bunker. Maybe you'd come collect it.'

But it was not till Lil found Tippy, already stiff as a
board, that she fully understood.

With Nibbles sorted, we're nearly set for Crete, day after

tomorrow. Katy finished waitressing today, and I just have to go over the roster with Mary O'Mara tomorrow, even if Mary says she's only doing it to humour me. Anyhow, I'm not anywhere as anxious about going off as I was last September to Boston on just a day's notice. Just worried we'll sleep it out Saturday morning and miss our flight. Meantime we had a laugh tonight, watching 'Shirley Valentine' on the telly.

'Are you sure you want to bring me along?' K teases, and I assure her I am.

Anyhow, with my luck, I'd probably meet another Stanley the Waiter.

'Are you taking your diary to Crete?' Katy asks before going up to bed.

'It's not really a diary,' I tell her, nor am I packing it either.

CHAPTER 71

DATE: 29 July 1988

WEATHER: Mediterranean

MOOD: Blissful

Well, I packed it after all, though I wrote nothing last week, beyond postcards to Orla, Brian, and the staff at the Home. The card that brought Pops to mind I plan to keep: a group of men playing cards outside a café under a massive bougainvillaea.

Fact is, had I opened this notebook sooner, I'd have wanted to record it all. Everything—the heat, olive groves, noisy cicadas, or hibiscus as big as small trees. But this isn't really that kind of a commonplace book—even if I'm not entirely sure what kind of book it is. If not for homework, as Sister Úna assured me, maybe for home truths? OK, I'm a long way from home, but maybe distance helps such truths to track you down? Home thoughts from abroad— as the poet put it.

It's funny how quickly routines spring up: Katy going down to the pool this time every day for one last swim, while I sit on our balcony overlooking a dusty hillside a few miles above the crassness of Hersonissos. Early evening being when the heat begins to relent, a breeze springing up as the sun slips slowly into a blood-red sea. Last night I sat on till the stars came out, watching a few bats, and admiring a green light that winked on the distant harbour wall. This evening I just sit however, thinking of Pops who never managed a proper holiday. Not even a week with Ma somewhere, say Cape Cod, whatever about Crete. Yet it's the leavings from his hard work, his bit of savings, that has helped give us this trip.

With that thought the old familiar ache starts up, somewhere behind my breastbone. But when I think how I too have never taken this kind of holiday, something else shifts inside—allowing me see how much like Pops I've maybe turned out? As if the struggle not to become my often impatient, sometimes diffident, and occasionally crazed mother has made me into my father instead—wedded to my work, keen to oblige, tending to everybody ahead of myself. Another tiny piece of the puzzle if so—which is why I fetched this notebook to fit it in.

CHAPTER 72

DATE: 4 August 1988
WEATHER: Mediterranean
MOOD: Ever More Blissful

Well, the coach arrives in an hour to take us to the airport at Heraklion. Meanwhile Katy's gone down to shoot a game of pool with a lad from Galway who arrived with his parents yesterday. Too late for a holiday romance, though romance may be budding back in Dublin. 'Who's Shay?' I casually inquire this morning after Katy mentions his name again. 'Oh, just one of the jiu-jitsu gang,' K answers every bit as offhandedly, opening her paperback against any further interrogation.

Yet K is why I reached for this notebook as our holiday winds up. Fact is, I was a bit worried about how we'd manage, living in each other's pockets for a fortnight. Never mind the free-fall age she's at—one minute you know everything, the next you want to be four again, sticking your tongue out at your mother. The worst was our first day at the beach when K instantly saw how unfashionably we were kitted out—our one-piece bathing suits like Victorian swimming costumes amid the bikinied bottoms and bare Continental breasts sunning themselves on all sides. 'We're like Nuns on Holiday!' K hissed, her face like a thundercloud.

Worse yet, we hadn't any drachmas to hire sunbeds or parasol, as I'd left my wallet behind. Instead we had to spread our towels over two large rocks above the ranks of French, German, English lazing comfortably on the sand below. I figured we'd do well to last the afternoon, whatever about the holiday, which suddenly stretched out like a prison sentence. As it was, we lasted just fifteen minutes before we hightailed it back to our apartment. But once off the beach, K brightened entirely. 'Mother Calcutta & Sister Mary-Make-Believe Do Crete!' she whooped as we trudged up the hill, making me laugh till I was weak. 'Coming Soon to a Cinema Near You!'

'I think you mean Mother Teresa?' I finally gasped, which saw K lose it altogether.

'What about him, Shirley?' K whispered that evening, pointing at the pot-bellied waiter in our taverna.

'Get da boat!' I kicked her underneath the table. 'Not Mrs. Valentine's type at all!' Yet another exchange that hints at the delightful prospect of my daughter growing up to be my friend. A sidekick once again—or 'sidecake' as Katy used echo it, toddling after me at age two. And a moment I want to write down here—to set against the next time I feel that stab of loss watching her go out the door. To remember this holiday hasn't to be our final shared outing, though it's likely to be one of the last for a while. 'Thank you,' I'd written on Sister Úna card, 'for telling me to seize this time.'

'Thanks for the memories,' I might've also scribbled— seeing it was Sister who set me to reclaiming the past here.

A past I want to share with her yet, as if this notebook were still an accessory to our sessions. Like the afternoon Katy asked, 'Oh, Mama, can we have watermelon every day?' as we bought yet another in the shop. 'Do you not remember, Pet?' I ask—then realise of course she can't! So I describe instead how she used screech like a gull that Somerville summer whenever she saw its bright-pink, black-seeded flesh. It's surprising, I want to tell Sister, the links you can find to your life in places you've never before been, memories like a trail of crumbs in a fairy tale to mark your way back home. How the bougainvillaea here is the same cerise of the rhododendron blossoms that carpeted the path K & I would take down to the lake at Balkill House. More home truths, I suppose, these moments of past happiness.

It's not every day you get to Greece, and I wish of course that I'd written far more here. Not the cradle-of-civilisation stuff we heard at Knossos—the first flush toilets and such— but sights like the amazing Cretan cats, skinny & sway-backed, that we saw among those ruins. Tiny heads on elongated necks and eyes like almonds set on end. Or the overnight trip we took to Paleahora, driving west in a hired car for hours through the mountains to arrive in late afternoon at the tiny village, where we found a second-storey room with a patio directly above the sea. I was awakened twice that night—first by a fishing boat whose winking red & green lights seemed at arm's length in the dark. And again, nearer dawn, by a strange, angel-shaped cloud beyond the patio doorway, filling me with a feeling akin to peace.

Too late now to embark on a travelogue, as Katy's already back from the pool. So I'll just have to entrust the rest to memory: the dusty red soil of the olive groves, or the swallows skimming the swimming pool. Or Katy pulling

335

me aside on the way back from the beach, as a noisy gaggle of tourists overtake us from behind. 'Never a good idea,' she giggles in my ear, 'to be in the path of a German advance!'

CHAPTER 73

DATE: 13 August 1988

THOUGHT FOR THE DAY: My Duty Towards My Neighbour Is To Love Him As Myself

We're home over a week now and back into the swing. There looked no loss on Nibbles, who even made out to be glad to see us. Katy, in bed early tonight with a headache, is waitressing again, and there's still no sign of the new owners next door, though the realtor's sign is gone at the front. Or 'owner' per Mrs. Mahon, who misses nothing on the road. 'A single man,' she informed me when I dropped her over a bottle of ouzo for looking after Nibs. A single man not given to late-night parties, I hope, as we rarely heard Mrs. Sheedy, apart from the odd night she fell asleep with her telly on.

It was all quiet on the Home front too during our holiday. 'Someone's stolen my teeth,' Kitty the Conductor announced my first morning shift, by way of saying welcome back!

Next came Constance Fitzgerald, whose mother was waiting on her at home. 'There's a new time-lock,

Constance,' I chanced, which seemed to do the trick. 'The door doesn't open for a key anymore.'

'We've all been divided into two groups,' Germany Calling informed me later, going down to dinner.

'What groups, Gemma?' I asked, though I figured it was more likely Allies & Axis than Fianna Fáil or Fine Gael.

'Don't be daft!' Gemma snapped as if the answer were obvious. Then, relenting, she offered me her best conspiratorial smile: 'Those who eat cattle fodder, and those who eat sweets!'

But dinner in fact was chicken & chips which Gemma only picked at, seated across from Eamon Kerr whose T-shirt suggested OLD AGE COMES AT A BAD TIME. A few residents who'd actually computed I'd been away, like Tom or Alice May, inquired about my holiday, and I'll show them the photographs when I get them.

'I need a six-letter word for "confused",' Alice May said as I poured her a sherry after dinner. 'With three "ds"?'

'Muddled?' I suggested, only Alice May pointed out that 'muddled' has seven letters.

'Leave it with me for a moment?' I said. And it came to me too, just after Mary O'Mara discovered Kitty's teeth in a box of chocolates under her bed. 'When did you get worse than you were?' I heard Mary ask Kitty, same as Pops would whenever Brian or I did something daft.

'Addled!' I went to tell Alice May.

Only she was dozing in her chair, which she does more and more, so I lifted her paper and filled it in myself. She's a sweetheart, Alice May, more friend than client now, even though she's only been here a scant six months.

'Addled,' I then tell Fiona Flynn who was doing the same crossword at tea break.

'Addled isn't the half of it!' rejoined Fiona, whose

mother Nelly mistook an old tube of hair-colouring for shampoo, and is walking around now like a founding member of Deep Purple. Whereas I need to pick up some henna for my mop which has definitely faded from that Mediterranean sun. However much I once hated it, I'm not ready to lose that red quite yet. 'Only 9% of the Irish are natural redheads!' Tom the Teacher declared yesterday, after Enda Glynn remarked how there seem to be more redheads around now, whatever the reason. To think I once believed there was *nothing* natural about red hair, disgusted by the redheaded Yahoos I discovered in 'Gulliver's Travels' at age twelve, who shat on you from trees. The same year Brian told me it was bad luck to meet a red-haired woman at the start of a journey—another thing Uncle Hughdy had told him never to tell his sister.

CHAPTER 74

DATE: 14 August 1988

'Get a cup of coffee,' Dr Jordan said. "And I'll send for you as soon as the lumbar results come back." I had a mad thought about racing home—to look up meningitis in my nursing texts—but I'd only terrify myself more. Thankfully I'd recalled enough when Katy woke this morning, still complaining of her headache, plus a sore neck. There was no sign of a rash yet, but as soon as I felt her feverish brow we were in the car. I managed to hide my panic too, even after we got to Temple St Hospital, and the waiting game began. They let me stay with her in an isolation room, where I'd reassured her everything would be OK, even as they pumped her full of antibiotics. Nor did I let K see how I was monitoring her, watching like a hawk for spots. As was the nurse who came in every fifteen minutes to examine her with a torch, even checking between her toes. K didn't get drowsy, another symptom, but she was starting to present a rash along her tummy just before they took her out for the lumbar puncture. I wanted to stay with her but Dr Jordan said no—that, even if I was a nurse, it'd be too distressing. I could feel myself starting to slip anyhow, so I just gave her a kiss and watched them wheel her away.

So here I sit in the hospital canteen, spelling out in plain English how I won't be able for it—should anything happen to her. So please, please God may she pull through. I can hear Mary O'Mara saying only yesterday how parenthood is really all about loss. But Mary was talking about how children grow up and leave, not the ultimate forfeiture—your child dying—which is more than I'd be able for.

There—now I've written it—the worst thing I can imagine. That any child is a hostage to fortune is something you sense from the first time you hold your first-born. And I make myself fortune's hostage too—by saying I couldn't survive her being taken from me. But it's the God's truth— and I pray God she'll come through.

It doesn't seem possible—a week after our wonderful holiday. Or was that the Master Plan—that we could have that time because this time was to come?? Oh please, God, don't let that be so. I think of waking up in Paleahora, staring out to sea at an angel-shaped cloud that seemed both cloud and angel, Katy breathing softly beside me, and thinking how blessed I am, before falling back asleep. Please God let it be so ....

CHAPTER 75

DATE: 15 August 1988

Unable to stay in the canteen, I went back up to Dr Jordan in his cubicle on the second floor. I waited for him to get up and turn his back—like Dr Alper had when I asked about Pops' chances. But he just looked up and said, 'It's acute viral meningitis, Mrs. Maguire. I just got the results. Katy's going to be fine.'

I looked it up just to be sure when I got home: 'Acute viral meningitis: a self-limited illness, common in summer, hospitalisation rarely required.' The very diagnosis I'd been praying for—only I was too scared to name it, afraid to lay down anything resembling terms & conditions.

Dr Jordan kept Katy overnight in case of sequelae, though that's rare enough with the viral strain. But she came home this morning and is upstairs now in bed. Still shaky, but strong enough to bemoan the loss of her waitressing wages. Count your blessings! I nearly echo Ma, but I bite my tongue in time. Remind myself she's still a

343

child, and needn't know just yet how lucky she is.

Meantime Shay-Just-One-of-the-Jiu-Jitsu-Gang is calling by tomorrow. He somehow turned up at the hospital this morning, only to learn no visitors were allowed. 'Are you Shay?' I chanced, after seeing a nice-looking lad by the lift.

'Yes, Mrs. Maguire,' he blushed, making me feel even older than his baby face already had. 'Nice to meet you,' he stammered.

His baseball cap was back-to-front, so I only saw the familiar red *B* as we went into the lift. I doubted he knew anything about the Red Sox—baseball caps over here being about fashion, not sport—but it happens an uncle in Boston had sent Shay it. Which gave us something besides Katy to talk about, as he unchained his bike from the railing outside.

'Call by the house?' I encouraged, before I walked over to the Gardiner St Church to light a candle in thanks.

CHAPTER 76

DATE: 28 August 1988

There's no way youth is wasted on the young. Not wasted on my Katy anyhow—who's bounced back no bother. Her second morning home, however, I awoke with my stomach so knotted I feared I might vomit. As if my head knew she was safe, but a chunk of that initial terror was lodged in my body yet. Which is why I have not only 'sat' each morning since, with a candle in my bedroom, but also why I went down Sunday to the Zen Centre on Exchequer St. There was a brief introduction beforehand for beginners, six of us, a few like myself more lapsed than absolute beginners. And nobody—not even after the regulars arrived—who looked even remotely like Steven from BU or Stanley the Waiter with his stories of half-naked monks. The room was lovely, apricot walls and lavender trim, even if we 'sat' so long I feared my knees would lock. But I managed to get upright when it ended, and I may even go back again.

I also considered calling Sister Úna last week, but didn't. Decided instead it was OK I felt a bit low, given my fright over K and how Pops' anniversary is just next week. I found a dead wasp yesterday, behind the pot of basil on the kitchen window, though hardly the same one that was buzzing there the morning Brian rang. It's hard to believe nearly a year has passed since Pops checked out, and I want to take his ashes up to Glenmore before a second Christmas passes. It's also time to put aside this notebook, seeing it's nearly a fortnight since I last scribbled in it. Still I'd like to finish up properly—not just trail away until some sentence proves the last. Had I a better grasp of the storyline, I might better know how to bring it home, a final line or two in the crossword puzzle before I lay it down.

CHAPTER 77

DATE: 5 September 1988

ACTIVITY: Being Here Now

I went into the Franciscan Church on the way to work today and lit a candle beneath a statue of St Joseph. Lord knows who the patron saint of Superintendents is, but carpentry being one of Pops' trades, I figured Joseph was near enough. And as I knelt, the last evening I saw Pops alive came flashing back—just before I caught the plane home that May. Pops was having trouble with buttons by then, so I sat beside him on his bed, giving him a hand with his pyjama top. The mood was a tad glum, but that didn't stop me from blurting out, 'I love you, Pops, more than I can say.'

'And certainly more than I need to hear,' Pops smiled wearily.

And smiled again, only brighter, at my 'Meet you under the apple tree!' as I let myself out.

My tears in church this morning were only the start, I figured, given the day, a year to the day. But I actually felt a kind of lightness as I left the church, a sense of reprieve that followed me to work and whose afterglow lingers yet. As if candle and memory had somehow shunted me back into the Here & Now of a day that I'd been dreading. Which is only how Pops would want it—a day in early September just like any other. A day spent grounded in the quotidian: the usual carry-on at work, plus K's excitement over the new school year that starts tomorrow. Or my first glimpse this evening of our new next-door neighbour, a fellow whose face I definitely know?

Or what seems like a true gift from above—as Katy shouts down that she's found her 'Encyclopaedia of Dreams'.

'What was it you wanted to look up, Mama?'

It takes me a moment, but then I have it.

'A peacock?'

'"Showing your true colours",' Katy shouts down again, which sounds good to me.

'"Or joy in the afterlife"'—which sounds even better.

CHAPTER 78

DATE: 9 Sept 1988

THOUGHT FOR THE DAY: The Pills that Mother Gives You, Don't Do Anything At All

'There's a corner boy hanging about!' Germany Calling tells me after dinner.

'Ain't nobody here but us chickens,' I gesture at the empty dining room. 'No boys anywhere, Gemma.'

'A corner boy!' Gemma insists. 'And I don't like the look of him.'

'We'll keep an eye out so,' I wink at Clodagh as Nurse Ethel takes Gemma off.

No sooner do they depart, however, than a 'corner boy' comes out of the laundry room, proving Gemma right. Mistaken she might've been about the Minister for Propaganda or the poor, light-fingered Pakistani, but Gemma was dead right about the corner boy. Nor do I like the look of him myself. Skinny, in a grey track suit, deadened adolescent eyes staring out from under a NY Yankees cap.

You often see junkies begging in the city centre, seated by

the ATM machine at College Green, or hunched down on the Ha'penny Bridge, oblivious to the drizzle. In hooded sweatshirts or anoraks, holding a Styrofoam cup and mumbling something. Only this kid's holding a syringe filled with what looks like blood. Nor is he mumbling, for I can understand him perfectly.

'Jus gizzus some fuckin' drugs. Jus' the fuckin' gear and nobody gets hurt.'

Thank God Ethel took Gemma off, I think, as this scenario would only rocket-fuel her fantasies. Another part of me wonders what we have that would mess him up real good. Like a cocktail of Maalox, Warfarin, and Temazepam, say. While yet another part of me is thinking what I think every time I see one of his tribe: how he's some mother's son, and how dreadful it would be to see your child end up like this. For he's the one shaking—like he's the one being menaced—not myself and Clodagh. Though Clodagh looks pretty shook, eyes bugging and mouth open, like she's going to faint.

'Sit down,' I tell her before turning back to our NY Yankee.

I want to say all drugs are locked away upstairs, but am afraid of provoking him. So I point instead towards the drugs trolley back in the corner, hoping to fob something off and get rid of him quick, before anybody else comes down and spooks him into doing God knows what.

'Come over here, you,' I order in my most matron-like tone, gesturing toward the trolley again.

He follows me at a little distance which suits me fine. 'I have to unlock it,' I say, slowly, in case he thinks I'm reaching into my pocket for a pistol. But then just what I'd feared actually happens—somebody walks in behind us: Nurse Ethel Lyons again, having come through the kitchen.

But Clodagh shakes her head slightly, and Ethel stops and cops it all: myself behind the trolley, our Drugstore Cowboy facing me, holding his syringe up like a tiny baton. I start to fumble in the trolley then, for Nurse Ethel is moving again, slowly towards us in those long Roscommon strides of hers—like she were down on the farm again, only more quietly in her rubber-soled nursing shoes. Meantime our visitor is bent over the trolley, studying the pharmaceutical cornucopia.

'Here's to you, Joe DiMaggio!' I shout.

'Wha'?' our corner boy says, straightening up, just as Nurse Ethel locks her fists together and hits him with everything she's got upside his ear, sweeping his feet out from under him on her follow-through, then sitting down on his pole-axed back.

You're as good as your Granny was, I want to tell Ethel, with that drunken wedding guest! Only I'm in the kitchen by now, tearing a tea-towel in strips to bind his wrists.

One of the two Guards who arrived in a squad car five minutes later turns out to be Sgt Breen. 'Never a dull moment at the Fairview Home!' he says as he admires Nurse Ethel's handiwork. 'How'd he get in?'

'Someone left the laundry window open,' I say, someone like Lil the Mop I suspect, sneaking another smoke.

CHAPTER 79

DATE: 10 Sept 1988

MEMORIES FOR THE DAY: Fuchsia, Whitethorn, Gorse

I offered Ethel and Clodagh today off, but both declined. Thankfully I wasn't rostered till evening myself, as I'm still something of a nervous wreck after yesterday's intruder. Enough so that I drove out this morning to Malahide for a walk along the shore. Which is where I stumbled across them—on that rocky stretch towards Portmarnock—what looked like thousands & thousands of starfish. More starfish than you could possibly imagine, piled up in drifts like seaweed. Every size of starfish, some seven or eight inches across, arms outstretched. Pink, pimply, and dead, every last one of them.

It was an amazing sight—which I've carried in my head since. Like the hundreds of earthworms that could litter the Common footpaths after a heavy April shower, having crawled out of the ground to avoid drowning, or so Manny claimed. Most of them drowned in the puddles anyhow, their desiccated bodies like tiny bits of string underfoot once the sun returned. Those worms fascinated me, but these starfish in their thousands were something else—like a huge mystery washed ashore. Nothing that would make the news, yet something truly worth pondering. Like Tom the Teacher's latest fact, which he exchanged for a cup of tea yesterday.

'Did you know, Maeve, there's a bush in Tasmania over 40,000 years old?'

'I did not, Tom.'

'Aye, they reckon it's the oldest living thing on earth.'

It's a bit late, I know, to be turning this into a Nature Notebook. Seated here in the kitchen before I head in for my evening shift, admiring the Heavenly Blues I planted last June in a huge pot just inside the sliding-glass kitchen door. I've never had much joy with Sweet Pea which Mrs. Sheedy grew next door, but Morning Glories I can surely grow. Over 400 blossoms last year according to Katy, who totted them up daily. Glorious trumpets that reign for a few hours before shrivelling away. Like a meditation they are, reminding me to be here now.

I finally placed our new next-door neighbour, whom I met across the back-garden hedge last week. Declan, who works in Chapters Bookshop on Middle Abbey St, where I sometimes browse the remaindered hardbacks. I never knew his name, but I had his face all right, the blue eyes mostly. Plus a widow's peak which I've always fancied on a man. And a wedding band too, because I can't help that reflex with any guy my age. I hate admitting that, nor do I want to speculate about his wife's whereabouts. That he seems as pleasant next door as he always did in the bookshop is all I have to add to today's Nature Report. Though maybe I'll begin that kind of journal next? Like the school copy I brought back from Donegal which listed all the wildflowers I found that first summer, or at least those whose names Aunt Chrissie knew, including the spray of whitethorn she wouldn't allow me bring indoors. And a separate page for the birds I saw, all of whose names Uncle Hughdy had, in Irish and English both.

CHAPTER 80

DATE: 18 Sept 1988
ACTIVITY: Á la belle étoile!
THOUGHT FOR THE DAY: Home, Sweet Home,
and the Fire Out!

Who knows, this may yet turn out more a Police & Fire log than Nature Notebook! Last week's break-in and now, of all things, a fire at the Home. And not just Lil's knickers this time—rather an electrical fault two nights ago in the storage room off the kitchen—which Valerie discovered, Deo Gratias, before it had time to spread. Val rang me at 2.00 a.m. and I was only minutes getting down. The fire brigade got there first however, and had the flames already doused—though not before the night staff had evacuated the new wing, wheeling and walking its eighteen residents through the lower day-room into the garden. The firemen needed another ten minutes before giving the all-clear, so I quickly checked the first-floor bedrooms. God knows what a four-alarm fire might do for Germany Gemma's equilibrium, but fortunately the fire doors either end had kept out the smoke, and Gemma and the others were all taking it in their stride.

I went downstairs then and into the back garden,

expecting some kind of pandemonium. What greeted me, however, was more like a late-night garden party: the old folks swaddled in wraps and blankets, scattered in wheelchairs, or seated on garden benches and dining-room chairs. Kitty the Conductor was keening softly to herself, while the others either chatted or quietly waited to go back in. I couldn't get over how calm they were—as if having lived this long and seen it all, a small fire in the wee hours was nothing to get exercised about. Least of all on such a lovely night—a quarter-moon peeping through the trees along the railway embankment, and a starry sky above.

'I don't know the last time I saw so many stars,' Alice May remarked when I got to her. 'Look, Maeve, isn't that Cassiopeia?' she pointed, sounding livelier than she has in weeks.

I looked and it was—hanging like a huge **W** embroidered on the black—my favourite of the few constellations you could make out against the lights of Boston when Pops took us out star-gazing. Miss Russell our French teacher had us memorise a line from Pascal—'Le silence éternel de ces espaces infinis m'effraie'—but there was nothing terrifying those nights on the Common. Nor was there the winter night I carried my one-year-old Katy up the back stairs in Somerville, when suddenly she went all rigid, startling me so that I looked down, perplexed, only to see her staring up, transfixed. Then, looking up, I saw it too, a magnificent starry night. What's more, saw it almost as she was seeing it: for the first time, literally star-struck.

'Keep those feet warm,' I tell Alice May, tucking her rug around her ankles before I move on to Tom the Teacher and Eamon the T-Shirt. Seated on a garden bench in bathrobes and slippers, like two old fellas out of Beckett. Behind me W^2 wheels out a trolley, the steam from its teapot like a tiny locomotive, while somewhere on the embankment a collared dove gives a muted hoot.

CHAPTER 81

DATE: 29 September 1988

THOUGHT FOR THE DAY: Good Fences Make Good Neighbours

'Don't just tail off, Class!' Miss Dewey cautioned back in Boston High whenever she set us an essay. 'Always craft your conclusion!' So is that why I'm back here once again? Not hoping for anything so tidy as a conclusion, but not wanting to simply tail away?

I took a rhubarb & strawberry tart next door a few evenings back. Just a neighbourly gesture, seeing Cadogan Rd hasn't a Welcome Wagon like American suburbia in the 1950s. I considered taking a bottle of wine too, but decided that might get misconstrued. Seán loved to tell how he'd ask a girl out for a drink when he worked in the States. 'Ohh ...?' she might hesitate, eyes widening. Until a pal explained how in America you ask a girl out to dinner. That was OK—except Seán forgot to switch back when he returned to Dublin. 'Would we go for a meal?' he'd ask a girl he fancied. 'Ohh ...?' she would look at him, eyes widening.

Anyhow Declan insisted I stay for a coffee and slice of tart. We sat in the kitchen as his sitting room is still filled with boxes. 'Mostly books,' he laughed. 'I'm thinking of quitting Chapters and opening a branch library here.'

It's funny how much larger he seems in his own house. Not your average 5' 9" Irish male; six-foot at least, and wide-shouldered like an American footballer.

I didn't stay long, a half-hour or so, just long enough to get some of his story. How he grew up in another terraced row just over in Marino. And how Janet, his wife, died a year ago, five years to the day they married, which explains the wedding band. They bought a small house in Drumcondra, but put off starting a family after Janet was diagnosed with lymphoma. He sounded OK talking about it, though my heart went out to him. Her photograph was on the kitchen counter, a lovely girl with a mass of blonde curls, but I didn't comment on it.

'You must come look at the books,' Declan said as he saw me out. 'Once I've them shelved.'

'I'll bring a bill with my address,' I laughed. 'So as to get my library card?'

'Ask him over for supper,' Katy says back home as she hands me her French verbs. I checked to see is she teasing Shirley Valentine, but she simply parrots 'Je vois, je voyais, je verrai' and takes herself off to bed.

It's been quiet on the Home front too, no crime nor conflagrations. Jim brought in an electrician and a builder to reconfigure the storeroom which gives us some more badly needed kitchen space. A few residents, Veronica Egan and Constance Fitzgerald, had trouble sleeping a night or two after the fire, but the break in routine once again seemed to take years off Tom the Teacher. And even Eamon the T-Shirt had a few words to offer the next day—along with: I INTEND TO LIVE FOREVER—SO FAR, SO GOOD!

Alice May, however, is definitely failing. No longer really able for her crossword puzzle, never mind a book. She doesn't feel up to the day-room either, so I try to visit her room a few minutes at least twice each shift. 'On the top shelf,' she instructed me today, pointing up at her wardrobe from her easy chair. 'The hatbox.'

'I never knew you to wear a hat,' placing the box on her lap.

'I never did,' she smiled, 'except when I went out to Tucson to see Johnny.'

She's told me before of visiting Johnny her only brother, but I didn't mind hearing it again. Of the train journey she took out to him each spring, before the hot weather arrived. Taking two weeks' vacation from her St Louis library job, and booking herself a sleeper on the Southern Pacific with a change at Kansas City to the Santa Fe line. Describing for me an America I've yet to see: first cornfields, then wide grassy plains when the train got as far as Oklahoma, and finally the Arizona desert.

Her brother first lived in Tucson before he got his ranch, and they walked out into the desert one visit with a picnic supper. Only they lost their way back, going in circles till they finally pointed themselves towards a glow on the horizon, which turned out to be Tucson. A few years after Johnny got his ranch, a huge rattlesnake crawled out from under the porch as Alice May came down the steps.

'I screamed,' Alice May told me, 'and Johnny came running from the barn. Struck its head off with a long-handled spade, then skinned all six feet of it atop his kitchen table.'

I shivered slightly at that.

'Yes,' said Alice May, 'it was messy. But he spread

newspapers over the oilcloth first.'

It wasn't a snake on a kitchen table that had made me shiver, but I just smiled, 'No, go on.'

Johnny offered her that skin, but Alice May asked for another he'd found the previous year and hung on a nail in the barn, probably shed by that same snake. And she took it back to Missouri in her small trunk with red-leather straps. The trunk was stolen a few years later, but the St Louis police came upon it in a residential hotel, not far from the Mississippi.

'Empty except for this,' Alice May said, handing me the hatbox.

Lifting the lid, I saw the snake coiled asleep inside. At least that's what I first thought, though it was only its shed skin. I didn't dare lift it for fear it might break—walked over instead to the window for a better look. 'It's beautiful,' I said—and it was. All milky grey with darker diamond patterns, its tiny sun-lit scales linked in an endless mosaic.

'Imagine shedding your skin every year like that?' Alice May laughed.

'That's one way to make a fresh start,' I said, which made her laugh again.

'I want you to have it,' Alice May said as I replaced the lid.

'Oh, I wouldn't take that away from you,' I protested.

'You're not taking it away, Maeve. I'm giving it to you.'

CHAPTER 82

DATE: 30 September 1988

THOUGHT FOR THE DAY: Wreaths on Shortest Notice

I thanked Alice May as I put the hatbox back into her wardrobe yesterday. 'For safekeeping,' I said, not wanting to acknowledge what she else was likely saying with the gift. But this morning she spoke it outright, after I brought her the last of the mums from my garden.

'I've elected to die,' she smiled, after thanking me for the flowers.

'Has it come to that, Alice May?' I smiled back. Not fobbing her off so much as hoping to shift her mood.

'I believe it has,' she nodded, like we were talking about the weather.

'Are you not getting up this morning?'

'Oh, later perhaps,' she said, lifting a hand from the bedclothes.

She's said this kind of thing before of course. 'Here's to a final breath!' one Sunday, holding up her glass of sherry.

'Ripeness is all!' I proposed in turn, knowing 'Lear' to be

her favourite Shakespeare.

'I might just walk out into Dublin Bay,' she says sometimes too, when feeling a bit disconsolate. But I wonder if this time she doesn't mean it? As if she senses a denouement coming on, like a cloud shadowing the horizon, or the lassitude that precedes a particularly nasty flu. 'Some yogis can open the bottom of their spine,' Stanley the Waiter had informed me in the Parker House laundry room, 'and let their life drain away like water from a tap.' Was it some kind of surgical trick? I wondered, until like most of what Stanley told me, I forgot all about it. Nor was it the kind of thing Alan the Yogi talked about either in that Boylston St loft. 'Follow your breath' was most of what he advised instead. 'Take note how you sit or stand.'

'You don't know the where, when, or how,' Uncle Hughdy used to say. 'Who it is will take off the clothes you put on in the morning.' Like Auntie Chrissie, who was planning a trip to the hairdresser in Killybegs the day she died. WREATHS ON SHORTEST NOTICE said the sign in a Sligo flowershop that Katy and I passed later that afternoon on the drive up to Donegal.

Yet some folk seem to get an inkling, like Manny craving a chocolate éclair. And Mary O'Mara's grandmother who always insisted she'd die in November—the month she was born, married and widowed—and did.

Or the story Leo the Porter told last week, how his father one night told a neighbour he'd return in the morning to collect for a tiling job he'd done. 'And if I don't call by,' he quipped, 'I'll send an angel to your door.'

'I'm going up to bed,' his Dad announced when he got home. Which is where Leo's mother found him shortly after, sleeping the sleep of the dead.

'He had lots of sayings,' Leo said, 'but nobody'd ever

heard that one about an angel before.'

'Be sure to call round for what I owe,' the neighbour told Leo at the funeral.

CHAPTER 83

DATE: 4 October 1988
GRAFFITO FOR THE DAY: 'I have the body of a God!'—Buddha

I started 'Siddhartha' last night, a mere twenty years after Stanley the Waiter recommended it. It's a bit of a fairy tale—handsome prince with keen intellect goes off on a spiritual quest. Like wide-mouthed frogs and six-toed sloths, you don't see many of them round here. But I liked how he leaves his palace 'to investigate the causes of suffering, old age, and death'. A pity he never called at a nursing home, as we could have told him a thing or two.

Of course, suffering isn't reserved for the elderly alone. Take, for example, what Declan Next Door told me last night at the supper chez nous which Katy had suggested. It proved an easy evening, not at all awkward as I'd worried. Katy was in great form—doing impressions of her French teacher, Miss LeBlanc, who sounds daft as a brush—and Declan praised her enthusiasm and confidence after she went up to study. I usually demur when somebody commends K, not wanting to play the proud parent. But last night I ended up telling Declan about her meningitis, as if I still needed to exorcise the terror of those first hospital hours. Even so, it was a lot to unload on someone you hardly know. The kind of thing we Yanks are known for doing, but something I try not to practise.

But maybe it enabled Declan to tell in turn over coffee about his previous house in Drumcondra. How his Janet had been after him to paint the floors, as she hated both carpet and bare boards. 'We were always going to pick out a colour,' Declan smiled. 'Dark green or navy—but we never got around to it.' Then, six months after her death, Declan brought home a five-litre tin of high-gloss black paint, and by evening had painted himself out the front door. Oil-based paint takes hours to dry, so he just locked the door and started walking. He wasn't fifty yards down the road, however, before he fell apart.

'I spent the night at my brother's,' pushing his coffee cup away, 'and put the house on the market the following morning.'

His voice caught just slightly once in the telling as I held my breath. But he finished up OK, just shook his head at the end.

'A house holds a lot of memories,' I said—to say something.

'A lot of memories,' Declan smiled. 'But you'd have wanted to see the estate agent's face when he saw black floors everywhere.'

'How's the New Man on the Block?' K teased this morning at breakfast. But I just pointed to the night-shirt Orla gave me for my birthday. A knee-length flannel jersey that lists TEN REASONS WHY A BOOK IS BETTER THAN A MAN.

CHAPTER 84

DATE: 6 October 1988

I took Katy in to Alice May on the spur of the moment this afternoon, after she dropped by work to get money for new shoes. It was lovely seeing Alice May brighten up, and Katy—who hadn't the benefit of growing up in an apartment building full of older folk—seated chatting with her. Well, experience if not benefit, given how skewed life as the Super's daughter sometimes felt. Still, it heartened me to have the pair of them meet.

'You forgot to take something with you last week,' Alice May said as we were going out.

I looked blank, until she pointed to her wardrobe.

'Are you sure about that?' I asked, but Alice May assured me she was sure.

And so I took the hatbox down and opened it for K.

'Oh, Mama, that's beautiful!' she gasped, though not before taking a half-step back—as if the snake were once again just sleeping.

CHAPTER 85

DATE: 7 October 1988
THOUGHT FOR THE DAY: Home Is Where the Heart Was

Last night I read up to where Siddhartha meets the old ferryman Vasudeva, who patiently listens to his life's story. Just as Sister Úna had mine, despite my thinking that all she <u>did</u> was listen. But I know better now—how if somebody listens, you get to speak. And getting to speak helps to get it out: both what you've experienced and what you feel. And its validity. Validation. Plus you get to hear your own voice—find it even. Lord knows how Sister Úna will feel about being compared to a Buddhist boatman, but I copied out a few words from the novel on the postcard I sent to her today: 'And Siddhartha felt how wonderful it was to have such a listener who could be absorbed in his own life, his own strivings, his own sorrows.'

Nor had what Sister offered, when she did speak, always sunk in straight away. Like an early session in which I spoke of feeling like an orphan, now that Pops was gone. 'I know that's silly,' I said, but Sister Úna shook her head.

'Most of us feel that, Maeve, once we lose both our parents. But it also clears a way for us to look back at our childhood, and view some of the painful things. Our lives turn toward nostalgia as we revisit our past, not unlike emigrants returning home.'

Only I didn't know last February how I was already on that journey—just dead certain 'nostalgia' wasn't what I was talking about. But when I looked it up last night, I saw Sister Úna had it dead right. Not just the dictionary definition, 'homesickness', but its root too. From the Greek 'nostos', a return and 'algos', pain. A painful return, a return to the pain. Had Boston High still allowed Mr. Barry to teach Greek, I might have known that already. Or I might've recognised 'algos', the painful bit, rooted in lingo like neuralgia, coxalgia or glossalgia which we had to master at college. Not to mention all the Distalgesic we dispense at the Home for pain relief. "Those Disco Jesus tablets" as Lil the Mop, our Mrs. Malamop, recently rendered them.

CHAPTER 86

DATE: 11 October 1988

THOUGHT FOR THE DAY: Mother is the Necessity of Invention

'Sure, what good's a key to anybody?' Constance Fitzgerald muttered this morning, after I fibbed again how we've lost ours for the front door. It's nothing Constance hasn't told me a hundred times before, but how differently I heard it this morning—now that I know what key she means. Marty, her nephew, having told Mary O'Mara the story yesterday—Constance's story. How she was bound for London, aged twenty-five, when her mother threw down the key to her uncle's house onto their Galway kitchen table. 'Take you that,' her mother declared. 'Take you that, and the house will be yours.'

'She used to cry telling me about it,' Marty told Mary. How her mother had told Constance the uncle needed minding, and she should go down to him. So Constance went down to the uncle, but she never got over handing over her life like that. 'You'll get the house,' her mother had promised—but Constance was fifty-four before she got it, as the uncle lived to ninety-six. And he needed some minding too. Doting, irascible, and incontinent, he ended up needing to be nailed to his chair.

'So Constance cared for her mother after that?' I asked.

'Would you believe Constance never ever cared for her mother?' Mary said.

I didn't believe it—not at first. Not the way Constance frets daily over her. But it turns out her mother died in a nursing home a few year years before the uncle. Which is why Constance cares for her mother now, with almost every breath she takes. As if to say: 'I'd have minded you, Mam. Whatever about the uncle, I'd have gladly minded you.'

CHAPTER 87

DATE: 14 October 1988

LYRIC FOR THE DAY: C'est La Vie (Say the Old Folks)

Were this a Nature Notebook, I'd note down the tropical oranges and reds of the sumac in Mr. Declan Next Door's garden, same as those sumacs which flaunted their autumn colours all over Somerville during our two years there. And were this a diary, I'd no doubt return to Mr. Declan, who called over last night. Confess that yeah, I like him, and feel like maybe I could like him a lot? Not just the boxes of books but those strong lines to his face, nose like a Roman Centurion. Or Roman Caesarean per Lil the Mop. Plus his laid-back manner. And a sense of humour too—which I find vital. Something Seán surely had, as did Peter the Landlord, for all his formality. 'Why did the Buddha never vacuum?' Declan asks last night. 'Is the dust that obvious?' I wince, but Declan just points at 'Siddhartha' on the coffee table. 'Because he hadn't any attachments, Maeve.'

There's a gravity about him I also like, unlike Seán who sometimes seemed to lack sufficient ballast. Not that losing a partner as Declan did wouldn't either ground or finish you. Indeed I can't imagine how you begin to get over that kind of loss.

And there's that, too, to keep an eye on—that we don't end up pooling our losses, much as Peter and I did our loneliness. Even if it's far too soon be thinking our neighbourliness is necessarily headed anywhere that way. Or that it ought—given that Declan's likely to be next door long after any fire dies down and we go our separate ways. Better to stay with a strictly boundaried Good Neighbor policy, methinks, as FDR advised.

Not that I wouldn't fancy a man in my life again. Or in my bed as I was feeling last night. Like the nun atop a ladder who enthused aloud: 'I feel like a fireman!' Or a lovely man in any uniform? And having journeyed this far, who knows, I might even manage to commit to a lover next time. But I'm not madly looking for a happy ending—for Declan to turn out my Captain Corelli, a kind of deus ex Italia, or in this instance, Hibernia.

'Did you ever think of marrying again after Dad died?' Fiona Flynn asked her mother recently.

'No way!' Nelly retorted. 'And have to put up with that sex thing again?'

'Sex thing?' Fiona said.

'You know—what they want to do now? Stick it in your mouth and all!'

'She must be getting that from "Oprah",' Fiona said once we all stopped laughing.

But it's not just the sex thing I miss—there's also the simple comfort that comes with it. A cuddle can be as nice as the whole nine yards—though there was no persuading poor Seán of that when he couldn't get hard after a pint too many. 'Olives'll put lead in your pencil!' I overheard

Manny telling Brian once, though I don't think Seán would've laughed had I advised him to switch to martinis. Same as I didn't when he told the one about your man who answered 'Not a wink!' when asked had he ever slept with a redhead? Still I used to love just holding him—his skin soft as a baby, smoother than the wrinkled flesh you bathe, dry and powder in the Home.

Anyhow, who knows how much longer I'll be on Cadogan Rd? I'd never crowd Katy, but I can't imagine living an ocean apart, and she's already talking about America after college. You can count on change far more than you can a happy ending, and autumn always feels like a veritable symphony of change.

I've a note at work to talk to Jim about replacements for Wang Wei and Leo the Porter. W^2 is starting a nursing course at the Mater, and Leo a job with the Buildings & Grounds Dept at Trinity College. 'You'll make a super Super,' I told him, though they probably have another word for it here. And Lil the Mop is also leaving, to look after her grandson when her daughter returns to work. It's as well too—seeing I should have sacked her after our corner boy came in the laundry window. 'That drug attic!' as Lil dubbed him.

And while I haven't put my own name down on the list, Jim may well need to look for a new matron by next year. Time for a change—if not high time—as I've been in something of a holding pattern the past year. Lingo like 'holding pattern', 'stacked up' and 'clear to land' a legacy from my time with Seán the Tower. I'm half-thinking of doing the paediatric course at Temple St—sick children's nursing it's called over here. But I also wonder might I leave nursing altogether—as if like Katy I've a wide-open future too?

Time, anyhow, to be thinking of moving on from the Fairview Home of Happy Retirement—which seems even less happy of late—as if I'm finding it harder to bear witness to the inevitable, inexorable changes. Like Enda Glynn's confusion, her bright blue eyes filling with tears as she only remembers every second day how her sister Eva passed away last month. Or poor Pat the Pope who suffered a stroke and now bawls like a baby when washed.

Time so to move on, methinks, lest I leave it too long and end up stranded myself here in Hotel California with the Escape Committee—what Mary O'Mara calls Constance Fitzgerald and Nora Doorstop, who try all the doors just before bedtime, hoping for a way out. 'We'll leave it so,' I overheard Nora tell Constance the other night, 'and get a fresh start in the morning.'

Only Happy-As seems as happy as ever. A case of when you don't know where you are, anywhere will do. 'Give us a few bob before you go,' he asks his wife when she visits. 'For my bus-fare home.' Then five minutes later he's home already, asking W^2 to draw his sitting-room curtains for a quick nap before the racing results come on.

CHAPTER 88

DATE: 16 October 1988

WORD FOR THE DAY: Tesserae

THOUGHT FOR THE DAY: If the shoe fits, get another just like it!

Another memory upon awaking, another piece of the mosaic. The evening Ma put a slice of meatloaf and some peas in front of us, said Pops' plate was in the oven, and walked out the door. Pops arrived home an hour later from a painting job, and rang his pal Officer Feeney, who waited in his cruiser, blue lights flashing, while Pops went into any shops still open along Tremont St, asking had they seen his wife? Until he found her, huddled in a booth in Hayes-Bickford on Boylston St, weeping over a cup of stone-cold coffee. Ma went into hospital shortly after, but it often seemed as if she were still on walkabout in the years that followed.

Maybe a mosaic is what I'm pasting together here: each memory like a bright bit of coloured glass; this notebook no less an aide de memoir than the turf bank onto which Hughdy inscribed 'Brenda Lee'. The same Hughdy who hushed Aunt Chrissie when she scolded us for jumping off the loom shed: 'Sure they're only making memories!' Memories like Ma also surely made—only to find herself years later unable to entertain them. Memories of a Donegal childhood, I mean, whatever about those memories she lost to electro-shock.

And pasted in here are more memories than mine alone—Mrs. L's Maine salt-water farm, Durca W's Cracow childhood, or Wang Wei's disco-dancehall nights. All the memory—and its loss—that plays out daily at the Home, where Eamon's T-Shirt only yesterday puzzled DOES THE NAME PAVLOV RING A BELL??

CHAPTER 89

There's no doubt Alice May is dying, be it by election or otherwise. In bed over a week now, and only a little ice cream or yoghurt taken in the past twenty-four hours. Her speech comes and goes, and most of it as if she too is speaking memories. Other times, God love her, she's doing a crossword. 'Four letters,' she puzzles aloud, eyes shut. 'Beginning with L?'

'How about "love"?' I offer. 'Or "luck" or "life"?' To think it was only last month she gave me 'Nemo' for Captain of the 'Nautilus', which I couldn't recall. Though I remember diving under my seat between Brian and Pops when the giant squid grabbed the submarine on the Orpheum screen.

It wasn't a crossword troubling her yesterday however. 'Oh, I should've left this,' she fretted in her sleep. 'The roll's finished and I'm short at the bottom.' Wallpapering, I decided, either in St Louis or the Killester cottage she came

381

home to. Or had she once helped her brother Johnny to paper the parlour of his Arizona ranch?

'Leave the decorating for now,' I advise, wetting her lips with a cloth.

It seems a fit way to leave a life—by tidying up the quotidian. She's asleep when I go in to her this evening, but she wakes as a DART train rattles by outside, carfuls of yellow electric light in the autumn dusk. Eyes open, she smiles at me and asks, 'Are you here to see my right mind takes the right turn?'

'Just keep the river to your right,' I laugh as she smiles, then shuts her eyes again.

I leave word for Val on the night shift to call me if she gets worse. Only because Alice May has nobody else, I tell myself, though she wouldn't be the first tribal elder to check out with just a night nurse by her side. We learned at college how patients will sometimes trigger intense responses in a nurse—anger, over-involvement, or feelings of helplessness as they continue to fail. But that's all a shade too clinical, I think, for what I'm feeling here. Something more like one of those four-letter words—love, loss, and the like.

CHAPTER 90

DATE: 20 October 1988

THE HERE & NOW: My Kitchen Table @ 6.00 a.m.

SONG FOR THE DAY: 'Sweet Rose of Sharon, Abide in Me'

It was nearly the same dream from last spring that woke me just minutes ago—Katy and me on a bus journey—the same errand as the Greyhound pulls into a terminal. Once more I walk across the waiting room—only this morning I woke before I reached that door. I lay for a moment, listening to the early traffic out on Fairview Road, before it came back to me—what I'd found the previous time upon opening it! I got up then and came downstairs—to hunt here for that entry which describes that dream: the rows of shelves and a counter behind which Ma stands, smiling her answer to a question I want to ask but can't.

I thumb back then a few months to an earlier entry—where I'd noted down a suggestion of Sister Úna's, and how nothing had come of it. Nothing, that is, till that first dream—only I didn't cop it last May even after I wrote it down. A question of idiom perhaps. 'Imagine you're in the Lost Property Office of Your Life,' Sister Úna had said.

'Looking for something you've lost or misplaced.' Had she called it the Lost & Found as we do in Boston, I might've recognised that dream for what it was. For I believe that's where I'd found myself after getting off that bus. And found my mother in attendance—the attendant if you like—behind its counter. And smiling at me—sadly, yes, but no less sweetly for that. Smiling before I can even inquire after something—like a mother's love—I thought I'd lost along the way. Lost & found. Or reaffirmed at least—which this morning feels enough. No matter how long buried, just knowing it's there will do for me. Like that other family treasure buried in a Donegal hill behind a cottage.

CHAPTER 91

DATE: 21 October 1988

All we got into Alice May today was some 7 Up, spoonful by spoonful. Her swallow reflex is all but gone, which usually marks the end of the line. I managed to sit with her again for a few minutes at the end of my shift—only this time she merely stirs when the DART ratchets by. Recalling, who knows, her Pullman sleeper on the Southern Pacific, which took her each spring out to the Arizona desert?

After work I walk Katy down to our dentist around the corner, which she hates as much as I. 'Did you hear about the Zen master who refused Novocain?' I try to jolly her and myself up. 'He wanted to transcend dental medication!' Back home I ring Valerie, tell her again to ring me tonight if needs be. Though the need, I accept, is my own.

CHAPTER 92

It's usually dead slow on the graveyard shift, which is why I brought this tome into work tonight. As if I'm only a piece or two shy of the entire jigsaw, a few final words to the crossword puzzle, or as close as I can to completing it.

I asked Pops once, who'd worked his share, why it's called the graveyard shift. And I must have outgrown my nightmares too—otherwise he'd have never explained about the late-night watch mounted at London cemeteries to discourage grave-robbers. Pops didn't mention how the robbers were most often Irish—something I read years later. Yet how like Pops that was—to gauge how much I was able for. Informing me of such ghoulish practice—if only to harden me up, however gently, for life ahead.

It's funny what comes suddenly into focus—like movies used to in a cinema after the audience whistled and stamped their feet. The way loose strands finally come together, tying everything up. Not that everything is anyways that clear for me—not by a long shot. But it feels like enough has fallen into place for me to lay down this notebook and cap my pen. Like how Pops hadn't the leading role here—even if losing him is what took me to Sister Úna. Instead it's Ma who came stage-centre over these months and pages. Róisín O'Byrne Maguire, the mother of necessity. Summoned from the wings by Sister Úna who insisted from the start: 'And what about your mother, Maeve?'

Which is why, seated by Alice May's bed, I see myself like Constance Fitzgerald just down the hall, still dancing the mother/daughter pas de deux. Only in my case, I attend to Alice May's final hours because I couldn't monitor my mother's own. As if to say I'd have done this for you, Ma. For you, gladly. Not just a death-bed vigil, but whatever care you might have needed at the end of your day.

Nor do I feel anyways culpable in seeking out Alice May like this: none of the old guilt I used feel sneaking up to Apt 3C, wishing Mrs. Lunenberg could be my mother. No doubt Alice May has helped fill some of that long-ago gap too. But, listening to her ragged breathing, I tell myself I don't have to finger that old wound tonight. That I can sit here for Ma and Alice May both. And for Mrs. L and Aunt Chrissie too, all elders of the one tribe. A quartet of Boody Women, one for each point of the compass, with my mother at true North.

CHAPTER 93

DATE: 23 October 1988

THE HERE & NOW: 5.23 a.m.—the nurses' station

Six hours on, and I'm back at the nurses' station. Wang Wei, who finishes today, came down at half-four to say Alice May's heart was racing, so I went up and took her pulse which had slowed a bit already. She felt cold however, so I placed her reading-chair rug over her blankets. I went back downstairs then, where I heard Gemma Dunne calling out for her shoes. I told her she reminded me of the old woman Chrissie told us of in Donegal, who kept a bag of sheep's wool in bed for her feet. But I also put her shoes on her beneath the blanket.

Having settling Gemma, I told W² I was going up to sit with Alice May again—whose breathing sounded the same: laboured, shallow, ragged. And doesn't it all come down to the breath at the end? 'I have arrived' Alan the Yogi told us to think on our inward breath. 'I am home' on the outward. She has a great heart, Alice May, and it's hanging in there yet as hearts do, sending the blood round and round. Watching her chest rise and fall beneath the blanket, I think again of Ma who keeled over in her Boston kitchen twelve years ago. Gone forever—or so I've thought all these years since. But now I'm not so sure—now that I've maybe mastered the task I now see Sister Úna set me at the start. To reclaim my mother and redeem her love, such as it was. The best she could muster, yet every bit as much as she could give.

I see Ma furiously sweeping her kitchen, all that anger spilling out: yet never once did she strike Brian or myself. There are also things I'll never see or know—like exactly what it was that fuelled such rage? What hand was she dealt up in Donegal, where the deal was done? And what precisely was it that prevented her from clasping me as hard to her heart as I can my Katy? As soon seek roses in December as think you'll find answers to it all. But what I've teased out here is enough to be getting on with. What I know now—and what I accept cannot be known. Time so to shut the door on that Lost & Found and re-join Katy on the bus. Get on da bus at last! Resume the journey as it were, keeping my eye on the Here & Now. I may be taking the long way home, but I doubt many of us get there as the crow flies. Funny, too, how it can all round back to where you started from—how roundabout life is—the circularity of things.

I see, too, how long and hard I've run from my fear of going under the same way Ma did. And how running from it kept it somehow always there at my shoulder. Until last April when on my knees in my own kitchen, I finally open my eyes—and see not the blackness I'd dreamt as a child, but a bright splash of sunshine on my own fridge. No clockwork gears behind its white door, nor Templeton III scuttling out from behind. On my knees in my <u>kitchen</u>, of course! Lear, being a guy, gets a windswept heath with the heavens raging overhead on which to work it out. But Ma, being a woman, had only her kitchen—with a dead crow, live rat, and her sweeping brush as props.

'Safe home,' I told Alice May just minutes ago, kissing her brow and fixing her pillow. What Aunt Chrissie always said whenever Katy and I departed Donegal for Dublin. I head for the kitchen then, to switch on the Burco for the breakfast tea—only I step out into the garden instead. Step out and stop short at the sight of a DART train: silent, stationary, awaiting its first run of the day on the railway embankment above the garden wall. Suspended there, carriage windows lit, like some sweet chariot. Behind the train, beyond the sycamores, are the first colours of a new day. An incipient pink flush, like a wash of water-colour across the gauzy clouds. Only warmer than pink—more like rose. Yes, rose, of course! I stand there, knowing to catch it while I can, having learnt that much my first Donegal summer. How dawn colours are subtler, fleeting, unlike a sunset's deeper, lingering stain. You have to look sharp mornings, to see them before they vanish.

ACKNOWLEDGEMENTS

Heartfelt thanks, firstly, to the large cohort of friends and colleagues who read the narrative in various drafts and whose feedback was immeasurably helpful. Likewise to the Arts Council which awarded me a Literature Bursary to work on the novel. Full-hearted thanks also to Paula Campbell, publisher, and to Gaye Shortland, my inspired and inspiring editor, and to the rest of the unwavering Ward River Press team. Final thanks go to Adrienne and our three children whose immense support could not be tallied up.